END of the AGES

Fred DeRuvo

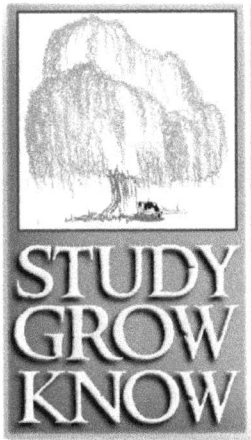

STUDY
GROW
KNOW

Published in Scotts Valley, California, by Study-Grow-Know
www.studygrowknow.com • www.adroitpublications.com

Scripture quotations unless otherwise noted, are from The Holy Bible, King James Version. This version is in the public domain.

Cover Design and Interior Layout: Fred DeRuvo

Edited by: Hannah Richards

Library of Congress Cataloging-in-Publication Data

DeRuvo, Fred, 1957 –

ISBN 0977424499
EAN-13 978-0977424498

1. Religion – Eschatology

Contents

"He which testifieth these things saith, Surely I come quickly. Amen. Even so, come, Lord Jesus. The grace of our Lord Jesus Christ be with you all. Amen."

– Revelation 22:20-21 (KJV)

Charts and Diagrams

• FOREWORD •

I have wanted to write a book like this for some time, but other things had to be done or written first. The book of Revelation, probably more than other, is a portion of the Bible that causes the most debate, argumentation, and even *ill will*.

Certainly, God does not want us to beat each other up (emotionally *or* physically) over areas of the Bible in which we disagree. It is important to understand that even if we disagree over aspects of Eschatology, it should not bring us to the point of harboring anger, resentment, or especially hatred toward one another.

I have chosen to cover the book of Revelation from chapters five through twenty-two. I wanted to walk us through the events that begin in chapter five to the end of the book. I hope you gain something from this endeavor. If you disagree with my findings, that is certainly fine. I would hope you would give them a fair hearing and if we disagree, then we disagree.

The most important job every Christian can accomplish is to introduce people to Jesus Christ as Savior and Lord. Some may feel that I am wasting my time dealing with Eschatology. I do not see it that way. I see Eschatology as *promoting* Jesus Christ and Him alone as rightful King and Lord. When rightly understood, aspects of prophetic discourse *should* cause us to focus on Jesus Christ, the Author and Finisher of our faith.

I have frankly grown extremely tired of all the arguing over Eschatology to the exclusion of everything else. I have long grown tired of being referred to as "deceived" because I have the temerity to believe that the Rapture occurs before the Tribulation. I am also very tired of people never couching their words with the phrase "*in my opinion.*" I have grown to thoroughly dislike the hype, fantasies, and arguing that occurs among all the various cliques and groups regarding the prophetic calendar. It serves no good purpose whatsoever.

For instance, though I firmly believe that the Rapture will occur prior to the Tribulation, if I am wrong, then I am wrong. It makes no difference to me. If the Lord has chosen that I go through the Tribulation (provided I am alive when it occurs), then so be it. I pray only that my life will glorify Him in all things and through all situations. I know beyond doubt that whether or not the Rapture happens any time soon, I *will* one day die. My death is inevitable and it is always imminent. Whether or not I am alive at the Rapture or the Tribulation or something else is not inevitable. At the point of my death, as Paul says, to be absent from the body is to be present with the Lord! What a blessing *that* will be to experience! There will be no more sin, and we will worship Jesus *face* to *face!*

The reason I am writing this book has everything to do with the fact that people are so enamored with prophecy. The plain fact of the matter, though, is that most of our disagreements over aspects of it do not matter because what is destined to occur *will* occur regardless of our opinion on the matter. I do not say this to be flippant about Scripture or what I believe Jesus has revealed to us. I say it because from my perspective, if the study of Eschatology does *not* either 1) bring to our minds the *need* for salvation, or 2) bring us *closer* to the Lord and a greater desire to fulfill the Great Commission, then the study of it is 100% worthless. We can talk about the Rapture or other aspects of prophecy until we run out of breath and be no better off at the end than when we began. I believe Satan has had a field day turning Christians against one another and involving them in worthless discussions that bear no fruit whatsoever. Of course, God has allowed this because we know Satan does not have free reign and can only do what he is allowed to do.

It will undoubtedly surprise the reader to understand my position on this area. For me, the study of Eschatology is a study about Jesus

Christ. Our conversations *should* begin *and* end with Him (not the Rapture, or the Tribulation, or the Seven Seals or whatever). Obviously, prophecy was extremely important to Him since He fulfilled a great deal of it already and will fulfill more of it. Beyond that, He took the time to address specific situations with His own disciples, showing us how important it is for us to understand.

The purpose of *End of the Ages* is to accomplish two things:

1. *to help the AVERAGE person grasp the book of Revelation*
2. *to help people understand that above ALL things, they need salvation*

In my view, there is no book in the Bible that provides a more dire reason for wanting to know Jesus as Lord and Savior than the book of Revelation. It is a book that promises great blessing to those who study it. I believe this is because to properly study Revelation, many other books of the Bible must be studied with it (Daniel, Ezekiel, Joel, Amos, Isaiah, etc.). Too often, the main goal of Eschatology is simply to know *information* in order to debate someone else. While knowing Scripture – all of it – is worthwhile, that in and of itself does not necessarily do anything for the person. There are many individuals in cults who study Scripture but they are no closer to the Author of salvation than my dog.

In other words, **salvation is *the* most important decision a person can make in this life**. If not *every* biblical topic I discuss or write about is drenched in discussion of the need for salvation, then it is pointless to discuss or write about it, in my opinion.

Because we focus on Him, we want others to come to know Him. Focusing our minds on the things above keeps us from spending too much time focused on what is happening here on earth. Our job is to *preach* Jesus Christ and *Him* crucified. Whether or not the Rapture will happen before, during, or after the Tribulation is beside the point. The actual point is that we do not know the day or the hour of our own *death*. Yet, we are often way too comfortable here in this life. That needs to change. It can only change when we learn to raise our eyes above our own life and learn to look to Jesus.

If Eschatology can bring us to that point, then it is serving its purpose. If it becomes a hostile forum, then people should drop it and focus on the Great Commission from another perspective.

The reality is that fulfilling the Great Commission through which people learn of the free gift of salvation is the most important aspect of being a Christian. Certainly, Christians need to grow in grace, and that can only come through the study of His Word, since God Himself wrote it. Our growing in grace occurs over the remainder of our lives from the time we become an authentic believer. During this process of growing we also need to be witnessing, evangelizing for Christ.

If you are a person who picked up this book because the topic interests you but you are not sure if you are a Christian or not, I pray that you will take the time to find out. While you read this book ask yourself about Jesus, who He is and what it is He has accomplished for you.

Jesus is the source of all Scripture. He is the Author and Perfecter of the Christian's faith. He died and rose again in order to *give* us salvation. This salvation He offers comes with no strings attached. You cannot earn it or buy it. You *receive* it through faith in Jesus and His sacrifice on Calvary's cross on your behalf.

Paul tells us in Romans 10:9-10 *"That if thou shalt confess with thy mouth the Lord Jesus, and shalt believe in thine heart that God hath raised him from the dead, thou shalt be saved. For with the heart man believeth unto righteousness; and with the mouth confession is made unto salvation."* In order to do that, you must come to grips with the Man Jesus. Who is He? What did He do for you? Is He who He claims to be? Paul says that you must believe that Jesus is Lord, and from that belief will come a verbal confession.

Like the thief on the cross who one moment was ridiculing Jesus and the next *embracing* the truth about Him, you can also have salvation (cf. Luke 23:39-43).

Between the time the thief hurled insults at the Lord of Life hanging next to him on the cross and the time he asked Jesus to remember Him, something had changed. Something or Someone opened the thief's eyes to the truth. The thief *learned* the truth and then *embraced* that truth and came to believe that Jesus was actually the King of the Jews (like the sign above His head stated). When the thief asked Jesus to remember him when He (Jesus) came into His kingdom, he was saying, "*I believe that you are He who came to set the captive free! Save me, Jesus! Help me to embrace this truth! Please give me the smallest portion of your kingdom!*"

Jesus gave the thief what He gives everyone who calls upon His Name in faith, based on truth: *salvation.* The salvation that God bestows on those who trust Him is eternal. It never ends from the moment we receive it.

The first step is in believing that Jesus came into this world to die for you. After He died, He rose three days later because death could not hold Him. Do you believe that? Do you believe that He is God in the flesh, who came to do what you and I cannot do? I pray that the Lord will open your eyes to see the truth about Jesus.

The book of Revelation is not merely about prophesy or future issues. It presents some of the greatest reasons why every person should have no hesitation in receiving the free salvation that Jesus offers. There are many times throughout Revelation that we see situations occurring on earth that *should* bring people to their knees in repentance. Instead, they only harden their hearts against the Lord.

I would beg you not to do this if you are one of those who have a difficult time believing in Jesus. I would implore you to consider the future. Do not allow your pride to dictate to you. Just as in the book of Revelation Jesus reveals to us through the apostle John the very things that *will* occur to this planet and the people on it, so also does He reveal to John the many times in which people are given the opportunity to receive salvation but refuse. Please, do *not* be one of those people described in the book of Revelation.

As we go through Revelation together, I will be pointing out any number of times the need for you – the reader – to receive salvation from Jesus Christ. If you are already saved, I pray that this book would promote a great desire within you to serve our Lord by dedicating yourself to the Great Commission. If you are not saved, then I pray the Lord would open your eyes – as He did to the thief on the cross – to the truth that He is and the salvation that He offers you.

There is way too much acrimony in the study of Eschatology. People argue about this timing or that, the Rapture or not, and a million other things. Satan laughs and the Lord is saddened. If the study of Eschatology (end times) does not bring us closer to the Lord (for those who know Him) or open our eyes to the truth of salvation (for those who do not know Him), then the discussion is pointless.

My greatest desire as you study this or any biblical topic is that you come to embrace the truth about Jesus Christ and the fact that He and He alone died for your sin. Your sin and mine is something that neither one of us could take care of and eradicate. It is impossible for us to do so because we are fallen people, wholly unable to rectify our situation.

Do not fall into the error of thinking that you are not as bad as (so and so). It is easy to say, "*I'm not a murderer. I have not robbed a bank,*" etc., and believe that this exempts you from eternal damnation. Try this test:

1. *ask yourself if you have ever been so angry with someone that you wanted to murder them or at least see them die*
2. *ask yourself if you have ever lusted after another human being, or a better job, or a more expensive car, etc.*
3. *ask yourself if you have ever told a lie...ever in your life*

If you can answer "yes" to any of the three statements above, then you have sinned. The Bible tells us that sin is *"falling short of the glory of God"* (cf. Romans 3:23). If we sin (and we *have* and *will*), God says that because of this, any righteousness we might *think* we have is absolute *filth* (cf. Isaiah 64:6). If because we have sinned we are now filthy, then it should be obvious that it is impossible to cleanse ourselves enough for God. No matter what we do, we will remain filthy. For one thing, we will continue to sin in this life, so even if it was possible to fully cleanse ourselves it would only last until the next time we sinned.

Only God can and has offered the real solution. He took the form of humanity, lived a sinless life, died a criminal's death, and then rose again. Here are Paul's words from Philippians:

"Who, being in the form of God, thought it not robbery to be equal with God: But made himself of no reputation, and took upon him the form of a servant, and was made in the likeness of men: And being found in fashion as a man, he humbled himself, and became obedient unto death, even the death of the cross. Wherefore God also hath highly exalted him, and given him a name which is above every name: That at the name of Jesus every knee should bow, of things in heaven, and things in earth, and things under the earth; And that every tongue should confess that Jesus Christ is Lord, to the glory of God the Father."

Please notice that God the Son became a human being in order that He would become the perfect sacrifice for you and me. Paul tells the people at Colossae these words:

"In whom we have redemption through his blood, even the forgiveness of sins: Who is the image of the invisible God, the firstborn of every creature: For by him were all things created, that are in heaven, and that are in earth, visible and invisible, whether they be thrones, or dominions, or principalities, or powers: all things were created by him, and for him: And he is before all things, and by him all things consist.

And he is the head of the body, the church: who is the beginning, the firstborn from the dead; that in all things he might have the preeminence. For it pleased the Father that in him should all fulness dwell;

And, having made peace through the blood of his cross, by him to reconcile all things unto himself; by him, I say, whether they be things in earth, or things in heaven. And you, that were sometime alienated and enemies in your mind by wicked works, yet now hath he reconciled" (Colossians 1:14-21).

Paul is saying that Jesus took on the form of humanity but *retained* the fullness of God within Him. In other words, according to both Philippians and Colossians, Jesus *added* humanity to Himself and only used His deity when it coincided with the Father's will. Jesus humbled Himself to become human, and voluntarily placed Himself in a position of servitude to the Father as an example of how we are to live.

It is impossible for us to live this way without Jesus. When we begin to understand that Jesus is God the Son, and that He took on the form of humanity in order to live a sinless life that made Him the perfect sacrifice for us, we begin to realize just how *impossible* it is to live a perfect life as He lived.

Once we begin to see the truth about Jesus Christ, we then have the chance to embrace that truth. Once we embrace that truth, we become new creatures. Paul tells the believers at Corinth that *"...if any man be in Christ, he is a new creature: old things are passed away; behold, all things are become new"* (2 Corinthians 5:17).

Therefore, it is the act of *seeing* the truth about Jesus and *embracing* that truth that creates within us a completely new creation, and everything old is passed away. This is what Jesus refers to as being born again, or being born from above, in chapter three of the gospel of John.

In John 3, Jesus is talking to Nicodemus, a Pharisee (who should have known what Jesus was talking about already), and there He tells Nicodemus that unless a person is born from above, there is no salvation. Please take the time to read the entire chapter of John 3.

Jesus is talking about a spiritual transaction that takes place within us when we receive and embrace the truth about Jesus Christ. Once this occurs, the Holy Spirit comes to dwell within us and as Paul tells the believers at Rome, not only can nothing ever separate us from God's love, but also we are no longer condemned for anything!

"There is therefore now no condemnation to them which are in Christ Jesus, who walk not after the flesh, but after the Spirit. For the law of the Spirit of life in Christ Jesus hath made me free from the law of sin and death" (Romans 8:1-2).

"For I am persuaded, that neither death, nor life, nor angels, nor principalities, nor powers, nor things present, nor things to come, Nor height, nor depth, nor any other creature, shall be able to separate us from the love of God, which is in Christ Jesus our Lord" (Romans 8:38-29).

To sum up:

1. there is nothing you can do to save yourself
2. Jesus became a human being to do what you cannot do for yourself : gain salvation

3. Jesus lived a sinless life, making Him the perfect One to offer Himself as a sacrifice for lost humanity
4. Jesus died a criminal's death on the cross
5. The shedding of His blood while on the cross is for the remission of your sin and mine
6. Jesus rose three days later because the grave could not hold Him
7. You must *see* the truth, and then
8. *Embrace* that truth
9. Once you embrace the truth about Jesus and what He did for you, you become a new creation
10. The Holy Spirit takes up residence *within* you and *cleanses* you from every sin – *past, present*, and *future*
11. Your name is written in the Lamb's book of life
12. From the moment you receive the truth about Jesus Christ, you receive eternal life

Don't worry. If you forget what I am talking about as you read this book, you will meet up with these truths again. I pray you will take the time to honestly look at your life and what Jesus has done for you. I pray that you will ask God to open your eyes to the truth. I pray that once you *see* the truth, you will *embrace* it and you will be embracing eternal life along with it.

I hope you enjoy this book and I hope you gain much from it. It is my prayer that more than anything else, your desire for others to come to know Christ will be the most important thing in your life as a Christian.

Fred DeRuvo, January 2011

PICTURING THE JUDGMENTS OF REVELATION

©2011 - Study-Grow-Know

SEVEN SEALS OF REVELATION

White Horse   Red Horse   Black Horse   Pale Horse

1	2	3	4	5	6	7
ANTICHRIST *Conquering Politically* (Rev 6:1-2)	WAR *Removal of Peace* (Rev 6:3-4)	BALANCES *Famine/Crop Failure* (Rev 6:5-6)	DEATH/HELL *1/4 of World Dies* (Rev 6:7-8)	MARTYRDOM *Persecution to Death* (Rev 6:9-11)	COSMIC SIGNS *Earthquake, Black Sun, Red Moon* (Rev 6:12-17)	SEVEN TRUMPETS *30 Minute Silence, Trumpets* (Rev 8:1)

SEVEN TRUMPETS OF REVELATION

1	2	3	4	5	6	7
HAIL/FIRE/BLOOD *1/3 Trees Burned Up* (Rev 8:7)	FIERY METEOR *1/3 of Sea - Blood* (Rev 8:8)	ASTEROID *1/3 of Rivers - Bitter* (Rev 8:10-11)	CELESTIAL SIGNS *1/3 of Sun, Moon, Stars Turns Dark* (Rev 8:12-13)	LOCUSTS *Demons from Pit* (Rev 9:1-11)	FOUR DEMONS *1/4 World Dies* (Rev 9:13-20)	SEVEN BOWLS *All Kingdoms Are Now God's* (Rev 11:15-19)

SEVEN BOWLS OF REVELATION

1	2	3	4	5	6	7
LOATHESOME SORES *For Those with Mark* (Rev 16:2)	SEA TO BLOOD *All Remaining Seas* (Rev 16:3)	FRESH WATER TO BLOOD *Remaining Fresh Water* (Rev 16:4-7)	SUPER HOT SUN *People scorched* (Rev 16:8-9)	PAINFUL DARKNESS *Beast's Throne* (Rev 16:10-11)	EUPHRATES DRIES *For Armageddon* (Rev 16:12-16)	EARTHQUAKE *Worldwide/Hailstones* (Rev 16:17-21)

1

ABOUT THE RAPTURE...

I agree. The Rapture subject has been done to death and I do not see anyone changing his or her mind, do you? You should probably know up front that I am a PreTrib Rapturist, meaning that I believe the Bible teaches that the Rapture will occur prior to the start of the Tribulation. This will instantly whisk the Invisible Church, aka Christ's Bride, off the planet and into His waiting arms.

I am not going to spend time debating the merits of the PreTrib Rapture position. I have covered the subject in numerous books I have already written and people much more capable than I have done so before me. In spite of this, the debate rages on, with no letup in sight.

I refuse to be part of that debate. I have better things to do with my time, such as *evangelization*!

I *do* want to take this chapter to point out a couple of things to my brothers and sisters who have recently taken up the cause and have begun referring to people like myself with less than charitable names. Shame on all of us who stoop to that level of debate.

"No Persecution" Clause

First, it is said that one of the *main* reasons I believe what I believe is because I want to escape persecution. Wrong. The main reason I believe as I do has everything to do with Scripture. I did not come to the Bible and go, *"Hmmm, let's see, I really don't want to be here when it gets tough so I'm hoping to find some passages that I can twist in favor of a PreTrib Rapture position."*

No, that was not it. Consider this: *IF* the PreTrib Rapture position is the correct one (just humor me for a moment), then it must be in the Bible, correct? If it is in the Bible, then any excuses that are thrown at me for believing it actually wind up denigrating God.

While I do not like the prospect of physical persecution, that fact is *not* why I believe the PreTrib Rapture position is *the* biblically viable position. It is based on Scripture, not my presuppositions or wants.

Tremendous persecution exists in this day and age and has existed for some time. Those Christians are not getting an "Escape Persecution" card, so why should I expect one? The plain and simple answer is that I *don't* expect one. I could be persecuted tomorrow or the next day. God could send me to Asia, or India, or some other God-forsaken country where Christians are killed in numbers that are unbelievable. Persecution is alive and well across this planet. The PreTrib Rapture position does not include a "No Persecution Clause," and that is not why I have adopted that position. You are only kidding yourself and puffing yourself up at the same time, as if *you* have no qualms about being physically persecuted yourself.

C. I. Scofield

The other reason that people say I am a PreTrib Rapturist is because prior to Scofield the theory did not exist, so therefore what I have done is merely read what Scofield taught and said, "*YES!! This is my ticket outta here!*" Again, wrong.

I have actually *studied* the various theories and proposals, and the one that makes the most sense to me is the PreTrib Rapture. It is not as if I was *born* a Dispensationalist. I spent *many* years not believing in any particular form of Rapture. It did not matter to me, and in some ways it *still* does not matter to me!

The reality is that either the PreTrib Rapture is based solidly on Scripture or it is not. If it is, then shut up. If it is not, then shut up. I am just not interested in debating with anyone who believes I only adhere to the PreTrib Rapture theory because I do not want to endure persecution (as if that belief actually changes anything) or that I am too dim to study on my own to assess the situation. Those who make these claims are really in danger of puffing themselves up, and we all know what happens when we puff ourselves up, don't we?

Deceived

This is similar to the last one. I am said to be fully deceived, therefore I believe the deception I am under. Because of believing this deception, if I am alive when the Tribulation begins, I will lose faith in God because I will wake to the fact that the Rapture did not happen as I thought it would! Because of this I will mistake the Antichrist for the Real Christ and take the mark, doomed to be ever segregated with those other poor souls in the Lake of Fire.

So far, every objection is based on something *other than the Bible*. These are very nearly ad hominem attacks. Obviously, God cannot do anything about it because apparently my "free" will supersedes His, so He is powerless. Simply not true.

The Thessalonians Passage

Ah, we finally come to something that has to do with the Bible. The text reads, "*Let no man deceive you by any means: for that day shall not come, except there come a falling away first, and that man of sin be revealed, the son of perdition; Who opposeth and exalteth himself above all that is called God, or that is worshipped; so that he as God sitteth in the temple of God, shewing himself that he is God*" (2 Thessalonians 2:3-4).

Here's what I read and hear constantly from people who deign to come down from their high horse to even give me the time of day. They say that it is *obvious* that the Rapture cannot happen before the Tribulation because of this verse! So I listen intently, as if they are performing the greatest magic trick ever. I wait patiently so that I can applaud when they finish and then return to their high position.

Paul says that "that day" cannot arrive until a falling away happens (which is where I believe we are now as far as this world is concerned). Then he says "and that man of sin be revealed."

The person I've listened to stops and tries to hide the smug expression on his face while silently waiting (*daring*, actually) for me to say anything to negate his words. I cannot. There is nothing I can say that would negate his words, because all he has done is quoted Scripture.

Pitifully, he looks at me, sighs a bit, and then explains that the text *means* that it is when the Antichrist *is revealed*. However, when is he revealed? He is revealed at the midpoint of the Tribulation, three and one half years into it when he breaks the covenant with Israel. Again he stops –this time the smugness is a bit more obvious – and waits, assured within himself that I can say nothing to counter his superior intellect. Sure I can, and in fact it is very easy to do and I will do it now. Yes, Paul says *"that day"* cannot occur until the Antichrist is revealed. I agree with that. It cannot happen.

However, *when* is the Antichrist actually *revealed?* Isn't the Antichrist revealed when he brokers an agreement with Israel in the first place? Isn't this when we know that the Tribulation has *begun?* Yes, this is the event that kicks things off.

Now, why do mid-tribbers take this verse to mean the time when the Antichrist reveals himself as a *liar*, which is when he breaks the covenant he makes with Israel by going into the Temple and setting himself up as god? Is it because the rest of the verses following point that out? To me, it appears as if that is merely Paul's extended description of the man of sin. Yes, this is what he will do, but surely the Antichrist opposes God from the beginning!

He *eventually* sets himself up as god by sitting in the Temple, which alerts the Jews to the fact that he is nothing but an imposter. The real Messiah would never desecrate the Temple. However, when the Antichrist actually brokers the deal with Israel and the surrounding nations in the Middle East is when we actually find out who the Antichrist *IS*. He is the guy! That's him right there, as he signs the paper with the leaders of the other nations.

Look, people can think what they want about the Rapture, except they need to stop thinking that I am deceived or cannot think for myself or whatever. I listen to many Posttribbers who seem unable to think for themselves either. It is as if there are thousands of carbon copies of Dave MacPherson running around, all parroting his words, while at the same time accusing me of parroting Scofield's.

Christians need to get along and realize the most important thing we can do in this life is *serve* God and *evangelize* the lost. We are not to enter into insipid, time-wasting debates about aspects of Eschatology.

Here is a list of things that I think most authentic Christians can agree upon:

- *No one knows when they will die*
- *No one knows when the Rapture will occur*
- *No one knows when the Tribulation will start*
- *We DO know the event that actually starts the Tribulation*
- *The Rapture will occur sometime in the future*
- *We do not know HOW far in advance of the Tribulation the Rapture will occur ("no one knows the day or hour")*
- *We do not know how bad things will actually become prior to either the Rapture occurring or the Tribulation starting*
- *Chances are excellent that life on this planet will become hellish **before** the Rapture occurs and **before** the Tribulation starts*
- *We do not know when the Tribulation will begin, we only know how long it will last*
- *Many Christians could die before either the Rapture occurs or the Tribulation starts, or both*

Whether you can agree with all those bulleted items or not, you would probably agree with a number of them. The one I think all people can agree upon is the bullet that states that no one knows when they will die. Do you? No, you do not. Even if you are now dying of cancer, you do not know the exact day or hour or moment of your death. You just know that your days are numbered, like all the rest of us. You simply have an idea of how many days you have left and we do not. We are all stuck in the dark, though.

Not knowing when our death will occur should make us want to use our time here wisely. How is that accomplished? It is done by living our life *for* God and not for ourselves. We are to see the Great Commission as the *highest form of worship* because by involving ourselves in evangelization we will be obeying Christ to the fullest.

So why am I writing this book, which is not *directly* about evangelism? Because the book of Revelation elevates Jesus Christ by showing Him as He is *now*! It is as simple as that. Understanding Jesus and seeing Him in His rightful context, as Ruler of the universe and *beyond,* is what every Christian needs to see.

Jesus is *God.* He is immaculate, deserving of our constant worship. We need to on a daily, moment-by-moment basis bow the knee to Jesus, our Lord, our Savior, and our God. We need to love Him with an undying love that is so much in union with Him that if circumstances call on us to die for Him, we would do so in a split second.

The book of Revelation is about Eschatology, but more than that it is about the King of Kings and Lord of Lords! The more we know about Jesus, the greater our communion with Him will be. Do I hear an amen? I hope so.

— ◆——————— 2 ——————◆ —

THE TRIBULATION

As usual, there are many disagreements over the subject of the Tribulation, as well as various other aspects of Eschatology. Some believe it will not happen, some believe it already *did* happen, yet others believe it will be 3 ½ years in length, while still others believe it to be a full 7 years in length. Who is right? Obviously, not all opinions are correct, so while you are left to make up your own mind about it, the chart on the next page highlights our position.

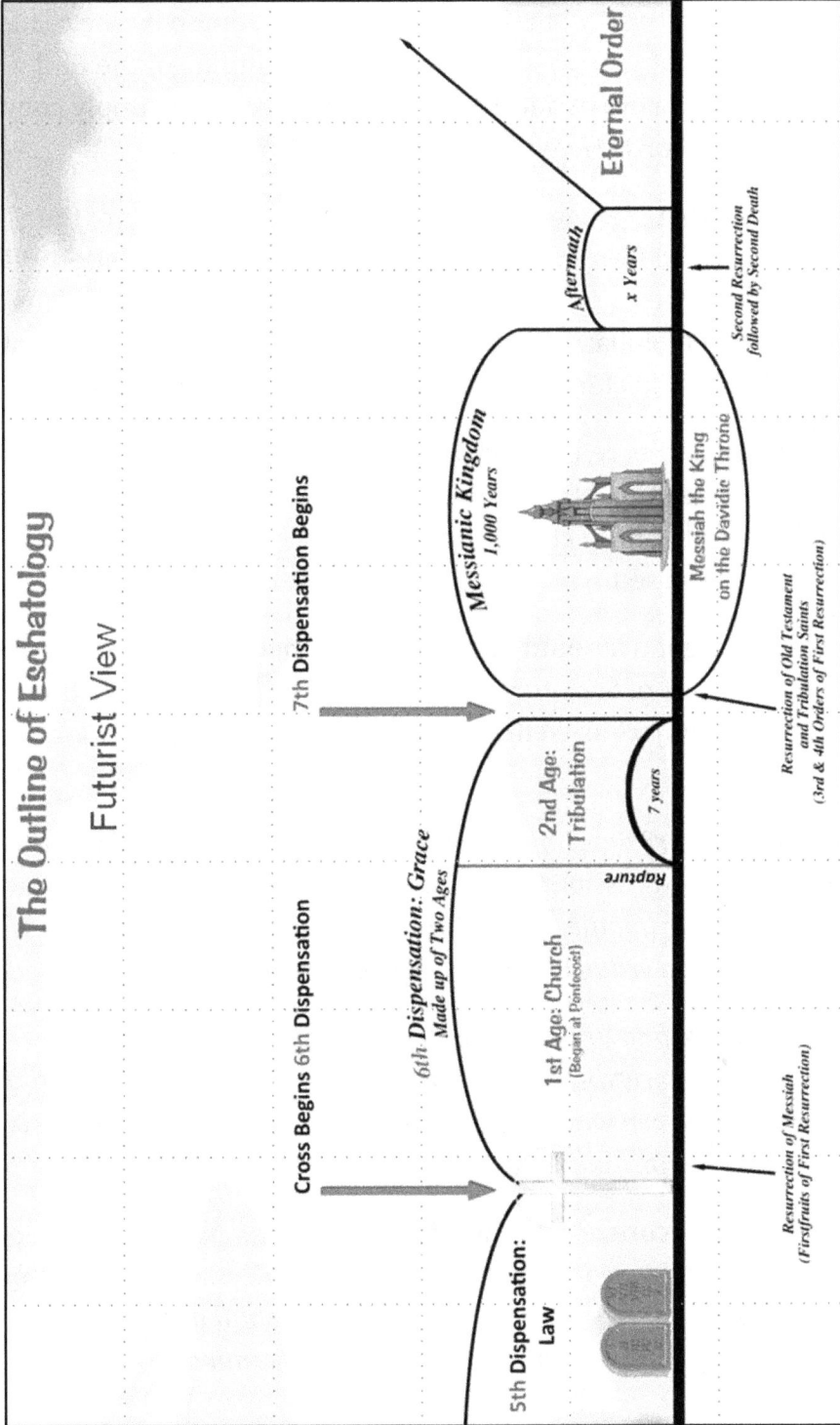

The Outline of Eschatology

Futurist View

Cross Begins 6th Dispensation

7th Dispensation Begins

Eternal Order

Aftermath

x Years

Messianic Kingdom
1,000 Years

6th Dispensation: Grace
Made up of Two Ages

**2nd Age:
Tribulation**

7 years

Rapture

1st Age: Church
(Began at Pentecost)

**5th Dispensation:
Law**

Messiah the King
on the Davidic Throne

*Second Resurrection
followed by Second Death*

*Resurrection of Old Testament
and Tribulation Saints
(3rd & 4th Orders of First Resurrection)*

*Resurrection of Messiah
(Firstfruits of First Resurrection)*

It is certainly not critical that this position be adopted by the reader. If you believe that you arrived at your understanding of the End Times through an impartial study of God's Word, then simply commit yourself to the Lord. He will most definitely direct you.

I will tell you that I believe there will be a full seven years of the Tribulation in the future. The first 3 ½ years is the Tribulation, while the second 3 ½ years is the *Great* Tribulation. Again, though, I am not interested in debating anyone about it. It is not that important to debate it. It is important to know why *you* believe the way you do.

As for me, all of this refers back to Daniel 9. There, the angel Gabriel explains the meaning of the "70 weeks" to Daniel. This subject is only found here in the ninth chapter of Daniel. There is no other place where it is discussed.

I have spent a good amount of time in other books discussing and explaining this part of Scripture. Many others have written their own books on the subject as well. Here is the text to which we are referring:

"Seventy weeks are determined upon thy people and upon thy holy city, to finish the transgression, and to make an end of sins, and to make reconciliation for iniquity, and to bring in everlasting righteousness, and to seal up the vision and prophecy, and to anoint the most Holy.

"Know therefore and understand, that from the going forth of the commandment to restore and to build Jerusalem unto the Messiah the Prince shall be seven weeks, and threescore and two weeks: the street shall be built again, and the wall, even in troublous times.

"And after threescore and two weeks shall Messiah be cut off, but not for himself: and the people of the prince that shall come shall destroy the city and the sanctuary; and the end thereof shall be with a flood, and unto the end of the war desolations are determined.

"And he shall confirm the covenant with many for **one week***: and in the midst of the week he shall cause the sacrifice and the oblation to cease, and for the overspreading of abominations he shall make it desolate, even until the consummation, and that determined shall be poured upon the desolate"* (Daniel 9:24-27; emphasis added).

To break this down quickly, we need to realize that a "week" here is actually a period of seven years. The word that was translated "weeks" *should* have been translated "sevens" (as it was in the New American Standard Bible). Ultimately, the translators thought they were doing everyone a favor by simply placing the word "weeks" instead of "sevens" in the text because it ultimately turns out to equal a period of seven years anyway. We know that because of the context.

For instance, the text that says, *"Know therefore and understand, that from the going forth of the commandment to restore and to build Jerusalem unto the Messiah the Prince shall be seven weeks"* should really say *"Know therefore and understand, that from the going forth of the commandment to restore and to build Jerusalem unto the Messiah the Prince shall be seven* **sevens.***"* The sevens eventually translates into periods of seven *years.*

Gabriel is saying that when the decree to rebuild Jerusalem is given to the Messiah (Jesus) the time will be seven *sevens*, or 49 years (seven x seven). Immediately following that is a period of "threescore and two" or "sixty-two weeks." This sixty-two weeks translates to 434 years (62 x 7). There is now a total of 434 + 49, which equals 483 years. Essentially what Gabriel is telling Daniel is that the time from the decree to rebuild Jerusalem *until* the Messiah reveals Himself to the Jews would be 483 years total. The math has been figured out by others and it brings us to the time that Jesus entered Jerusalem on the colt of a donkey to offer Himself as Messiah. Space does not permit me to break this down further, but you can read all about it in my book *Between Weeks* or any number of other books written by individuals who prove the point.

Notice that there has not been any type of break between the first 49 years and the 434 years. One happens immediately after the other. However, once Jesus presents Himself as Messiah He is *rejected*, and that very week He is crucified. The very next part of the passage in Daniel 9 states, "*And after threescore and two weeks shall Messiah be cut off, but not for himself.*" Gabriel is saying that "after the 483 years passes, the Messiah is *killed* (cut off). Then notice that two other things happen after Messiah is crucified:

- *The people of the prince who is to come will destroy the city and the Temple, and*

- *Desolations will continue until the end*

After 483 years, Messiah presents Himself and is then killed. Then after that, *people* destroy the city and the Temple. There are wars and desolations until the end. The people who destroyed Jerusalem and the Temple were *Romans* and they were also *Gentiles*. This means that the prince being referred to cannot be Jesus Christ because Jesus is Jewish. Therefore another "prince" is being referred to here, which can only mean the Antichrist.

Proof of this (as far as I'm concerned) is found in the very next verse: "*And he shall confirm the covenant with many for **one week**: and in the midst of the week he shall cause the sacrifice and the oblation to cease, and for the overspreading of abominations he shall make it desolate, even until the consummation, and that determined shall be poured upon the desolate.*" It is this same prince that the pronoun "he" refers *back* to here. Therefore, that prince is the one who causes the sacrifices to cease. How? By doing exactly what Paul says he is going to do in 2 Thessalonians 2:3-4, which we previously referred to already. The Antichrist will waltz into the Temple and declare himself to be God. This will defile the Temple, and at that point the Jewish Remnant will know they have been deceived and they will literally run for the hills!

Please note also that this Antichrist will confirm a covenant with the many for *one week*. We *must* apply the same principles of interpretation here that we did with the previous uses of the word "week." If those represented *years*, than this one also has to represent years. One week, then, would be seven years. Since there has been an obvious break between the 483 years and this final seven years we can conclude that it has not begun yet, because as I look back through history, I see no point in time where *anyone* has made a covenant with the Jewish people and the nations in the Middle East for seven years, have you? Since this has not happened, then we must conclude that this final "week" or seven years has not begun yet.

We know then that the starting point of the Tribulation is the covenant or agreement that Antichrist makes with Israel and the other nations in the Middle East. It is that simple, but some would like to make it really complicated. It is not complicated at all.

Now, am I trying to convince you that *my* way is the right way? No, I am simply trying to explain how I have arrived at this understanding regarding the Tribulation as it references this passage of the Bible. You are still free to think that I am wrong, but please understand that I am not interested in debating it with you or anyone else. It is not that important in reality. What is important is evangelizing the lost and looking forward to the day when we will be with Jesus and without any vestiges of the sin nature! Imagine, finally being able to worship Him as He *deserves* to be worshiped!

—◆————— 3 —————◆—

BIRTH PANGS

Prior to the Tribulation beginning, Jesus pointed out in His Olivet Discourse (Matthew 24, Mark 13, and Luke 21) that when the world begins to experience certain things – and He listed them – we would know that this was the beginning of what He termed *birth pangs*. Birth pangs are just that, pains and cramping in the abdominal area that signals to the mother she is very close to giving birth.

At long last, the nearly ten months in which a human being needs to gestate is nearly over, and soon the husband and wife will be proud parents of a new and hopefully healthy baby.

This is exactly what is going to happen throughout the earth and in fact *is* happening now. Things will take place that will be very much like the birth pains that signal to the mother she is near to giving birth.

The Olivet Discourse, which is recorded for us in Matthew 24, Mark 13, and Luke 21 all say the same thing *essentially*. There are a few differences, so it is important to read all three versions to determine what is missing from one to the other. These are not contradictions or mistakes. They are simply the vantage point of the individual human author.

In *Footsteps of the Messiah,* Fruchtenbaum points out nine birth pangs that we are to note. These are important events and signal things that are not to be missed. If we look carefully at the narratives, we note that the disciples asked Jesus three questions about the timing of the things that He had just finished discussing.

The reader will hopefully recall that as Jesus began His dialogue with the disciples about the End Times he was referencing the Temple, because the disciples had just marveled about how beautiful it looked. Jesus pointed out that there would come a time when not one stone would stand upon another (cf. Matthew 24:1).

The disciples then asked their questions, which were:

1. *When will these things be? (cf. Luke 21:20-24)*
2. *What will the sign of your coming be? (cf. Matthew 24:29-31)*
3. *What is the sign of the end of the age? (cf. Matthew 24:1-8)*

The entirety of the Olivet Discourse answers these questions (but note that question number one is only answered in Luke). Fruchtenbaum points out that Jewish people and especially rabbis thought in terms of *this age* and the *next age*. These were the two ages: the one we live in now and the one when Messiah comes.

In essence, then, the disciples were asking Jesus what *the* sign was that signaled the end of this age (the one we are living in) and the beginning of the Messianic age.

In verses four through six of Matthew 24, Jesus points out two things to be aware of:

1. *False messiahs*
2. *Wars and rumors of wars*

Jesus immediately follows this up with, "*be not troubled: for all these things must come to pass, but the end is not yet,*" in verse six. While false messiahs and local wars will happen, these do *not* signal the end of the age.

Birth Pang #1 – World Wars, Famines & Earthquakes

Jesus then goes on to point out what *does* signal the *start* of the end of the age. Two events or scenarios are important for us to grasp here.

1. *Nation shall rise against nation; kingdom against kingdom*
2. *Famines with earthquakes*

Fruchtenbaum points out that the phrase "*nation shall rise against nation and kingdom against kingdom*" is a Jewish idiom that refers to a *global* conflict, not merely a local one. In other words, the nations rising against nations and kingdoms against kingdoms are happening *at the same time*. This, he believes, clearly points to the First World War. Few, with the possible exception of Richard Abanes (see his book *End Times Vision*), would argue with that.

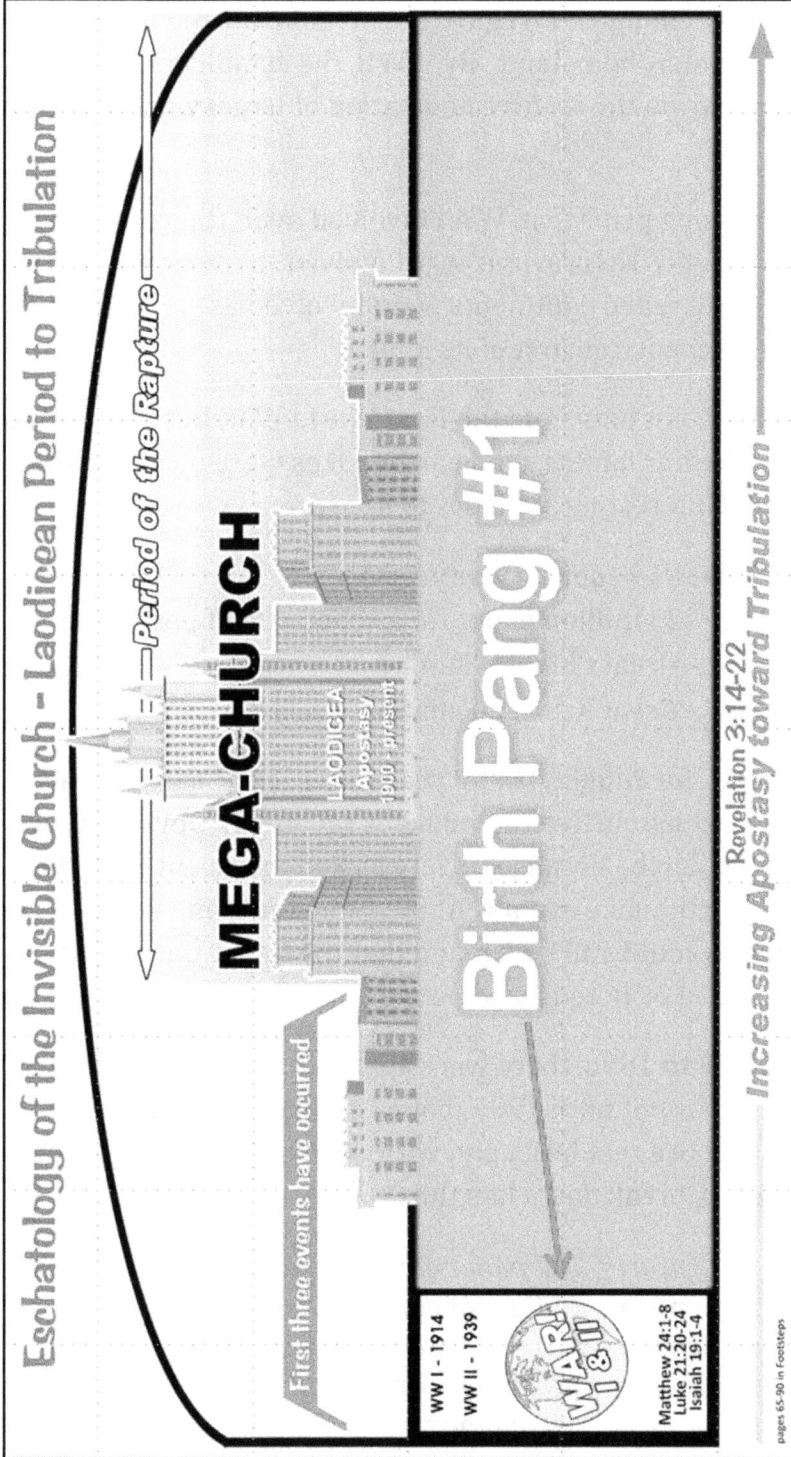

Eschatology of the Invisible Church – Laodicean Period to Tribulation

Period of the Rapture

First three events have occurred

MEGA-CHURCH

LAODICEA
Apostasy
1900 - present

Birth Pang #1

WW I – 1914
WW II – 1939

WAR I & II

Matthew 24:1-8
Luke 21:20-24
Isaiah 19:1-4

Revelation 3:14-22

Increasing Apostasy toward Tribulation

pages 65-90 in Footsteps

Interestingly enough, WWI gave rise to Zionism and a desire by Jews to return to their homeland. By WWII, the establishment of the Jewish homeland via the resurrected nation of Israel was soon to be underway.

Unlike anything prior to it, WWI involved over 100 countries around the entire globe. No previous war involved that many nations or countries. All seven continents were involved as well. This was a truly global event, the first of its kind.

However, we not only note the First World War, but also need to determine whether famines and earthquakes were near that time as well. Some interesting statistics to note are:

- 1918-1919 (during war years)
    - 23 million people killed because of pestilence
- 1920 – Great Chinese Famine
- 1921 – Great Russian Famine

Beyond this, for roughly 1,000 years after Jesus' earthly walk there were approximately five earthquakes recorded. Obviously, at least some of this can be because society lacked the scientific technology to record earthquake events. At the same time, one would think that earthquakes could still be felt and that the larger ones would have been recorded or noted by someone.

From A.D. 63 to 1896, there were approximately 26 recorded earthquakes. It was not until 1905 that earthquakes began happening with much more regularity and with the loss of thousands of lives. The statistics break down like this:

- *14th Century   157 major earthquakes*
- *15th Century   174 major earthquakes*
- *16th Century   253 major earthquakes*
- *17th Century   278 major earthquakes*
- *18th Century   640 major earthquakes*

- *19th Century   2,119 major earthquakes*
- *20th Century   over 900,000 earthquakes*

The above information is according to the United States Geological Survey, National Earthquake Information Center, Earthquakes with 1,000 or more deaths from 1900 (May 12, 2000). Even though Jesus never said that earthquakes would *increase* during the time of nations and kingdoms rising against one another, it is clear that this is exactly what happened.

In 2009 and into 2010 earthquakes have gotten even more destructive, moving entire cities off their foundations and compacting the earth's crust. It should be obvious that since WWI earthquakes along with famines have been part of the scene. The first birth pang, then, is World War I with accompanying earthquakes and famines, and this was initially fulfilled between the years 1914 to 1918. Remember, Jesus said that these were merely the *beginning of birth pangs*.

Birth Pang #2 – Israel Becomes a Nation
Zephaniah 2:1-2 speaks of something that Israel will do *before* the Tribulation. The text reads, "*Gather yourselves together, yea, gather together, O nation not desired; Before the decree bring forth, before the day pass as the chaff, before the fierce anger of the LORD come upon you, before the day of the LORD's anger come upon you.*"

Many conservative scholars believe this refers to the beginnings of the re-established nation of Israel. Both Isaiah and Ezekiel refer to a worldwide regathering that would occur *prior* to the day of Jehovah (cf. Ezekiel 20:33-38; 36:22-24; Isaiah 11:11-12). Together these passages indicate that God Himself will bring about a return of His people to Israel, from which He will take His final remnant.

The phrase "*day of Jehovah*" is always used in the Old Testament to refer to the Tribulation period at the end of the age just prior to Messiah's return.

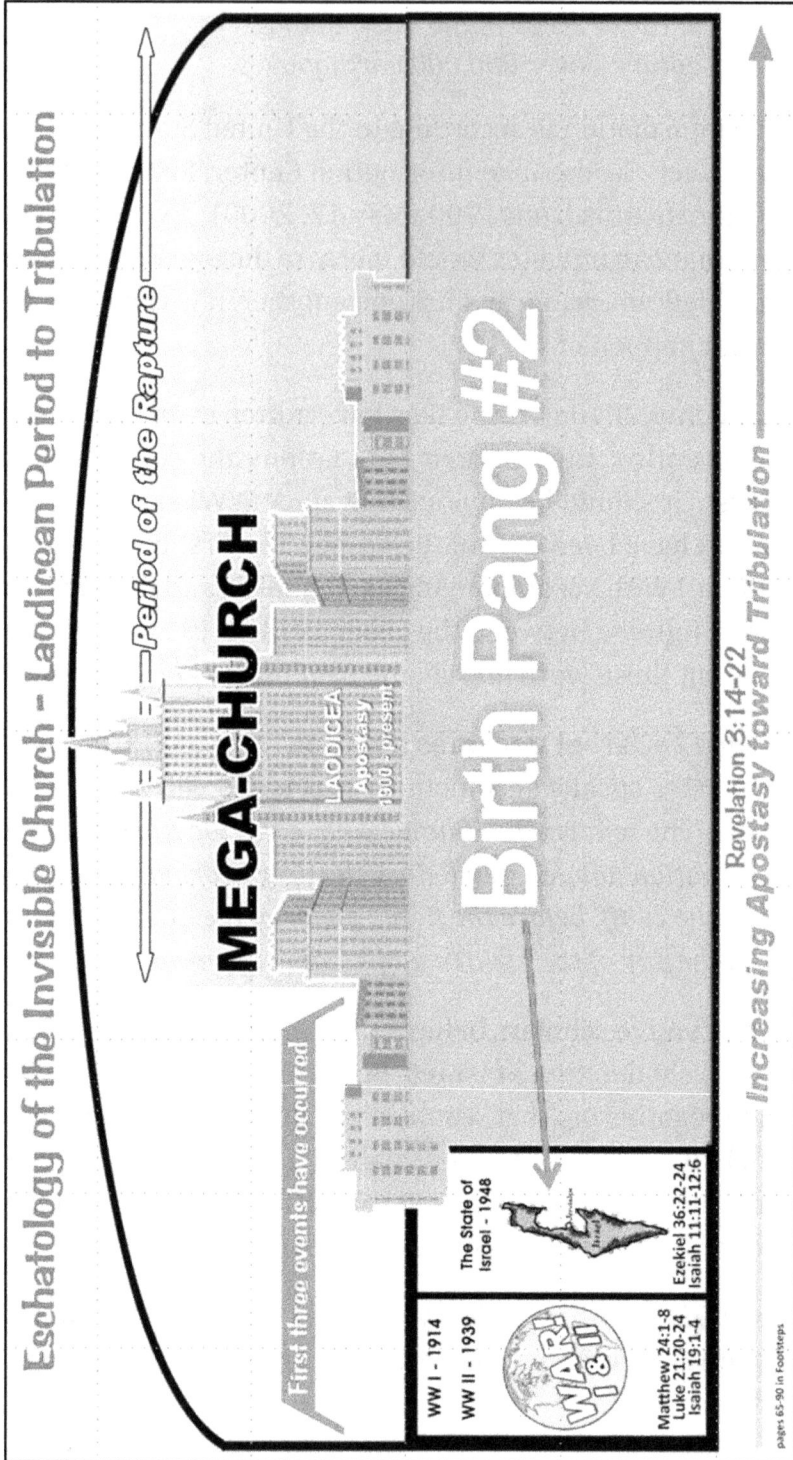

Eschatology of the Invisible Church – Laodicean Period to Tribulation

Period of the Rapture

MEGA-CHURCH

LAODICEA
Apostasy,
1900 - present

Birth Pang #2

First three events have occurred

WW I – 1914
WW II – 1939

WAR I & II

Matthew 24:1-8
Luke 21:20-24
Isaiah 19:1-4

The State of
Israel - 1948

Ezekiel 36:22-24
Isaiah 11:11-12:6

Revelation 3:14-22

Increasing Apostasy toward Tribulation

pages 65-90 in Footsteps

This regathering occurred in 1948 officially, when Israel again became a nation. See chart on the previous page.

Birth Pang #3 – Jerusalem No Longer Divided

It is interesting to note here that at the time Israel became a nation again, Israeli forces controlled:

- *West Jerusalem*
- *Newer Jewish section*
- *Old City of Jerusalem (the biblical city):*
    - *Fell into hands of Jordanian Legion*
    - *Later annexed into the Hashemite kingdom of Jordan*
    - *Jerusalem was divided city for 19 years*
    - *OT prophecies speak of Old City of Jerusalem falling under Jewish control*

On paper, when the Six-Day War ended, this gave Israel control of all of Jerusalem, which had remained divided for 19 years since the 1948 independence. During this war, Moshe Dayan led his troops into the Old Jerusalem sector and after intense fighting gained control of the Western Wall *and* the Temple Mount.

Though the Temple Mount *remains* under Israeli sovereignty, shortly after the close of the Six-Day War in 1967 Israel left the control in the hands of Islamic groups. This continues to be a source of problems for both Jews and Arabs since Jews are generally not allowed to pray on the Temple Mount, in spite of the fact that the area comes under the auspices of Israel's government.

So this third birth pang is a once again unified Old Jerusalem as indicated in Daniel 9:27, Matthew 24:15, and 2 Thessalonians 2:3-4. Not only is Jerusalem unified, but it remains under Israeli sovereignty.

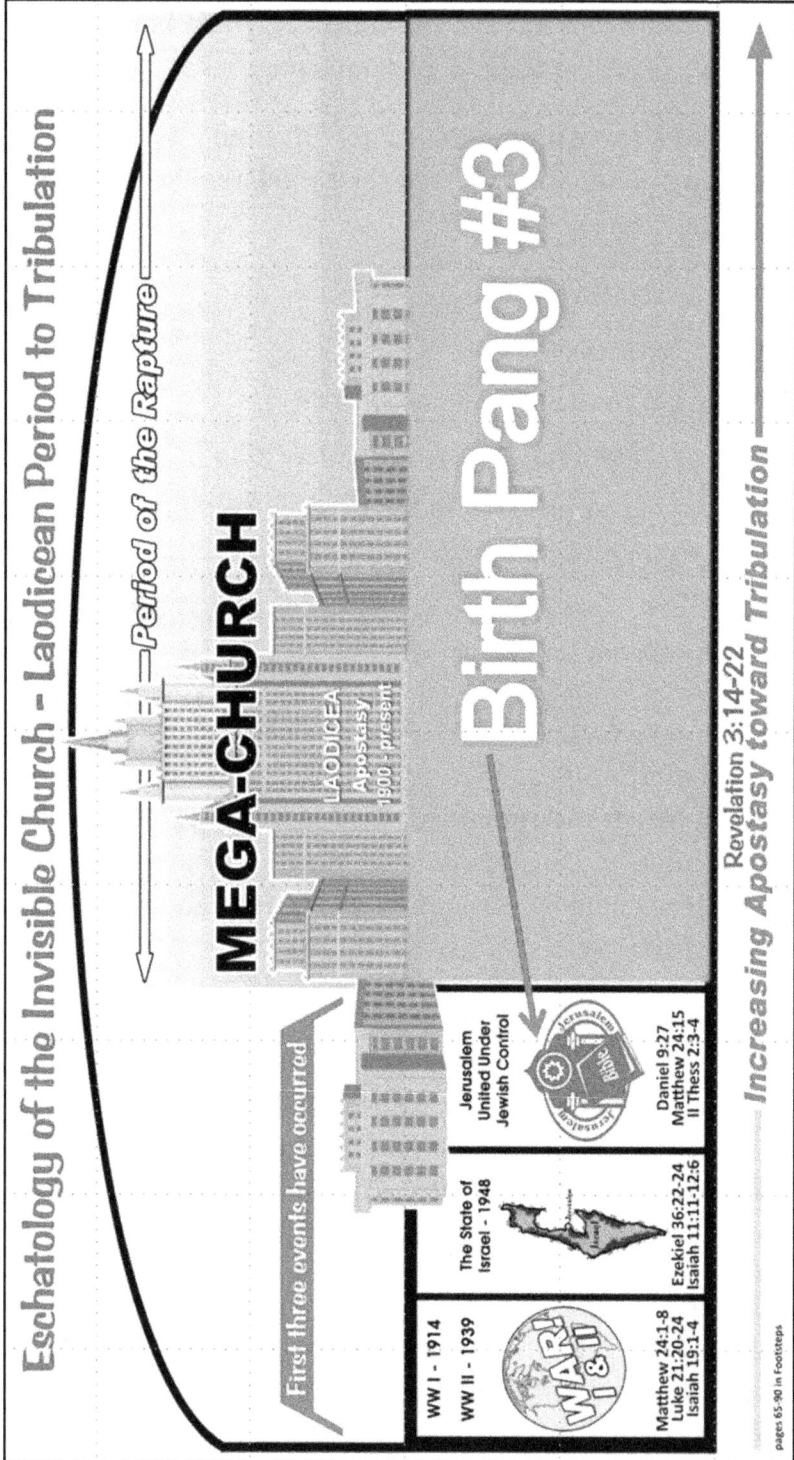

Eschatology of the Invisible Church – Laodicean Period to Tribulation

Period of the Rapture

First three events have occurred

MEGA-CHURCH

LAODICEA
Apostasy
1900 - present

Birth Pang #3

Increasing Apostasy toward Tribulation

WW I - 1914
WW II - 1939

Matthew 24:1-8
Luke 21:20-24
Isaiah 19:1-4

The State of
Israel - 1948

Ezekiel 36:22-24
Isaiah 11:11-12:6

Jerusalem
United Under
Jewish Control

Daniel 9:27
Matthew 24:15
II Thess 2:3-4

Revelation 3:14-22

pages 65-90 in Footsteps

Birth Pang #4 – Northern Invasion of Israel

Numerous scholars believe that prior to the beginning of the Tribulation an invasion of Israel will occur by a group of five nations, led by a leader referred to in Scripture as Gog. This title – not a name – may refer to the leader of this group from the north of Israel.

The main passage of Scripture referenced here is Ezekiel 38:1-39:16, which describes how God will actually bring the invasion about through the nations who have gathered together to overcome Israel. Not only will He bring the invasion about but also will do the fighting *for* Israel.

> *"And the word of the LORD came unto me, saying, Son of man, set thy face against Gog, the land of Magog, the chief prince of Meshech and Tubal, and prophesy against him, And say, Thus saith the Lord GOD; Behold, I am against thee, O Gog, the chief prince of Meshech and Tubal: And **I will turn thee back, and put hooks into thy jaws, and I will bring thee forth**, and all thine army, horses and horsemen, all of them clothed with all sorts of armour, even a great company with bucklers and shields, all of them handling swords: Persia, Ethiopia, and Libya with them; all of them with shield and helmet: Gomer, and all his bands; the house of Togarmah of the north quarters, and all his bands: and many people with thee."* (Ezekiel 38:1-6; emphasis added)

The interesting thing here is that though God Himself brings this attempted invasion about, the players will still be held responsible for their actions, just as Judas Iscariot was for his. You have to appreciate the imagery when God says that He will *"put hooks into thy jaws, and I will bring thee forth."* Who can resist God? At the same time, all He will be doing is causing Gog to act on what is already in his heart.

As we continue in this narrative, note God's viewpoint recorded in verse fourteen through sixteen of Ezekiel thirty-eight.

> *"Therefore, son of man, prophesy and say unto Gog, Thus saith the Lord GOD; In that day when my people of Israel dwelleth safely, shalt thou not know it? And thou shalt come from thy place out of the north parts, thou, and many people with thee, all of them riding upon horses, a great company, and a mighty army: And thou shalt come up against my people of Israel, as a cloud to cover the land; it shall be in the latter days, and I will bring thee against my land, that the heathen may know me, when I shall be sanctified in thee, O Gog, before their eyes."* (Ezek 38:14-16)

God is, at the same time, laying the blame squarely on Gog's shoulders, but also crediting Himself with making this happen. Why will He do this? For one simple reason: *to sanctify Himself before all the heathen.* In other words, God will create the problem that He will solve in order for the very world He created to know that He is God.

The remaining text of this chapter in Ezekiel provides us with an even heightened view of God's perspective.

> *"And it shall come to pass at the same time when Gog shall come against the land of Israel, saith the Lord GOD, that my fury shall come up in my face. For in my jealousy and in the fire of my wrath have I spoken, Surely in that day there shall be a great shaking in the land of Israel; So that the fishes of the sea, and the fowls of the heaven, and the beasts of the field, and all creeping things that creep upon the earth, and all the men that are upon the face of the earth, shall shake at my presence, and the mountains shall be thrown down, and the steep places shall fall, and every wall shall fall to the ground. And I will call for a sword against him throughout all my mountains, saith the Lord GOD: every man's sword shall be against his brother. And I will plead against him with pestilence and with blood; and I will rain upon him, and upon his bands, and upon the many people that are with him, an overflowing rain, and great hailstones, fire, and*

brimstone. Thus will I magnify myself, and sanctify myself; and I will be known in the eyes of many nations, and they shall know that I am the LORD." (Ezek 38:18-23)

Can God be any clearer here in the text? Here is what He promises to accomplish when Gog leads the coming invasion:

- A major earthquake throwing down the mountains and noticed by
  - The fish
  - The birds
  - The creatures of the earth
  - Humanity
- Nothing shall be left standing
- Soldiers will turn on each other
- Pestilence (disease) and blood
- God will join the fray by lobbing the following on the invaders
  - Hailstones
  - Rain
  - Fire
  - Brimstone

Again, why does God do this? So that no one will misunderstand, Ezekiel tells us again that God does this to glorify *Himself*! Amen! This creates a time when the nations and the people of the earth will *know* that He is God! However, how long will this last? Certainly, many within Israel will begin to come around to the fact that Jesus Christ was and remains the true Messiah, but certainly not all of Israel. God has just begun calling His remnant.

It reminds me of the few times (thankfully) when I knew my dad was going to be angry with me. I had blown it and was now waiting for the other shoe to fall. I became the politest kid around in an effort to show my dad that I had really changed and that I had all of a sudden

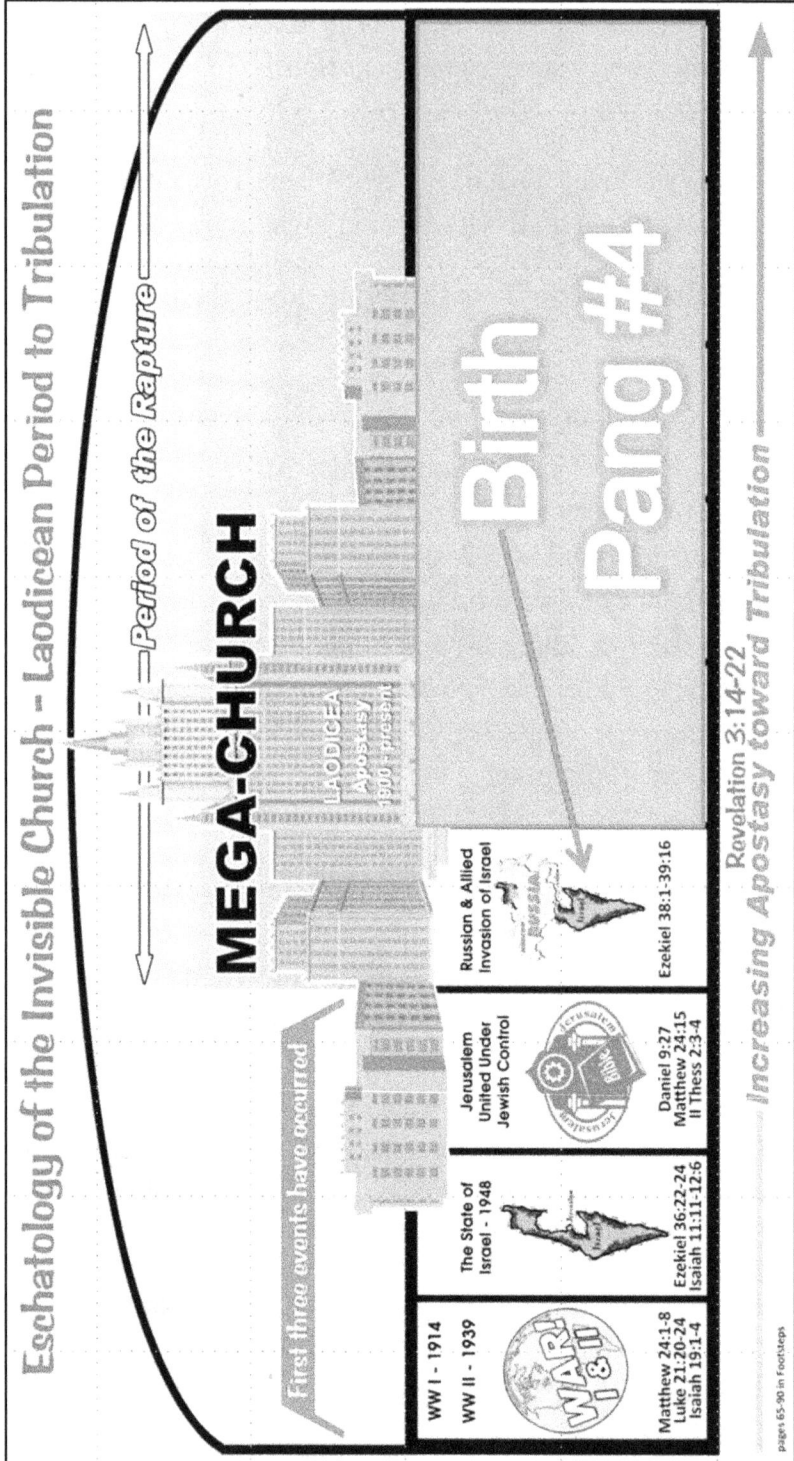

Eschatology of the Invisible Church – Laodicean Period to Tribulation

Period of the Rapture

First three events have occurred

MEGA-CHURCH

LAODICEA
Apostasy
1900 + present

Birth
Pang #4

Increasing Apostasy toward Tribulation

Revelation 3:14-22

WW I – 1914 WW II – 1939	The State of Israel – 1948	Jerusalem United Under Jewish Control	Russian & Allied Invasion of Israel
WAR I & II			RUSSIA
Matthew 24:1-8 Luke 21:20-24 Isaiah 19:1-4	Ezekiel 36:22-24 Isaiah 11:11-12:6	Daniel 9:27 Matthew 24:15 II Thess 2:3-4	Ezekiel 38:1-39:16

pages 65-90 in Footsteps

grown past the ability to do something stupid again! It was not long, though, before the punishment came; then it was over, and within a few days things returned to normal. I do *not* consider myself to have been a bad kid, but there were certainly times when I acted very stupidly and got what I deserved. Thankfully, my father loved me enough *to* discipline me.

This is likely the way it will be during the time just after this attempted invasion. God will prove that He deserves our praise and adoration. He will sanctify His Name because Israel certainly has not done it.

What people fail to realize is that Jerusalem is God's Holy City and the Land that He gave Israel is *His* Land. In fact, stop and consider how often people who become dictators treat parts of this world as if they own it. I do not recall God ever giving that dictator the title deed to earth.

Based on the Scriptural text, numerous Bible scholars believe that the following nations or groups are involved in this attempted invasion of Israel:

- *Russia*
- *Iran*
- *Ethiopia*
- *Somalia*
- *Germany*
- *Armenia*

Are the above the nations who will be after Israel? It could be, though some are not as sure. In either case, it looks as though the surrounding nations will be the perpetrators of this act of war, and God will preempt it before it even gets off the ground.

Birth Pang #5 – One World Government

This birth pang is related to the world and its governmental process. In today's world (mid-2010), there are major economic upheavals throughout. America is reeling from debt, joblessness, and an unsure future, with little confidence in our leaders.

This is happening throughout the world, and what will likely occur is a total devastation of world economies. This will prompt people to call for governments to do something – *anything* – that will cause people to regain confidence in their governments.

The only answer for this will be a one-world government. This one-world government will be touted as the only way to solve earth's problems. We will have become a global village, no longer separated by borders. The only reasonable solution to the problems our world faces is to have one government that rules over all of it.

This is outlined for us in Daniel 7:23-24, when the last Gentile kingdom – the 4th kingdom of Daniel 7 – will grow until it "devours" the world. Once the East-West axis of power derails, it will give way to a One World Government. In light of Ezekiel 38:1-39:16, the eastern balance of power will collapse with the fall of Northern forces (possibly Russia) and her Muslim allies in Israel and the destruction of the Northern area itself.

Birth Pang #6 – Ten Kingdom Stage

Once the one-world government is firmly in place it will divide into ten districts, with a leader over each district. The entirety of the ten districts will fall under the rule of one leader.

This ten-district unity will continue into the Tribulation period. It is from this ten-district system that the Antichrist will make his move to rise to the top of the heap.

Prior to the actual start of the Tribulation, the two things that must occur according to 2 Thessalonians 2:1-3 are:

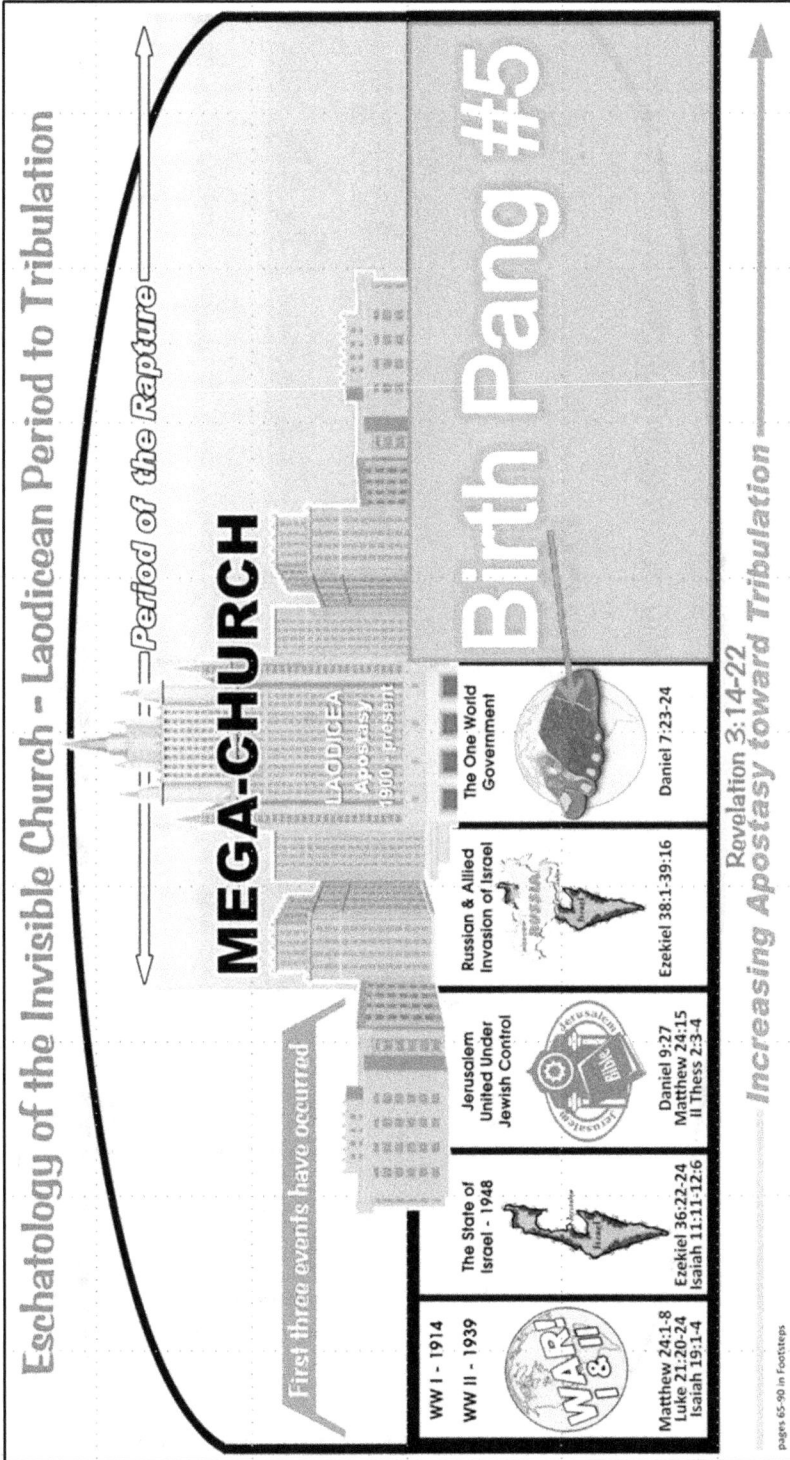

Eschatology of the Invisible Church – Laodicean Period to Tribulation

Period of the Rapture

First three events have occurred

MEGA-CHURCH

LAODICEA
Apostasy
1900 + present

Birth Pang #5

Revelation 3:14-22

Increasing Apostasy toward Tribulation

WW I - 1914 WW II - 1939	The State of Israel - 1948	Jerusalem United Under Jewish Control	Russian & Allied Invasion of Israel	The One World Government
Matthew 24:1-8 Luke 21:20-24 Isaiah 19:1-4	Ezekiel 36:22-24 Isaiah 11:11-12:6	Daniel 9:27 Matthew 24:15 II Thess 2:3-4	Ezekiel 38:1-39:16	Daniel 7:23-24

pages 65-90 in Footsteps

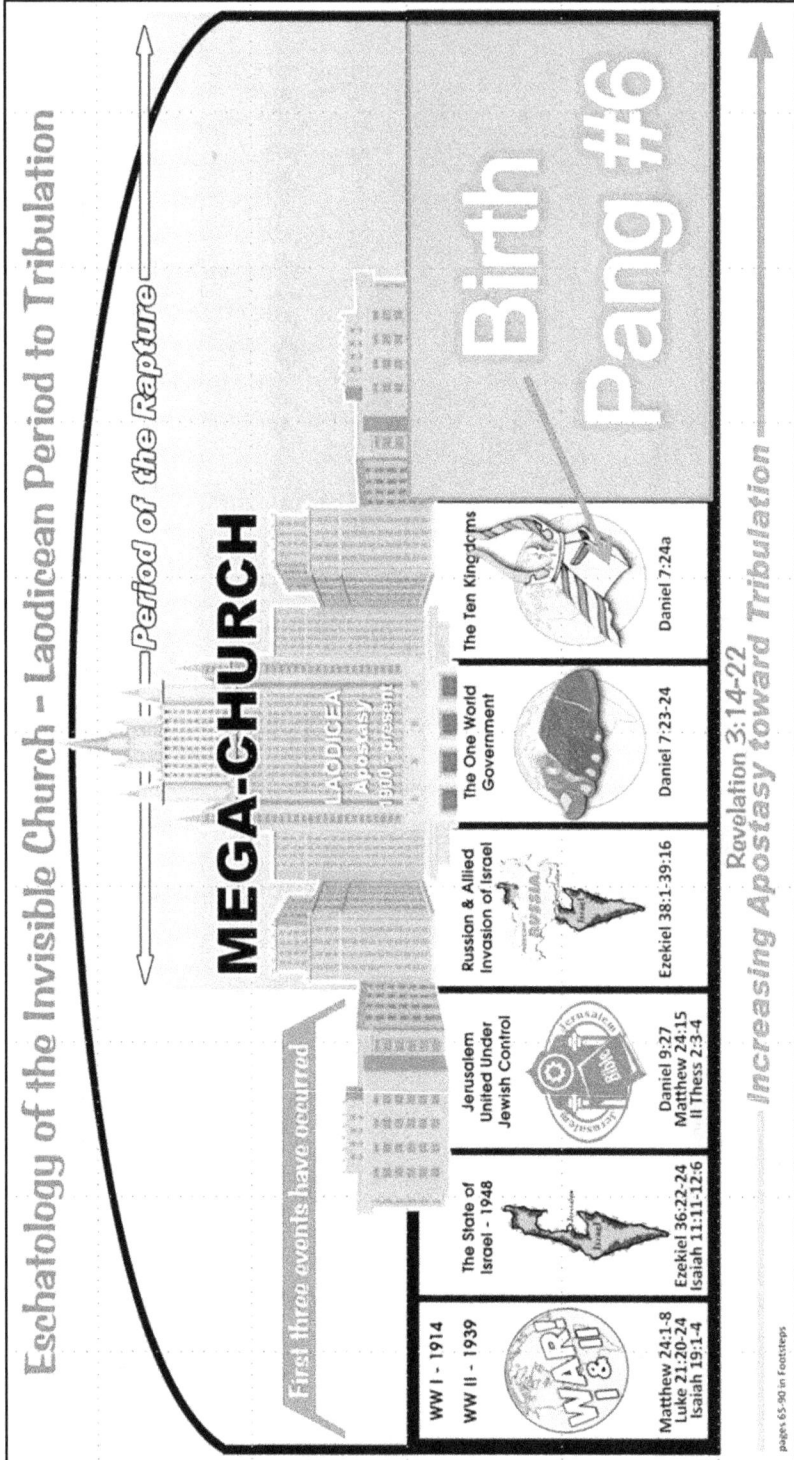

Eschatology of the Invisible Church – Laodicean Period to Tribulation

Period of the Rapture

First three events have occurred

MEGA-CHURCH

LAODICEA
Apostasy
1900 - present

Birth Pang #6

Revelation 3:14-22

Increasing Apostasy toward Tribulation

WW I - 1914 WW II - 1939	The State of Israel - 1948	Jerusalem United Under Jewish Control	Russian & Allied Invasion of Israel	The One World Government	The Ten Kingdoms
Matthew 24:1-8 Luke 21:20-24 Isaiah 19:1-4	Ezekiel 36:22-24 Isaiah 11:11-12:6	Daniel 9:27 Matthew 24:15 II Thess 2:3-4	Ezekiel 38:1-39:16	Daniel 7:23-24	Daniel 7:24a

pages 65-90 in footsteps

- A great apostasy, or falling away
  - o This does not mean that actual Christians will cease to be Christians. It means that those who have *professed* to be Christians will deliberately move away from the faith they once claimed to possess.
- The man of sin must be revealed
  - o As stated earlier, the man of sin will reveal himself prior to the Tribulation as the savior of the world

We do not know just exactly *how* the Antichrist will be known because the Bible does not tell us. It is possible that a numerical value of his name could be applied (Hebrew naturally has a numerical system for each letter).

Birth Pang #7 – Rise of Antichrist

Ultimately, it is simply not known how the world will know him. His rise to power is a biblical *necessity* because the Tribulation cannot begin until Israel signs a 7-year agreement with him. This, then, is the seventh birth pang: the covenant with Israel for seven years.

When this occurs, Israel will believe she is safe from assault for at least the seven-year period that they have agreed upon with the Antichrist. The other nations that will agree to this will also give Israel a sense of security; however, it will be a false sense of security that is ultimately undermined by Antichrist himself.

As we will note, during the first half of the Tribulation Antichrist keeps a relatively low profile. He rides in on a white horse pretending to be a savior, but is actually the devil incarnate. He promises peace, but brings anything but peace.

Aside from God's judgments being poured out onto the earth during the first half of the Tribulation, Antichrist will be busy waiting for his moment of self-glorification when he enters the rebuilt Temple, sits down in the Holy of Holies, and declares himself god. He will demand

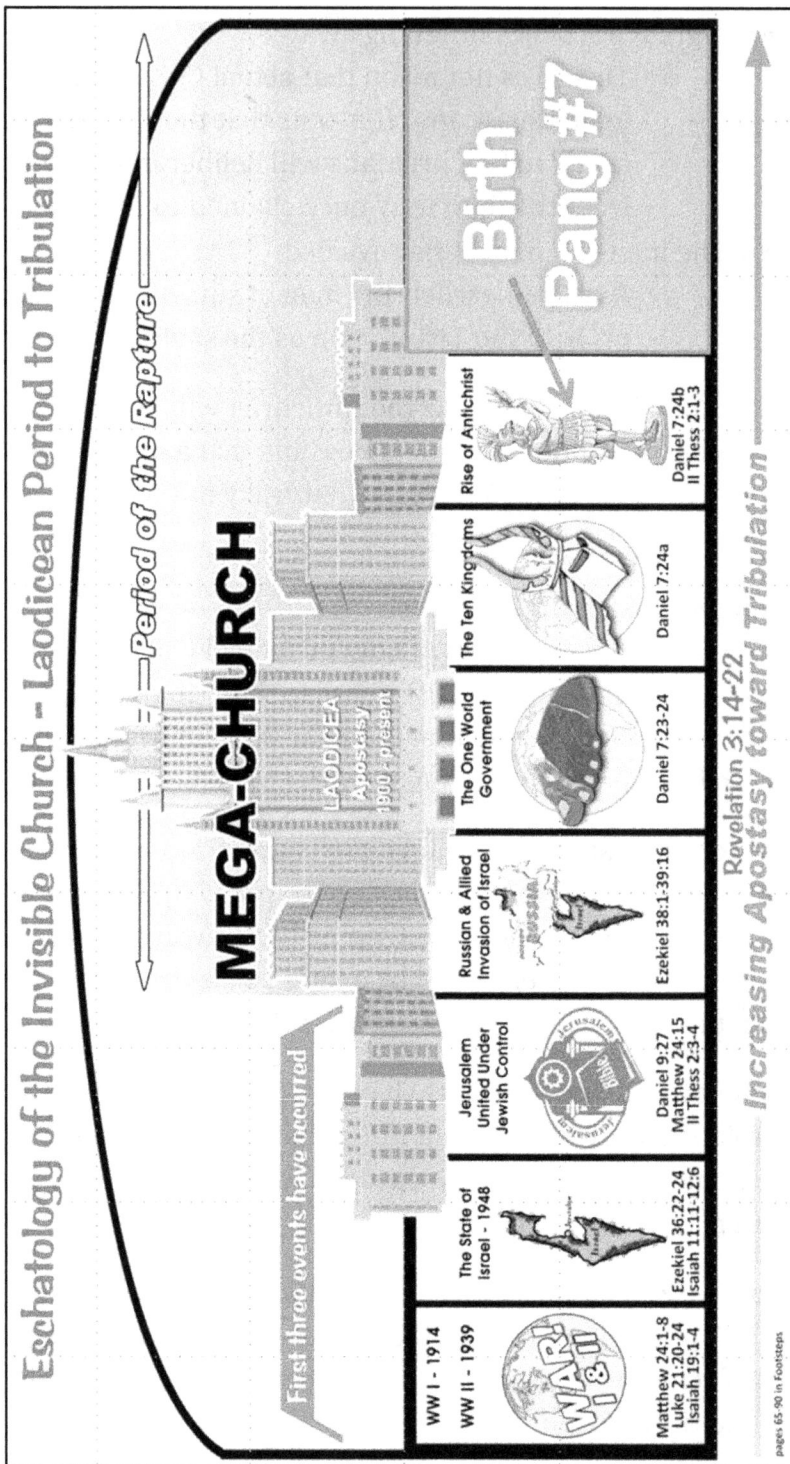

Eschatology of the Invisible Church – Laodicean Period to Tribulation

Period of the Rapture

First three events have occurred

MEGA-CHURCH

LAODICEA
Apostasy
1900 - present

WW I – 1914	The State of Israel – 1948	Jerusalem United Under Jewish Control	Russian & Allied Invasion of Israel	The One World Government	The Ten Kingdoms	Rise of Antichrist
WW II – 1939						
Matthew 24:1-8 Luke 21:20-24 Isaiah 19:1-4	Ezekiel 36:22-24 Isaiah 11:11-12:6	Daniel 9:27 Matthew 24:15 II Thess 2:3-4	Ezekiel 38:1-39:16	Daniel 7:23-24	Daniel 7:24a	Daniel 7:24b II Thess 2:1-3

Birth
Pang #7

Revelation 3:14-22

Increasing Apostasy toward Tribulation

pages 65-90 in Footsteps

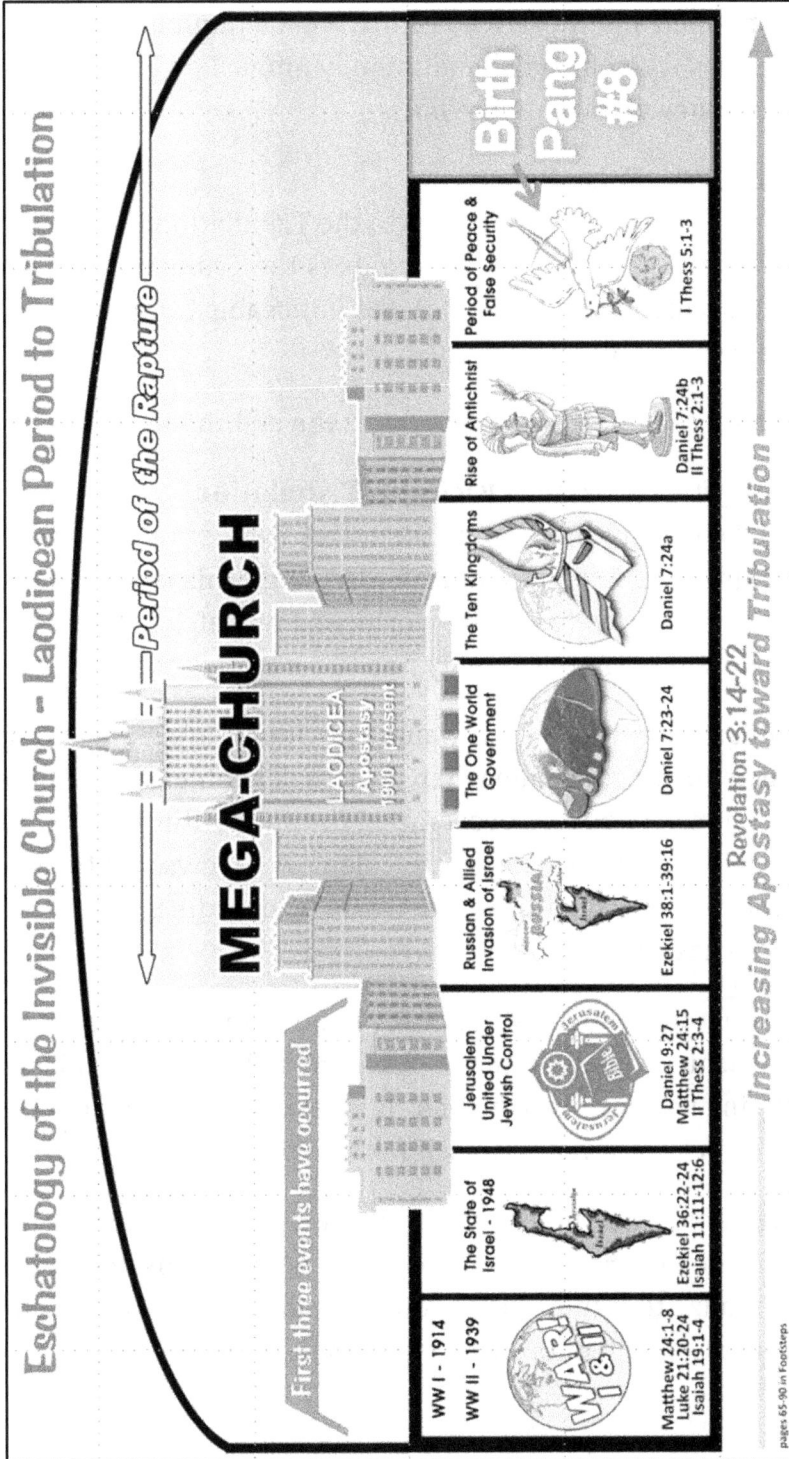

Eschatology of the Invisible Church – Laodicean Period to Tribulation

Period of the Rapture

First three events have occurred

MEGA-CHURCH

LAODICEA
Apostasy
1900 - present

Birth Pang #8

WW I - 1914 WW II - 1939	The State of Israel - 1948	Jerusalem United Under Jewish Control	Russian & Allied Invasion of Israel	The One World Government	The Ten Kingdoms	Rise of Antichrist	Period of Peace & False Security
Matthew 24:1-8 Luke 21:20-24 Isaiah 19:1-4	Ezekiel 36:22-24 Isaiah 11:11-12:6	Daniel 9:27 Matthew 24:15 II Thess 2:3-4	Ezekiel 38:1-39:16	Daniel 7:23-24	Daniel 7:24a	Daniel 7:24b II Thess 2:1-3	I Thess 5:1-3

Revelation 3:14-22

Increasing Apostasy toward Tribulation

pages 65-90 in Footsteps

to be worshiped and those who refuse will be hunted down and killed. This is when he will be ultimately unmasked to the Jewish people and they will run to the hills.

Birth Pang #8 – False Peace
However, even though building up to the Tribulation there may appear to be a time of security, the events of the Tribulation will destroy that security. As we will see, the noticeable ramping up of intensity of events will be made clear.

The false sense of peace and security is the eighth birth pang.

Birth Pang #9 – Covenant Kicks off Tribulation
The actual covenant that Antichrist makes with Israel and other nations surrounding her is the ninth birth pang. This is of course where the Antichrist is revealed to the world, and we refer to Paul's words in 2 Thessalonians 2:1-3, already noted.

The problem, of course, is that some individuals are *assuming* that he is revealed for the first time when he actually defiles the Temple by declaring himself god and desecrating the altar within the Temple. This is when his true identity is revealed to the Jews, but the world has already recognized him as *the* world leader, the Savior of the world who has come to right all wrongs.

The idea that the Antichrist is *not* revealed to the world through his efforts to achieve peace with the covenant he brokers with Israel and surrounding nations is erroneous. It is at this point – birth pang #9 – that the Antichrist *reveals* himself to the world as its savior.

When he defiles the Temple, he will be revealing his authentic character – the devil incarnate – to the *Jewish people*. This will cause them to realize that they have been conned. They will then run to the hills, where God will offer his protection to them.

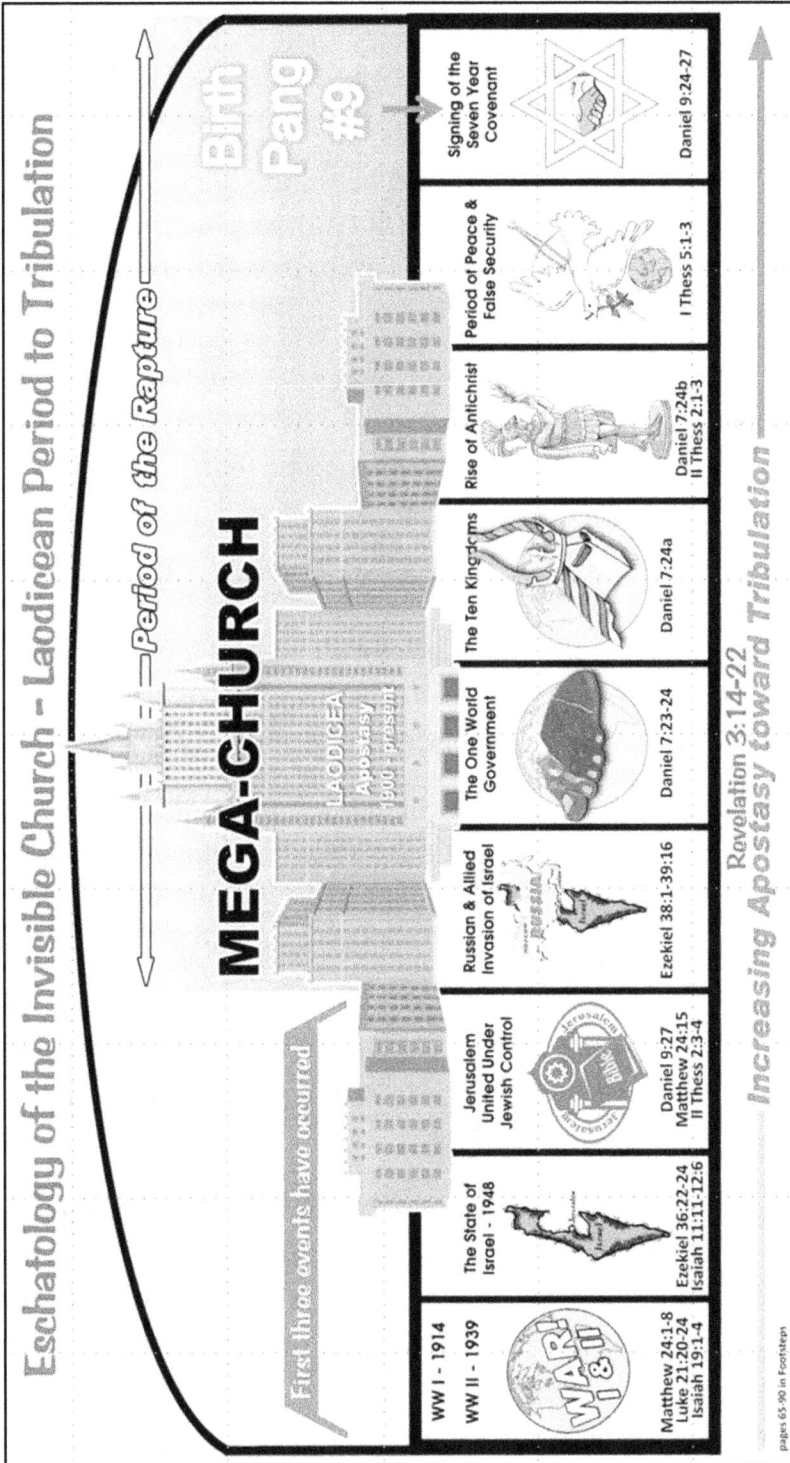

Eschatology of the Invisible Church – Laodicean Period to Tribulation

Period of the Rapture

MEGA-CHURCH

LAODICEA Apostasy 1900 - present

Birth Pang #9

First three events have occurred

Increasing Apostasy toward Tribulation

Revelation 3:14-22

WW I – 1914 WW II – 1939	Matthew 24:1-8 Luke 21:20-24 Isaiah 19:1-4
The State of Israel - 1948	Ezekiel 36:22-24 Isaiah 11:11-12:6
Jerusalem United Under Jewish Control	Daniel 9:27 Matthew 24:15 II Thess 2:3-4
Russian & Allied Invasion of Israel	Ezekiel 38:1-39:16
The One World Government	Daniel 7:23-24
The Ten Kingdoms	Daniel 7:24a
Rise of Antichrist	Daniel 7:24b II Thess 2:1-3
Period of Peace & False Security	I Thess 5:1-3
Signing of the Seven Year Covenant	Daniel 9:24-27

pages 65-90 in Footsteps

Because Antichrist is unable to spend his anger on the Jews, he will instead turn his terror on those who have rejected him as savior of the world.

The event of defiling the Temple occurs in the middle of the Tribulation and begins what Christ in the Olivet Discourse calls "great tribulation," (cf. Matthew 24). From this point onward, three and a half years remain of unbridled terror.

The Antichrist will release his own anger on God's people (along with all who refuse to receive him and his mark), while God will continue to pour out His wrath-filled judgments on the earth. It will be the most horrific time this earth and its citizens will have ever known.

It is clear that a number of these birth pangs have already occurred:

- *WWI with earthquakes, pestilence, and famines*
- *Israel becomes a state in 1948*
- *Jerusalem is united under the sovereignty of Israel*

The remaining birth pangs are still in the future, and it is possible that we may see the Invasion of the Northern Alliance soon. Daily in the news we read of the potential of Israel's preemptive attack on Iran in an effort to destroy Iran's nuclear capabilities.

If this preemptive strike occurs, it may well cause other countries to retaliate against Israel. If they retaliate, it may well be this Northern Alliance that does the retaliating on behalf of the nations in the Middle East.

If the Northern Alliance takes place God has promised to intervene, and it appears according to Scripture that if He does so He will personally defend Israel without Israel's armies having to raise a finger. He does this for the sake of His Name and for His own glory. Before we get into Revelation proper, we will deal briefly with the power that Satan has and the limits God has placed on him.

4

SATAN'S POWER

The sad fact is that Satan has been busy for centuries doing all that he can to bring his own takeover plan to fruition. In fact, if you read books by those who are doing their best to wake up the church to see the dangers that we have fallen into, it becomes clear that the world is quickly adopting the lies that Satan has been telling for eons.

There is a good deal of confusion out there today and we know that God is *not* the Author of confusion. In the many books related to the Illuminati, Freemasonry, and the coming one-world order we read about use of Black Magick (spelled with a "k" when it refers to *Satanism* or the *occult*). From what these authors tell us, it *appears* as though these supernatural beings *must* do the will of the person performing the magick. If we stop to consider this it really makes *no* sense whatsoever. Why would *any* supernatural being (that is far stronger than any human being) be *required* to follow the dictates of any person even if that human being said the "correct" words, in the "correct" order, under the "correct" positioning of the stars, at the "correct" time of year?

There is absolutely no reason at all why any of these supernatural beings would be required to do the bidding of anyone except *God*. To believe and state that by performing certain rituals human beings can somehow bring supernatural beings under their mastery is the height of arrogance and stupidity on the part of people. There can be only *one* reason why Satan would cause human beings to *believe* that this is the case – to serve *himself*.

Therefore, it appears that with respect to malevolent spiritual entities, including Satan, there are only a few options:

1. *These beings do not have to do the bidding of human beings, but they only make it appear as if they have to do it because it suits Satan's purposes.*
2. *These beings must do the will of the person invoking them through (occult) magick because that is the law of the supernatural realm.*

If we consider the Scriptural possibilities, only a few things make sense. First, while it might *seem* as though Satan has limitations with people in this world, the fact of the matter is that any limitations he has are placed on him not by people, but by *God*. We know this from the book of Job alone. This is clear throughout Scripture. While Satan and his minions likely have greater freedom with those who are not saved, the demons were *required* to obey the commands of Jesus and any of His disciples who approached or came across demonic entities in the power of His Name. There is no recorded biblical case where demons were *not* subject to the authority of Jesus Christ.

Certainly, Satan is the prince of the power of the air, and yes, he owns the major kingdoms of the world (or at least controls them, but he *still* controls them under God's *absolute sovereignty*). To this, there is never a question or a doubt. Yes, Satan is the prince of this world. The question, though, seems to be whether he is *bound* or *limited* by people's *incantations* in this world/realm. Once people begin contacting the lord of darkness, what is required of him, if anything?

For instance, those who are Satanists, or those who fill high posts in the Illuminati or Freemasonry, *know* that they are essentially worshiping Satan. This is what they *want* to do because of their view that Satan (Lucifer to them) is really their friend, and God Almighty, being a jealous God, wants to hide the truth from people. This is their belief system. Once these people make contact with the enemy of their souls, even though what they believe to be true about him is a lie, Satan gains free *access* to their minds, their actions, and the people they can influence. He has literally been invited into their lives. Because of this, he *already has* these people for the time being (unless they eventually become Christians).

Other people who are *not* Christians, but also not directly given over to the power of darkness, are *not* people he can necessarily work in and through *directly*. He must wait to receive some kind of an invitation to do so. This can be through pornography, Ouija boards, or aspects of black magick. The invitation to him can come from any number of areas, including drugs and/or crime. Unsaved people who become *possessed* usually do because they open the door to Satan. He (or his underlings) comes in and starts working toward his own ends. The more people he has under his control, the better.

It stands to reason that *if* Satan already *had* control of ALL non-Christians *NOW* the world would be fully under his control with no opposition at all (from human beings, that is). This is what *will* happen during the Tribulation period, because the Restrainer (whom I believe to be the Holy Spirit as He works *in* and *through* the Church) will be taken out of the way. God's influence will still be here, but right now He works mightily through the invisible Church, Christ's Bride.

Once the Restrainer is taken out of the way (through the Rapture of the invisible Church), He will – *for a time* – not be working directly in and through people (Christians) on the earth. Because of this, all hell will literally break forth on the earth and Satan will nearly have carte blanche to do what he wants to do. Yet even here he *must* remain within God's preordered will with respect to what happens during the Tribulation. There is never a time when Satan is allowed to do what he truly wants to do. God never gives up His sovereignty.

In other words, Satan's field of influence will dramatically *increase* after the Rapture, but he is *still* limited by God Himself. The Masons, the Illuminati, and the rest of those people who believe they are actually *conjuring* up Satan and his power along with gaining the ability to *control* him, of necessity *must* be acting on ideas and impulses that SATAN has *given* them over centuries of time! Satan has spent generations perfecting his system. He has carefully laid the groundwork so that people have come to believe that they *can* control him, or at least free him to bring his "benevolent" plan to the fore. He is very willing to allow them to think this because it serves his purposes.

This is *how* Satan's plans become reality. He *knows* he is restrained under God's power, but in the meantime, he *also* knows that he can only go where *invited* to go. Because of this, he must put it in the minds of people to help *create* situations where his appearance (through Antichrist) will be completed as planned. Yet even here the Antichrist will only be revealed to the world during that specific moment when God has decreed it will happen. Satan then continues to work, but his freedom is and always has been severely limited, in spite of the tremendous power that he continues to possess.

We know that Satan's plan has *always* been to thwart God by setting himself up as god. He does so by turning as many people *against* God as possible. First, when people turn against God they wind up worshiping *Satan*. This serves his purpose because they are worshiping him (instead of God) while at the same time are helping Satan to "raise" his throne above God's, something he will never actually be able to do, though. Secondly, while he is turning people *away* from God, he is doing so by planting the seeds of a *one-world government* and *one-world religion*. Of course, it is merely the same lie he told Eve, but on a far grander scale.

The upshot of it is that the *greater number of* people Satan can work *through*, the greater his chances are of revealing the Antichrist to the world, at least from his perspective. This he has attempted to do for generations and generations. In some cases he has essentially had to start over with each successive generation of people (as he did with each successive generation of Israelites, raising up new rebels to *stand* against God). Some things he has been able to *carry* over from one generation to the next. He has done so through groups like the Illuminati and Freemasonry as well as other secret orders. This connects one generation of rebels to the next, and that is how he keeps his lie going.

The fact that we are drawing that much closer to the Tribulation means that God has *given* Satan a *greater area* with which to work. Notice God gives Satan a greater realm. God does this by literally *giving people over to themselves* so that they will believe the *lie* that Satan has been peddling since the Garden of Eden; that man is *already* god.

Satan's lie has been crafted with great complexities, and because of the secret societies, which are said to possess secret knowledge (*gnosis*), people's appetites for this knowledge *increases*. People always want something that appears to be "off-limits." They want to know how to self-actualize, how to release their own innate deity, so that they can control their destinies and the universe. There is nothing new under the sun, and in spite of the slight differences between secret societies and the New Age, it is all the same lie.

Satan is more than happy to create a system that allows people to think that they are special because they have gained some personal knowledge that is kept from others. This knowledge – though a complete lie – is available to those who rebel against God and seek their own purposes.

The members of the (high-ranking) Freemasons and the Illuminati firmly believe that they have achieved and attained something the average person has not, nor ever will. In spite of the fact that Satan has simply created a complex labyrinth that leads to the Garden of Eden *lie*, the people who willingly take part in this are enamored with it, because it feeds their *ego*. Do you see that Satan has merely led people down a path lined with flowers, yet they are unable to see the poisonous thorns barely below the surface? He has led them to suppose that through various incantations and spells they gain the ability to call forth the powers of darkness and actually *have power over* them.

If they do not come to believe that they control these powers, they conclude that they are *helping* to set these powers and Satan himself *free.* Because they are helping to set him free, they are confident they will be rewarded with great honor by the supernatural being they call *master*. The tragedy is that these human beings are in actuality relegating themselves to the same fate as Satan. Satan has – *through his multifarious system of lies* – caused them to believe that they are actually helping to redefine the future.

God has *not* at any point in the past given people over to themselves to the extent that He is doing now, as we move toward the Tribulation. This greater area for Satan to work in and through, created by virtue of the fact that more and more people are willing to believe and *embrace* his lie (*ye shall be as gods*), means Satan has a greater foundation from which to work.

All this magick and hocus-pocus is something that *Satan* created. He has done this so that people will be *enticed* to try it, use it, and then see the *results*. Satan has created this complex system of beliefs that allegedly lead to higher knowledge. By following his paths, the individual gains spiritual insight and believes the lies he is told that he learns on the way. Since Satan creates the game, the rules, and the outcome, it should be no surprise that all is in his favor.

It is no different from a con artist plying his trade. I read about one con artist who was said to have created a machine that printed McKinley $500 bills. Once every six hours, a new bill would come out of the machine. He would "prove" to people right there that his machine did what he said, and sure enough, a real five hundred dollar bill would be produced. People were convinced, so they paid as much as $30,000 to buy one of his machines.

They took the machine home, started it and waited the six hours for the next five hundred dollar bill to come rolling out. Wow, were *they* impressed! They waited another six hours for the next one to be produced only to see a completely blank "bill" come out of the machine. Thinking it to be a mistake, they would wait another six hours to see another blank bill come out! The realization that they had been taken for thirty grand hit them, but by then, the con artist had a twelve hour start with their money!

People have always been gullible. Con artists are believable because they have not only designed the game, but the *outcome*. They know what will happen and they present that to the unwary victim. Believing it to be the truth, the victim becomes hooked (in spite of any red flags that go off in the victim's mind) and before they realize it, they have become another in a long line of victims.

This is exactly how Satan works. He has designed a scheme that, in essence, gets people to *invite* him into their lives. He makes it seem like it is *their* idea and he promises power, riches, secret knowledge, and sharing the glory of his reign. He does tend to deliver at least somewhat, but only for those he really *needs*. While they are busy believing that *they* control the dark lord, he is not only laughing and mocking them behind their backs, but also fully using them for *his* gain.

Many of the people that Satan uses wind up becoming thoroughly evil themselves. In other cases, they wind up dying because of the stress that is related to being Satan's mouthpiece. This certainly seemed to be the case with Jane Roberts, who introduced (through channeling) the entity known as *Seth* to the world.

Roberts and her husband encountered Seth by using the Ouija board in 1963, and she died in 1984. Some believed that she had become "one" with Seth and the stress of that union brought her death about. Toward the end, she appeared unhealthy, stressed and under the tyranny of an entity that cared nothing for Roberts, but wanted only to use her until she died. Many attribute Roberts' contact and eventual teachings from Seth with having started the modern New Age movement.

Satan is under no obligation to obey anyone except God. Though *not* obligated to obey people who use magick, he *allows* them to think he must obey so that he can increase his sphere of influence. If people *really* knew that Satan would torment and kill every one of them in a moment, they would *not* be part of his plan. He hides his true malevolence well, behind a façade of "light" and "energy" that puts people at their ease yet marvelously enraptured by his "willingness" to be used of them.

Satan deceives people into thinking that they are able to *control* evil forces when in fact they are controlling *nothing*. The only thing people are doing is simply opening the *door* to the evil realm, through which fly evil entities, manifesting themselves in ways that people *want* to hear and see.

There is *no way* that Satan would allow himself to be used like a puppet by human beings (the very things he hates the most), because his ego is far too large to be subject to anyone. Consider the fact that Lucifer (Satan before his fall; Isaiah 14 and Ezekiel 28) loved himself so much that he rebelled against the living God! If he was/is completely unwilling to obey His own creator, why would he *possibly* be willing to be subject to the whims of human beings? He would *only* do this if it suited his higher purposes of ultimately *controlling* all people and things. This is extremely important to grasp and it cannot be stated strongly enough.

Satan is the father of lies, and he tells a tale like no one else. He convinces people that by using this magick they will have power over entities that must in turn do their bidding. The reality, of course, is that Satan has created the game *and* the rules by which people play. The entire thing, though, is based on a lie, in order for Satan to gain a much greater influence over this world. His outcome is guaranteed *under* the sovereignty of God.

If Satan cannot work *through* a person, he is relegated to working *around* them, or *indirectly* bringing things to bear on them. Imagine what this world would be like, though, if Satan and his minions *could* be in command of all of humanity. This is exactly what Satan through the Antichrist purposes to accomplish.

Fully empowering the Antichrist, Satan will weed out those who are not sold out to him. These will be eradicated through execution. Those remaining *will* be sold out to him and will receive the mark of the beast, whatever that turns out to be. This will seal the deal because once someone takes the mark there is no *undoing* it. We will get into that in the appropriate chapter of Revelation.

Can you imagine the absolute shock and mortification on a person's face when they realize they spent their entire life worshiping Satan, writing books about him at his behest, and doing things for him in order to achieve peace throughout the world, only to find out immediately *after* their death that it was all a gargantuan *lie*? They fully believed the lie so that they *conformed* to it. They became *one* with that lie. They firmly believed that theirs was a higher purpose and that they were doing everything good.

So solid was their belief in Satan's lies that they were unable to see the truth as *truth*. They gave themselves over to something that they thought was the answer to life, only to find out that it was no answer at all but merely a shell game, a shell game in which they *lost* their life forever. This is *tragic*, and there is no other way to say it. This is why God uses Christians to seek and save the lost by introducing them to the Truth of Jesus Christ.

In this life, people believe God because either He *is* Truth or they believe the lie that Satan perpetuates as truth. Of course, only one is actual truth. Think about people like Helena Blavatsky (Satanist) who spent her life believing the lies Satan foisted upon her. Think about others like her who wrote books allegedly dictated to them from higher or ascended masters. These were none other than Satan's henchmen, weaving a lie as masterfully as someone tells the truth. The only "reward" these people receive is to be given the same sentence as the one they worshiped in this life: *the Lake of Fire.*

Numerous books have been written on the Illuminati, Freemasonry, the occult, and Satanism. The one thing we must always remember is that God is fully in control. Many of the authors who write these books seemingly forget that, or do not emphasize it enough. God is in control of all things. What happens on this earth and in our universe does so because of God's sovereignty.

Just as Satan was only *allowed* to do certain things to Job, his family, and his holdings, so also is Satan kept constantly in check by God. There is nothing that Satan does that is not allowed by God, and as we read through and study the book of Revelation, we need to remember that constantly.

We need to realize and know that all the things that take place in Revelation do so at the direction of God Almighty in the form of the Lamb who was slain, Jesus Christ. Satan is used by God to achieve His own purposes. Satan does not have free reign. He is limited and, in at least some cases, *very* limited.

To God be the glory! Satan gains nothing unless God permits it. Ultimately, Satan is kept on a very short leash, though he wants people to believe that he is the one who controls things. Too many people believe that and wind up giving credit to the enemy of our souls, when in the final analysis Satan is a puppet – a very strong, diabolical, malevolent puppet. He is used in order that God will be glorified.

Never forget that God is *always* glorified. He is God, never abdicating His throne. He is worthy of our praise, adoration, and worship. As we go through the book of Revelation, let us with open heart and open arms seek to embrace His truth, giving Him all the glory that He so rightly and richly deserves!

Now, let's get into the book of Revelation, and may we be eternally blessed from the truth we find there.

5

REVELATION 5

As chapter five of the book of Revelation opens, we are partakers of a heavenly sight. Through the apostle John, we are brought right into the throne room of God Almighty. Here we see a number of things happening.

Revelation 5:1-3

"And I saw in the right hand of him that sat on the throne a book written within and on the backside, sealed with seven seals.

"And I saw a strong angel proclaiming with a loud voice, Who is worthy to open the book, and to loose the seals thereof?

"And no man in heaven, nor in earth, neither under the earth, was able to open the book, neither to look thereon," Revelation 5:1-3

The scene just described by the apostle John is in the *throne room of God*. We see a number of important things that we need to consider:

- *A seven-sealed book at God's right hand*
- *A question: Who is worthy to open it?*
- *During this brief silence, no man was found anywhere*

This appears at first to be a tragic scene. We first see God on the throne. Taking a moment to consider it, we can picture His majesty as He sits, fully in control of all things. All eyes are on Him awaiting His next command. To His right lies a book. This book has writing within on the front pages and the back pages (or possibly just one long page, as a scroll).

What do we know about the book? This book or scroll has been sealed with seven seals. We know that *seven* is representative of God because it is a perfect, completed number. In Genesis during the Creation there were a total of seven days, six of which God used for His creative purposes, and on the seventh, He *rested*. This seventh day is just as important as the previous six. In this same chapter of Revelation we will read of the *seven* Spirits, which are representative of the Holy Spirit. Prior to this chapter, Jesus dictates letters to John to *seven* churches in Asia Minor. The Bible is filled with references of sevens and their association with God.

MacArthur points out, *"This is typical of various kinds of contracts in the ancient world, including deeds, marriage contracts, rental and lease agreements, and wills. The inside of the scroll contained all the details of the contract, and the outside – or back – contained a summary of the document. In this case it almost certainly is a deed – the title deed to the earth (cf. Jer 32:7ff). Romans sealed their wills 7 times – on the edge at each roll – to prevent unauthorized entry. Hebrew ti-*

tle deeds required a minimum of 3 witnesses and 3 separate seals, with more important transactions requiring more witnesses and seals."[1]

Referring to the scroll the angel, strong and vibrant, asks the question, "*Who is worthy to open it?*" It is like a pageant is being played out in heaven. No one can be found. It is obviously an important scroll. Unless it can be opened, nothing can move forward.

What is so important about this particular book or scroll? Since only one individual is found worthy, it must be very important.

Revelation 5:4 – 7

"And I wept much, because no man was found worthy to open and to read the book, neither to look thereon.

"And one of the elders saith unto me, Weep not: behold, the Lion of the tribe of Judah, the Root of David, hath prevailed to open the book, and to loose the seven seals thereof.

"And I beheld, and, lo, in the midst of the throne and of the four beasts, and in the midst of the elders, stood a Lamb as it had been slain, having seven horns and seven eyes, which are the seven Spirits of God sent forth into all the earth.

"And he came and took the book out of the right hand of him that sat upon the throne."

The situation brought the apostle John to *tears*. As old as he was, even though sequestered as a prisoner to the Isle of Patmos, he was not too old to cry. He understood that the scroll was very *significant*. Without opening it, everything was at a standstill. God on the throne held the scroll, waiting for the worthy one to step up.

However, an elder – one of the 24 – came to him to ease his sorrow with good news. The Lion from the Tribe of Judah, the Root of David,

---

[1] John D. MacArthur *The MacArthur Study Bible* (Thomas Nelson 2006), 1969

had been found to be *worthy*. There can be no mistake here; the elder was referring to *Jesus Christ Himself*. Jesus is the Lion of the tribe of Judah, and He is the Root of David. The Messianic line comes *from* David *to* Jesus and the genealogies in the gospel accounts bear this out. Jesus is the Lamb that was slain and was raised to life again.

This is Jesus, God the Son, the God Christians worship. This view of Him as the Lamb explains in one image the work that He accomplished on behalf of the lost of this world. We know that Jesus lived on this planet in the form of a man roughly 2,000 years ago. We also know from many portions of Scripture that He lived without sin. One of the more well known passages is found in Paul's second letter to the believers at Corinth. There Paul says, *"For he hath made him to be sin for us, who knew no sin; that we might be made the righteousness of God in him"* (2 Corinthians 5:21).

The fact that Jesus lived His entire earthly life free from all sin put Him in the position of being able to offer Himself as a sacrifice for lost humanity. When He lived on earth, His glory was veiled from human eyes. People did not see Him as He was, and here in Revelation, John sees Him as the Lamb that was slain and risen from the dead.

During the event we call the Transfiguration recorded for us in Matthew 17:1-9, Mark 9:2-8, and Luke 9:28-36, for the briefest of moments, Jesus' deity and glorified body were clearly visible to those present. The Matthew account tells us *"And was transfigured before them: and his face did shine as the sun, and his raiment was white as the light. And, behold, there appeared unto them Moses and Elias talking with him."* This is Jesus' appearance He had *before* being born into this world. His humanity veiled His deity just as our human body veils our spirit.

Once we die, our spirit leaves what Paul refers to as this "earthly tent" (cf. 2 Corinthians 5:1-10). Our human bodies retain our spirit, and once dead our spirit floats free to be with Jesus. John saw the crucified, risen, and glorified Lamb of God in His throne room, in His natural environment. This is the way all authentic Christians will see the risen Lord one day.

In the text, *to be worthy* means to be *"of commendable excellence or merit."*[2] Strong's Exhaustive Concordance tells us that it means *"weighing, having weight, having the weight of another thing of like value, worth as much."*[3] The word "worthy" in Greek is *axios*, an adjective.

Certainly, Jesus is *that*, but how did He come to be worthy to open the book/scroll, and what is the *meaning* of the scroll? Jesus is worthy because of a number of things He accomplished (some previously mentioned):

- *He lived a sinless life*
- *At every step, He obeyed the Father's will*
- *There was never even a speck of evil or sin in Him*
- *He fulfilled every part of the Mosaic Law*
- *He was obedient even to death; the death on the cross*

Because of the things that Jesus accomplished without ever falling short in *thought*, *word*, or *deed*, He *became* worthy. When it came time for Him to be offered as the sacrifice for the lost of the world, He was found to be worthy because not once in His entire life had He ever fallen short of the Father's glory through sinning. He maintained that perfection throughout His entire life without ever faltering. Since He arrived to the point of death in that condition, He continued to be worthy to die for us. Had He ever succumbed to any sin at all, it would have canceled any chance He had to be the offering, and canceled any chance we have to receive salvation.

---

[2] http://dictionary.reference.com/browse/worthy
[3] http://net.bible.org/strong.php?id=514

IF Jesus had sinned, He would not have been able to die for us, and therefore would not have been able to offer salvation to us. We can be thankful above all things that He never sinned – *even once* – and was found to be the worthy sacrifice for us. Praise His holy Name.

Because of His perfection in obedience, He was elevated to the status of Supreme Ruler (Philippians 2:9-10). Initially, during His earthly life, He had been made a little lower than the angels (cf. Philippians 2:6-7; Hebrews 2:9), but afterwards, after He had completed everything that God the Father had given Him – God the Son – to do, He was again raised to His former position He had enjoyed prior to coming to earth (cf. Acts 2:23-24; 5:31).

Though Jesus came, lived, died, rose, and ascended into heaven roughly 2,000 years ago, there are people today who believe *they* are Jesus Christ. Jesus warned us that in the end times, these deceivers would come to us and try to cause us to follow them. One of these men is *Apollo C. Quiboloy* who, as a minister in the Philippines, states that He *is* Jesus Christ. He says that what Jesus *failed* to do during His earthly life, he is finishing. This is a common theme among false messiahs. They point to Jesus and use glowing terms when discussing Him, but they also always point out that He failed at something and now He is back (in them) to complete His mission.

Of course, the problem here is that Jesus proclaimed loudly and from the cross His dying words, "*It is finished!*" (John 19:30). He left nothing undone. Everything the Father gave Him to do He did (cf. John 5:17-47; 10:32). Had Jesus failed at anything, He would have canceled Himself out of the possibility of being our sacrifice. He did not fail, *ever*.

These are the words from Quiboloy himself about his identity: "*This is very important, because once this has been declared the Lord will have a residence here. Whoever He chooses to dwell in, automatically, that is the Son. That is the body. The Deliverer has come! The Father has come! He has come because He found Himself a body. He has come in a manner that they did not expect.*

"When He said, 'Now, You are My Son, you are My residence,' that meant He can live in man. His plan in the Garden of Eden, before the Fall was going to be accomplished.

"We thank the Father that on that day, He said, 'My Son...' I was made worthy not by myself, but by Him. I was made worthy to receive the inheritance – the Sonship and the Kingship. When you do that, a change happens within. A spiritual revolution happens within. The serpent seed is overthrown and you die. That's why when you repent, you die. You die to that human will. You are reduced to zero, but don't worry, because you'll rise again. Another spirit will be given to you so that you will live again. But when you live again, you'll live to do His will only. And I am your model."[4]

There are many places on Quiboloy's website where he states without equivocation that he is the Son of God. Of course, we know that Jesus Himself said, *"For many shall come in my name, saying, I am Christ; and shall deceive many"* (Mark 13:6). Someone is *lying.* Either Jesus lied to us, or Quiboloy is lying to us now. I am going out on a limb to say that *Quiboloy* is the one who is lying. In essence, Apollo C. Quiboloy is a *type* of Antichrist. He has the *spirit* of Antichrist. He is one in a long line of those who claim to be Jesus Christ. Between now and the time Antichrist is revealed to the world, many more will come. Quiboloy's words mix truth and error, just like his father, the devil.

Note that Quiboloy is actually saying he is *greater* than Jesus Christ, not only because he says that he is *finishing* the work that Jesus did not complete, but by other statements as well. His statements (*When*

---

[4]

http://www.kingdomofjesuschrist.org/2/PACQ/the_threefold_ministry_of_the_son7.html

He said, 'Now, You are My Son, you are My residence,' that meant He can live in man. His plan in the Garden of Eden, before the Fall was going to be accomplished,) are pure lies. Since the Holy Spirit birthed the Church on the day of Pentecost, He has taken up residence within authentic believers. That was roughly *2,000* years ago.

In other places, Quiboloy teaches that Christians can *be* sinless. Of course, this is the ideal and we will become sinless in the next life, but it is just not reality in this life because our sin nature has *not* been eradicated. It remains with us.

There is only *one* Jesus Christ and He – *as a Man* – lived roughly 2,000 years ago. He never sinned, and He *gave* Himself a ransom for many (cf. 1 Timothy 2:6). After His death, He was in the ground for three days and then rose again. He eventually ascended to the Father in heaven. Christ's ministry and mission to *fulfill* the Law and to *become* a propitiation for the sins of humanity were accomplished. He completed *both* of those things.

This is the Lamb that John sees in the heavenlies. This Lamb is worthy to open the seven-sealed scroll. This Lamb pleased the Father in every respect. It is also very important to note here that this Lamb – Jesus Christ – is the One who was found worthy to *open* the scroll. By doing so, it is important to understand what happens next.

Regarding this seven-sealed scroll, it becomes evident that opening it releases terrible judgments on the earth. Why would God do or allow this? How could He do this if this world was recognized as belonging to Satan? Jesus made this clear when He told His apostles, "*Hereafter I will not talk much with you: for the prince of this world cometh, and hath nothing in me*" (John 14:30; see also John 12:31; 1 John 5:18).

What did Jesus mean with that statement? If we go back to the time that Jesus was tempted by Satan, after the Holy Spirit guided Him out into the wilderness and just prior to the beginning of His public ministry, we begin to understand this comment from Jesus.

Immediately after Jesus was baptized by John the Baptist (cf. Matthew 3), the Holy Spirit leads Jesus into the wilderness for the express purpose of being tempted by Satan. The text states, "*Then was Jesus led up of the Spirit into the wilderness to be tempted of the devil*" (Matthew 4:1). I realize, of course, that the Bible tells us that God cannot be tempted with sin (James 1:12-18). The natural question, then, is if Jesus was/is God, how could He be tempted? Jesus was also fully human, and it was there that Satan attacked. He tried desperately to get Jesus to sin by illegitimately using His deity during the temptation process, but he still tempted Jesus' humanity.

As we read through the temptation process, please note that Satan kept well away from Jesus until *after* Jesus had been in the desert for forty days and forty nights. It was *then* that Satan came to Him (cf. Matthew 4:2-3). At His weakest point humanly speaking, Jesus was subjected to Satan's temptations.

Jesus passed each temptation with excellence, never stumbling at all. There was *never* a point at which He sinned. In Matthew 4:8-9 we read, "*Again, the devil taketh him up into an exceeding high mountain, and sheweth him all the kingdoms of the world, and the glory of them; And saith unto him, **All these things will I give thee**, if thou wilt fall down and worship me.*" I have added the emphasis because it is important to note that by *offering* these kingdoms to Jesus, Satan was claiming *ownership* of them. If he claimed ownership of them, and was *not* the actual owner, one would think Jesus would have called him on that.

Jesus does not correct Satan with this implied claim. He responds to Satan as if the implication of his claim is valid because it *is valid*. In essence, Satan owns the kingdoms of this world *for now*. He controls the earth. This does not mean that he is somehow not subject to

God's sovereignty, but it means that the *title deed* to earth is in Satan's possession.

Satan gained the title through deceptive means when he successfully tempted Eve – and through Eve, Adam – to sin. They did so by deciding that *Satan* was the one who was telling the truth, not God. Because they chose to believe Satan, he gained access to God's Creation from which he had been previously excised.

This is important to grasp because it helps us understand the entire reason for the *cross* along with the many results that are tied to the life, death, and resurrection of Jesus. It was not until Christ's death and resurrection three days later that not only had sin been atoned for, allowing people to exercise saving faith in Jesus Christ, but also the *title deed* to earth had changed hands. Though Satan is allowed to continue as if he still holds the title deed, the deed now rests with Jesus.

What Jesus *bought* through His death and resurrection was not only souls who had been held captive by Satan, but He also purchased the title deed to this world *back*. Adam and Eve were the human guardians that God had placed over His Creation. Humanity was the pinnacle of His Creation and it was their job to literally *rule* over it. This they did until the day they fell. When that happened, rule went from *Adam* to *Satan*. Satan gained control of earth legally. In order for God to regain possession of it, He must do that legally as well. Enter Jesus' life, death, and resurrection. Is it starting to make sense? There is a great deal in the book of Revelation that is far more than simply prophetic utterances and a timeline of future events.

The situation between Satan and Adam and Satan and God was very much like signing the deed of your home over to someone whom you lost it to as a *gambling* debt. Satan entered into a *huge* gamble with humanity. If neither Adam nor Eve buckled under the pressure of his temptation, Satan would lose. Had Adam and Eve not succumbed, there is an excellent chance that, having passed the test, they would have gained knowledge of good and evil without ever having to sin (just as God has knowledge of good and evil without ever sinning).

That was the gamble and the stakes were very high. Should Satan lose, he would be left with nothing except his ultimate fate. Since he won, he gained much. He gained the ability to intrude into humanity's world because we had literally invited him to do so. Since he was invited, he wasted no time in wresting control of this planet from humanity to himself.

Jesus was well aware of this when He made the statement that the prince of this world was coming and he had nothing on Him (Jesus). Jesus knew full well that this world belonged to Satan, which is why Jesus did not argue with him when Satan offered Jesus the kingdoms of the world in exchange for worship.

In other words, Satan was tempting Jesus to gain the world *without* having to go down the path that the Father had laid out for Jesus. Satan wanted Jesus to circumvent the Father's will. This Jesus refused to do, preferring at all costs to obey the Father every step of the way, even if it meant death on the cross and a brief time of spiritual separation from the Father, something Jesus had *never* experienced before.

Satan was offering a way for Jesus to become ruler of this planet if He would but only worship Satan. Of course, *if* Jesus did it this way He *would* have become ruler, but the cost would be terrible. Jesus refused to move from the path the Father set for Him. In the end, He would become ruler of this planet, but it would be accomplished through *legal* channels and without one speck of sin to sully the deal.

God is a God of truth and absolute morality, and because of that, He is legally bound to all the promises He makes. He can do nothing less. He takes none of this lightly. He cannot simply take control of this planet back from Satan without doing harm to His own principles and character. Therefore, He worked through the very legal system He created and *regained* the title to earth legally, by fulfilling the Law and never breaking one aspect of that Law through sin. That is what *earned* Him the right as the Lamb to take the book, or scroll. He had earned the right. He had been found worthy, though no one else had. Jesus literally retrieved the title deed to the earth, and He will eventually reign from David's throne in Jerusalem as absolute and undeniable proof that He *is* the rightful ruler of this planet.

It is clear that it was only due to the worthiness of the Lamb that the scene moved forward at all. Because of the Lamb, the seven-sealed scroll was unsealed by the Lamb Himself, each of the judgments fell to the earth in their preordained order, and its inhabitants experienced those judgments.

All the judgments within the seven-sealed scroll are tied *to* and controlled *by* the Lamb. It was all due to Christ's victory over all things including sin and His own death on the cross that made Him worthy to open the scroll at all. It is extremely important that we do not lose sight of this very important truth. Jesus *became* worthy through His absolute and unending obedience to the Father's will. Because of His worthiness, He was also found worthy to open the scroll. The Lamb is the One who directs all the action.

Those who argue about this judgment being due to God's wrath and another judgment representing man's or Satan's alleged wrath are thoroughly missing the point. Both man and Satan are fully under the auspices of God's sovereignty.

Had Jesus *not* been found worthy, not only would He not have been able to open the seven-sealed scroll, but He never would have been able to offer Himself as the propitiation for our sin! The book, or scroll here in chapter five of Revelation, represents the final aspect of God's plan to restore all honor and glory to Himself.

This is the last phase of the salvation project that was first revealed to humanity as a germ of an idea, way back in the Garden of Eden, following our first parents' sin. Everything God has done or directed has led to this last *playbook*. It is all God. It is all for His glory. It is to right all wrongs. The fact that it is the Lamb who is found to be worthy to reveal this final portion of God's will for our world, its people, the spiritual realm and all it contains should not surprise us.

Some believe that God's greatest purpose has been to *save* lost souls. While that is obviously incredibly important, it is only *part* of His overall plan. His actual highest purpose has been to showcase His perfect love to the universe and all its inhabitants, thereby glorifying Himself and no one else.

It is for His honor and His glory that God does anything and everything! This is the message of the entire book of Revelation. This is the only explanation for why the Lamb releases all of the judgments contained within the seven-sealed scroll.

As each rider moves across the landscape, as each judgment falls, as each demon obeys, it is all to *verify* the Lamb's sovereignty! He shares this with no one else, and for good reason. There is no other god besides Him! All praise, glory, and honor to the King of Kings, Lord of Lords, to God Almighty!

Revelation 5:8 – 14
"And when he had taken the book, the four beasts and four and twenty elders fell down before the Lamb, having every one of them harps, and golden vials full of odours, which are the prayers of saints.

"And they sung a new song, saying, Thou art worthy to take the book, and to open the seals thereof: for thou wast slain, and hast redeemed us to God by thy blood out of every kindred, and tongue, and people, and nation;

"And hast made us unto our God kings and priests: and we shall reign on the earth.

"And I beheld, and I heard the voice of many angels round about the throne and the beasts and the elders: and the number of them was ten thousand times ten thousand, and thousands of thousands;

"Saying with a loud voice, Worthy is the Lamb that was slain to receive power, and riches, and wisdom, and strength, and honour, and glory, and blessing.

"And every creature which is in heaven, and on the earth, and under the earth, and such as are in the sea, and all that are in them, heard I saying, Blessing, and honour, and glory, and power, be unto him that sitteth upon the throne, and unto the Lamb for ever and ever.

"And the four beasts said, Amen. And the four and twenty elders fell down and worshipped him that liveth for ever and ever."

If there is any doubt as to the identity of the Lamb, it should be eradicated with the information we read in verse 9b: *"for thou wast slain, and hast redeemed us to God by thy blood out of every kindred, and tongue, and people, and nation."* The Lamb was *slain* and by His death redeemed many from every kindred, tongue, people, and nation. This is Jesus Christ who died, yet lives! He is worthy of every form of praise our lips can *utter*, our thoughts can *think*, or our lives can *live*. There is no one who is as worthy as He is, and certainly no one who is *more* worthy. The devil has lost and he knows it. He is on borrowed time. Jesus is Victorious! He has gained salvation for us that we might live with Him forever. Is He not worthy of our unending praise because of it?

Notice verse 13, which says, *"And every creature which is in heaven, and on the earth, and under the earth, and such as are in the sea, and all that are in them, heard I saying, Blessing, and honour, and glory, and power, be unto him that sitteth upon the throne, and unto the Lamb for ever and ever."* Do you see what is happening here? *EVERY* creature…

- *In heaven*
- *On the earth*
- *Under the earth*
- *In the sea*

All these creatures *will* worship Him, whether they want to or not. This is at a time some point in the future when everything will bow the knee and give praise to the *only* God, our Savior and Lord Jesus Christ! All things will offer rightful praise to God, the Son! As authentic believers, we can and should be praising Him now for everything that comes into our life and for everything that He is to us! There is no reason to *wait* for the future.

Are you offering Him praise for the things that come into your life? Are you praising Him – even if it is a sacrifice of praise when things are difficult – because He is God, because He cares for you, and because He loves you enough to have died for you?

◆———————— 6 ————————◆

REVELATION 6

Revelation 6:1

"And I saw when the Lamb opened one of the seals, and I heard, as it were the noise of thunder, one of the four beasts saying, Come and see."

The fact that Jesus was found worthy to open the Scroll is one thing. The fact that opening the scroll *begins* a series of events that change the earth and its citizens forever is *another*. Please note that *Jesus* is the One who is opening the Scroll here. The contents of the Scroll represent *God's wrath* and no one else's because each *seal, trumpet,* and *bowl* represent God's judgment, which is poured out as wrath. If the contents were somehow *not* directly from God, why would Jesus open it?

Certainly, while the spirits of darkness and even Satan himself *are* utilized to bring about God's purposes for this earth and its people from the moment that the Scroll is opened, this does *not* mean that this is somehow *not* God's wrath that we are witnessing. It most certainly *is* God's wrath. The entirety of the scroll represents God's judgment and wrath on the earth and its citizens. It is the document that represents the culmination of the ages.

In his commentary on Revelation, J. Hampton Keathley III notes, *"This clearly shows that the seven-sealed book contains prophecies of all the judgments necessary to bring rebellious man to his knees, defeat Satan's kingdom, restore the kingdom of the earth under the visible authority of God, and to reestablish man as God had originally intended before the fall and the invasion of the tyrant, Satan* (Gen. 1:26 28)."[5]

As stated in the last chapter, there should be no question as to the identity of the Individual who controls *all* events that emanate from the seven-sealed scroll. The Lamb controls the *entire* scroll and its *contents*. He not only gains access to the scroll, but also has control over the opening of each seal within it. The Lamb *directs* each seal, trumpet, and bowl. It is as if each one *builds* on the one before it.

This *proves* that only one person was found worthy enough to *take* the scroll and open its contents. Everything that is revealed and pours out from each *seal, trumpet,* or *bowl* does so because of the Lamb. He opens each seal, trumpet, and bowl according to His *will* and His *timing*. He is dependent upon *no one*, and in fact, *all* are dependent upon Him.

---

[5] J. Hampton Keathley III *Studies in Revelation* (Biblical Studies Press, 1997), 89

Keathley quotes Wilber Smith as well, who states, "*what is to take place on earth is under the complete control and direction of heaven, so that we may safely say, judging from this book, as well as from other prophetic books in the Scripture, that everything that takes place on this earth only fulfills the Word of God. This principle is remarkably set forth in the preliminary announcements concerning the kings of the earth going forth to make war with the Lamb. Though we read of the ten kings satanically inspired, having one mind and giving their power and authority unto the beast (17:12, 13), nevertheless, it is God who 'did put in their hearts to do his mind, and to come to one mind, and to give their kingdom unto the beast, until the words of God should be accomplished' (17:17).*"[6]

In essence, the scroll is the title deed to earth. God will bring all humanity and the powers of darkness to their knees through the process outlined in the seven-sealed scroll, which we term the *Tribulation*. There are a number of reasons why the Tribulation is a necessary part of God's plan for this world *and* Israel. Some, like Covenant and Reformed Theologians, along with Preterists, argue that those of us who believe the Tribulation to be a coming reality are *making* it happen by *wishing* it to happen. This is absurd and is nothing more than New Age thinking. New Agers believe we are gods and can control our own reality. No matter how much a person wishes something to happen, it will *not* happen unless and until God wants it to occur. The chart on the next page briefly outlines the reasons for the Tribulation from a biblical perspective (cf. Daniel 9:24-25).

On Calvary, Christ defeated Satan and his minions. He said, "*It is finished!*" However, God has allowed Satan to continue to roam the earth, accusing,and harassing God's children in order that God's will would be accomplished.

---

[6] J. Hampton Keathley III *Studies in Revelation* (Biblical Studies Press, 1997), 99

God Will Accomplish Six Things with Israel (Dan. 9:24-25)

Finish the Transgression

Israel's rebellion needs to come to an end.

God will do that before the 2nd Coming of Christ

To Make an End to Sin

Unlike Christ, Israel committed sins daily, which stem from their rebellious attitude

To Make Atonement for Iniquity

While Jesus atoned for Israel's sins, it will not be applied until Israel accepts Him as Messiah (this refers to the NATION of Israel, not individual Jews)

To Bring in Everlasting Righteousness

When Israel repents and believes in Christ as Messiah at His 2nd Coming, she will be given lasting righteousness at that point.

To Seal Up the Vision & Prophecy

Revelation that comes through vision or prophecy will no longer be needed. All will have been totally fulfilled.

To Anoint the Most Holy Place

Consecrating the articles of the Temple or Tabernacle

Yet, we know that Satan is a fully defeated foe. There is no question of it. None at all. It is a done deal. On Calvary, *because* Jesus defeated Satan, He also regained the title deed to the earth, something that had been taken from the first Adam. It is not until the Tribulation that God actively works to disengage Satan from his long-standing rule of the earth and the air above it.

Through the twenty-one judgments of the *seals*, *trumpets*, and *bowls*, God will break Satan's hold on the earth. God will also break the power of rebellion that is inherent within His people, the Israelites. We need to understand that even with all of the judgments God pours out He is still *merciful*. That may be difficult to comprehend, but consider that God has the right (and the reason) to wipe out the population of this entire earth as He did during Noah's day. It is because of His mercy that He does not do that. His mercy *constrains* Him, even in the midst of all the judgments He pours out on the earth.

The judgments, born from God's own wrath, are designed to show just how feeble Satan and his workers of iniquity truly are as they work against God. This same holds true of all people. The rebellion that most people have toward God is nothing compared with God's ability. It is absolutely *nothing*, yet people think they are something and have the capacity to stand against the Living God. Absurd.

God's mercy *keeps* Him from obliterating us in order that the very last person to be saved *will* be saved. God is so merciful we cannot comprehend it. Yet too many think they know better than God. They believe they have it all figured out, and because they offer quips that Christianity does not answer to their satisfaction they believe likewise that God would have no retort. They are in for a shock when they stand before this Living God, who gave them every chance possible in this life to turn to Him for salvation. They refused repeatedly and have only themselves to blame, something they will unfortunately do throughout eternity!

<u>The</u> Lamb is Completely in Charge

While it is clear that <u>the</u> Lamb (not "a" Lamb; there is only One Lamb!) opens each seal, trumpet, and bowl according to His own desires, it is *equally* clear that throughout this chain of events, the Lamb *uses* many other beings to *perform* the very things within each judgment. They will carry out the specifics of each judgment, whether it is a seal, trumpet, or bowl. This is no different from God using the Babylonians to overtake the nation of Israel during the period of the Old Testament. The actual Babylonian army overcame and defeated Israel, but God *directed* it. Yet, the Babylonian army was held accountable.

One example we can point to (of many) is Ezekiel 38. Here, we see a group of nations who will come against Israel. Note, though, that God credits *Himself* with causing these nations to band together to attack Israel. He says, "*And say, Thus saith the Lord GOD; Behold, **I am against thee**, O Gog, the chief prince of Meshech and Tubal: And **I will turn thee back, and put hooks into thy jaws, and I will bring thee forth**, and all thine army, horses and horsemen, all of them clothed with all sorts of armour, even a great company with bucklers and shields, all of them handling swords*" (Ezekiel 38:3-4,emphasis added).

To the leader referred to as "Gog," the Lord says that He (God) is against *him*. Because of that, He will cause Gog to turn and decide to invade Israel. Why does God do this? It is to show the world *and* Israel that God has not given up on Israel. It is also to bring glory to Himself. Here are the verses: "*And it shall come to pass at the same time when Gog shall come against the land of Israel, saith the Lord GOD, that my fury shall come up in my face. For in my jealousy and in the fire of my wrath have I spoken, Surely in that day there shall be a great shaking in the land of Israel; So that the fishes of the sea, and the fowls of the heaven, and the beasts of the field, and all creeping things that creep upon the earth, and all the men that are upon the face of the earth, shall shake at my presence, and the mountains shall be thrown down, and the steep places shall fall, and every wall shall fall to the ground. And I will call for a sword against him throughout all my mountains, saith the Lord GOD: every man's sword shall be against his brother. And I will plead against him with pestilence and with blood; and I will rain upon him, and upon his bands, and upon the many people that are with him, an overflowing rain, and great hailstones, fire, and brimstone"* (Ezekiel 38:18-22).

In the above text, even though we have just read that God is the One who will *cause* Gog to invade Israel, God says that He will overcome Gog and the invaders through a variety of ways. God Almighty will turn the sword on the soldiers so that they will begin fighting each other. God will also send illness and bloodletting, and finally, God will pummel and overcome Gog and his armies with huge hailstones, fire, and brimstone! At first glance, that does not appear to be fair (since God is bringing the invasion about), but if we consider the fact that *all* men are incredible sinners, what God is really doing is *directing* that which is already resident within Gog and inciting Gog to do what he would do *anyway*. If you have a difficulty with that, then you will need to take it up with God. Good luck on that, by the way.

To Magnify Himself

As stated previously (and it cannot be stated *too* much!), the ultimate reason God brings this whole situation about is for one purpose only: *"Thus will I magnify myself, and sanctify myself; and I will be known in the eyes of many nations, and they shall know that I am the LORD"* (Ezekiel 38:23). God does all of this to magnify His Name. He does *not* do this for Israel or for individual *Jews*. He does it all so that His Name will be glorified in all the earth, among all the nations. Amen, and *amen*. God needs no other reason for the reason He does anything. It is to bring glory to Himself.

Let's talk about Satan for a moment. We know that Satan has a wrathful attitude toward all of God's creation. We also know that during part of this coming period of time in which the contents of the

Scroll are poured out onto humanity and the earth, Satan becomes even *more* wrathful. However, this does not mean that God's wrath is poured at one point, while Satan's is poured out at another point. This is not a tag-team event! Satan has and will continue to hate all of God's Creation! He hates mankind! He wants all of us to go to the Lake of Fire with him. His demeanor is always filled with wrath towards us, even when he is trying to make people believe he is some benevolent ascended master!

God *pours* out the contents of the Scroll, and God *controls* the contents. Satan has no absolute control over anything at all. If we consider Job as an example, we will note (or *should*) that Satan could do absolutely nothing to Mr. Job without God's permission. Even when Satan was *granted* permission, he still had limits. God at first allowed Satan to do what he wanted to Job's children and possessions.

Satan sent a tornado and marauding enemies who took Mr. Job's herds and his children. Was Satan filled with wrath then? Of course he was, because that is his normal *demeanor*! He can do nothing else *but* be filled with wrath because he hates God and the entirety of His Creation. God merely allowed Satan to be himself where Job was concerned, with limitations.

Can you imagine how Satan went about this? I can see him rubbing his ugly hands together in glee, believing that it would take little to knock Job off his high horse! Soon, he would be complaining to God saying, "*Woe is me! Why, oh why, God?*" However, to Satan's chagrin, Job did not do this. The text says that when he heard the news that his herds had been stolen or killed and that his children were all dead, his response was, "*Naked came I out of my mother's womb, and naked shall I return thither: the LORD gave, and the LORD hath taken away; blessed be the name of the LORD*" (Job 1:21).

The ENTIRE Tribulation Is God's Wrath

7-Years of Tribulation Signaling the End of God's Patience with Israel and Humanity

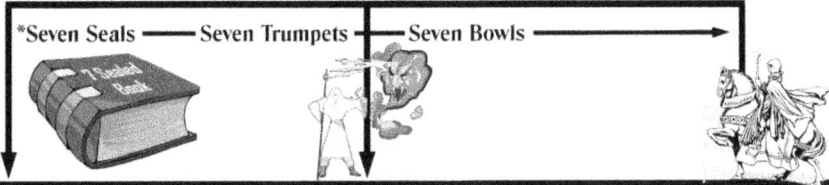

*Seven Seals —— Seven Trumpets —— Seven Bowls ——

Trib Starts with Israel signing Covenant with Antichrist	Midpoint when Antichrist Breaks the Covenant and Demands worship	Trib Ends when Antichrist is destroyed at the Coming of Jesus Christ!

(*Seals, Trumpets and Bowls All Come from Same Seven-Sealed Book, which is ONLY Opened by Lamb)

6 Reasons Why All of Trib is God's Wrath

Jesus Only is Found Worthy to Open the Seven-Sealed Book (Revelation 5)	Israel Signs Covenant w/Antichrist (Daniel 9:27 - 70th Week)	Earth Dwellers Speak of the Wrath of the Lamb (Revelation 6)
Tribulation Would Not Begin if Not For the Lamb Opening the Book	Antichrist REVEALED to the World	Petrified w/Fear of LAMB'S wrath!
Satan is NOT in Picture at Start of the Tribulation; Only **Christ**	Tribulation Begins with Command of Jesus (Revelation 6)	Tribulation Ends with the Return of Jesus (Revelation 19)

©2010 F. DeRuvo

When that did not work, Satan complained about not being able to touch Job's person, so God gave him permission with one proviso. God forbid Satan to kill Job. There is not a time when Satan can do whatever he wants to do whenever he feels like it. He is always kept on a leash and *God* holds that leash.

If at any point Satan were allowed to do what he *could* do, there would be no Christians left on earth. More than that, there would likely be no one left on earth! Satan wants *everyone* to join him in the Lake of Fire, but he has no control over the timing of each person's death! He does not know when I will die or you will die. He might be able to make an educated guess based on his vantage point from the spiritual realm, but he can't call it. Satan can *tempt* people to take their own lives (or someone else's), yet he cannot *decide* when they will die.

At no time does Satan ever have full control over anything. God uses Satan to accomplish His purposes, just as He uses the Assyrians or the Greeks or the Romans to achieve His purposes.

The idea – as some claim – that *part* of the Tribulation is God's wrath and *part* is Satan's wrath (or man's wrath) is absurd. God uses everything and everyone at His disposal to bring about His plans and purposes (cf. Proverbs 16:1-4, 9, 33; 19:21; 21:1, 31; Jeremiah 10:12-13; Amos 4:7; Daniel 1:2) .

Because God uses Satan does not mean that we can rightfully say that it is *Satan's wrath* (or *man's* wrath against men), as if he is allowed to do whatever he wishes. In some ways, yes, Satan evidences his wrath, but Satan is *always angry!* There is *never* a time when he is not angry because of his overwhelming hatred of God's Creation.

In some ways, men evidence their wrath against other men or, stupidly, against God. This does not mean that God gives up control and sits back, not caring or unable to control what happens here, and that man can do anything because he is filled with wrath.

Besides our example of Job and the references already provided, there are many instances in the Old Testament alone where God specifically uses a nation of people as an arm of judgment against Israel. Does that mean God is culpable? No, it means that whatever He does, or allows, is because He is righteous and holy. If God looked into Nebuchadnezzar's heart and saw that ol' Neb wanted to and was planning on attacking Israel, then if God *directs* that, allowing Israel to fall into Neb's hands, who is to be blamed? Nebuchadnezzar.

It is fair to say that God *used* Judas Iscariot to accomplish His purposes as far as God the Son, Jesus, was concerned. How did He do this? By simply *knowing* what was already *inside* Judas Iscariot and knowing that Judas would be *likely* to betray Jesus because of his own inner weaknesses and complete lack of understanding where Jesus was concerned.

Did God actually *cause* Judas to do what he did? He *oversaw* it, but He did not *directly* bring about Judas' sinful betrayal. Satan did that. In Luke, we read, "*Then entered Satan into Judas surnamed Iscariot, being of the number of the twelve*" (Luke 22:3). This occurred on the very night Jesus would be betrayed by this man.

On that same night, as recorded by Matthew, Jesus said, "*The Son of man goeth as it is written of him: but woe unto that man by whom the Son of man is betrayed! It had been good for that man if he had not been born*" (Matthew 26:24; Mark 14:21). Obviously, even though Satan entered into Judas, helping him do what he already was capable of doing, Judas is held accountable for it.

In the gospel of John, we read these words: "*And supper being ended, the devil having now put into the heart of Judas Iscariot, Simon's son, to betray him*" (John 13:2). Later in that same chapter, we read these comments: "*Jesus answered, He it is, to whom I shall give a sop, when I have dipped it. And when he had dipped the sop, he gave it to Judas Iscariot, the son of Simon. And after the sop Satan entered into him. Then said Jesus unto him, That thou doest, do quickly*" (John 13:26-27). It appears that Jesus was very aware that Satan had just entered Judas. Recognizing that, and knowing *why* Satan himself had entered into Judas, it seems that what Jesus says – "*That thou doest, do quickly*" – is directed *to* Satan, who now *possessed* Judas.

Note here that Satan had a plan and the plan was obviously to incite the crowds to crucify Jesus. Satan wanted Jesus dead and he had tried unsuccessfully on a number of previous occasions to have Jesus killed. For all his intelligence, Satan was not aware of the fact that it was for death that Jesus came, as one of His main reasons. Had Satan known that Christ's death on the cross fulfilled a number of prophecies (cf. Psalm 22), it is highly unlikely that he would have entered Judas in order to cause Judas to betray Jesus.

In all of this, though, Satan was *controlled*. There has never been a time (or even a moment) when he was *not* controlled! This is at least part of the reason he is so angry. He *knows* he is not God, and he also knows he will *never* be God. His doom is sure and he knows it is coming. Any anger he possesses is due to these things and the fact that God loves His Creation so much that He was willing to die in order to redeem it! These things *gall* Satan tremendously. This does *not* mean that Satan is allowed free reign.

What we will see as we continue to move through Revelation is an *ordered chaos*. In other words, what will *appear* to be chaos with no controlling aspects from the perspective of the people on earth is clearly and unequivocally ordained and controlled by God Almighty.

The Tribulation is *God's* wrath, not Satan's or man's. To say that Satan's wrath is one part and God's is the other part is to deny God's sovereignty. It takes away from the very character of God! Satan is *always* filled with wrath. That is the only emotion he has toward all of God's Creation. That is *not* God's response all the time. He has reserved the period of the Tribulation for pouring out of His wrath. This will be poured out in concentrated doses to those on this earth and the earth itself.

Satan is *used* by God. His anger is *used* by God. The depth of his hatred for mankind is *used* by God. That is the key, though. God *uses* these things that are already there to fulfill His purposes and His plans, all for His glory. By fulfilling these purposes, Satan winds up doing what he hates – *glorifying God!*

Revelation 6:2 – The First Seal

"And I saw, and behold a white horse: and he that sat on him had a bow; and a crown was given unto him: and he went forth conquering, and to conquer."

Immediately after the Lamb opens the very first seal, a white horse with a rider comes onto the scene. Theologians have disagreed (what's new?) over the identity of this individual. One thing we know for sure is that with this horse and rider come a type of *upheaval.* This rider has a bow and a crown. He goes out to conquer. There is no mention of arrows, just a bow, which could mean a number of things. It could mean that while this rider *seems* or *appears* to be on a peaceful mission, he does not have anything to back it up. He has no useful weaponry as a show of force. A bow is no good without arrows.

However, this rider goes out to conquer and he wears a crown. Dr. Arnold G. Fruchtenbaum points out that this particular crown is a *stephanos* crown (in the Greek), not a *diadem* as would be worn by Jesus, *the* Sovereign. In English, both words *mean* crown, so it is translated *crown.* This is why word studies as well as context are so important. As an aside, many of the illustrations throughout this book are based on parts of *Footsteps of the Messiah*, a book about the End Times, by Fruchtenbaum. This is a book well worth owning.

It would appear then that this individual:

1. *Does not possess weapons that will do any good (because the arrows are missing), and*
2. *Is a sort of imposter. He* <u>looks</u> *like a king of sorts, but he is not truly a king because of the type of crown he wears.*

Some believe that this rider is Jesus Himself, but as you can tell, this author disagrees with that based on the two things just listed. It would appear then that either this rider *is* the Antichrist, or the rider and horse *create* the situation in which the Antichrist *appears*.

A number of commentators have rightly pointed out that this cannot be Jesus for the simple reason that He arrives at the *end* of the Tribulation, not at the beginning. For those who prefer to allegorize the meaning of Scripture, then they often do what they prefer anyway. The truth of the matter is that this scenario does not *fit* Jesus.

As stated, when this horse and rider appear on the scene, there is a political *upheaval*. This rider is given the ability to *conquer,* and that likely has to do, not with war itself, but the ability to conquer men's *hearts*. This is probably why he does not have any arrows. His intent is not to kill, but to *rule over* people by conquering them *politically* and *ideologically*.

He wins the hearts of the people just as certain politicians have the ability to do the same thing with the populace from time to time.

Think about President Obama's run for president. There was a tidal wave of support for him that literally catapulted him into the Oval Office! He *conquered* politically, handily defeating his political opponents. He did not shoot anyone, and certainly did not kill anyone. Yet he was unequivocally victorious. President Obama *conquered*.

The First Seal – White Rider of Revelation 6:1-2

1. The Antichrist

White Horse & Rider
Revelation 6:2

The Rider on the **White Horse**

Man wearing a crown and conquering, and to conquer.

Stephanos Crown
Revelation 6:2

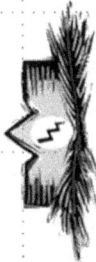

This is the crown of an over-comer, or victor. This is not the *diadem* crown, the crown of sovereignty or royalty.

Diadem Crown
Revelation 19

CHRIST KING

Messiah wears the diadem crown, signifying royalty.

2. Names of the Antichrist
Various Scripture

Seed of Satan	Genesis 3:15
Little Horn	Daniel 7:8
King of Fierce Countenance	Daniel 8:23
Prince that Shall Come	Daniel 9:26
Desolator	Daniel 9:27
Willful King	Daniel 11:36
Man of Sin	II Thess 2:3
Son of Perdition	II Thess 2:3
Lawless One	II Thess 2:8
The Beast	Revelation 11:7

Taken together, these names portray him as the epitome of evil in the human realm.

3. Will Not Be Jewish

Will have a natural origin
- Not Jewish

HALLELUJAH

Daniel 11:37:
"the God of his fathers"

Allows for a wider interpretation
Incorrectly translated "God" in KJV and should be translated:
"the gods of his fathers"

pages 204-216 in Footsteps

4. Will be Gentile

Biblical Typology (only 1):
- Antiochus Epiphanes

Biblical Imagery:
- the word "sea" is a symbol of Gentile nations (Rev 17:15)

Times of the Gentiles
- Ends at 2nd Coming
- Final ruler of Times of Gentiles will be a Gentile, not a Jew

Daniel 9:26-27
"the people of the prince that shall come" refers to the Roman army that destroyed Jerusalem in A.D. 70. Romans = Gentiles

5. Supernatural Origin

Counterfeit virgin conception found in Genesis 3:15

There will be enmity between Satan's seed and the woman's.

II Thessalonians 2:9 is another verse that deals with Antichrist's supernatural origin.

"working of Satan"

"all power and signs and lying wonders"

6. Character & Rise

Will always have access to the satanic and demonic realm.

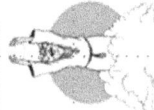

Will accept the offer the true Son rejected - worshiping Satan in exchange for the kingdoms. This begins his rise to political and religious domination of the world (Daniel 11:38-39; Revelation 13:2)

Rise to power is detailed in Daniel 8:23-25 and will give him:
- ability to solve supernatural riddles ("dark sentences")
- will have Satan's power
- will seek to destroy the holy people

White usually represents the good guy or peace. You may remember that symbolism from the old westerns. The good guy always wore a lighter colored hat, while the bad guy was always wearing a dark colored hat. This allowed the audience to know immediately which was which and not get them confused (in black and white movies).

Here, though, we have a bit of a sleight of hand, because though this rider is *white* representing peace, he actually goes out to conquer and to rule over. Because he wears a *stefanos* crown, he himself is under someone else's authority. He is under the authority of the *Lamb*. The average person of the earth will not know that, though. They will not be aware of that because they will simply be so grateful that *peace* has been achieved in the Middle East! No one will realize that this is not a lasting peace at all, not even lasting the seven years that it was designed (by Antichrist) to last.

Revelation 6:2-3 – The Second Seal

"And when he had opened the second seal, I heard the second beast say, Come and see.

"And there went out another horse that was red: and power was given to him that sat thereon to take peace from the earth, and that they should kill one another: and there was given unto him a great sword."

There is no real sequential timing that is revealed to us. One seal is opened and then it seems as the next is opened almost right away, though we do not really know how much time passes between the opening of each new seal, trumpet, or bowl. It could happen that the first seal is opened and then months go by before the second one is opened. We do not know. All we know is that these seals, trumpets, and bowls all occur within the framework of a seven-year period of time.

When the second seal is opened (again, by the Lamb), we see another horse. This one is red, and notice that the power to kill was *given* to this rider. He cannot kill by his own power. He is *given* the power *and* permission to kill, and ultimately, it is for a limited period of time.

The text states that the rider was *given* a great sword. Again, the ability to kill is granted to this rider, along with the means to do it. The fact that the sword is *great* may mean that there will be much death on the earth when the second seal is opened.

The first horse and rider (white) was given the ability to *conquer politically*. The first rider brings peace, albeit a tenuous and temporary one, as this second rider is given the ability to create war by *removing* peace from the earth. War robs the world or areas of it of peace and leads to casualties and *death*. This is what the second rider is able to accomplish. That is his sole mission, under the direction of the Lamb.

This is another reason why it is difficult to state that the first rider – though white – represents Jesus. When Jesus comes to this earth physically, He will address all things and will rule *supremely*. Nations waging war will not occur. It cannot happen under His rule.

Yet here we plainly see that after the first rider comes along a second one appears on the scene that brings war with him. The first rider brings political change leading to a false peace, while the second capitalizes on the political change caused by the first rider and from that ushers in *war*.

We can start to see that it is going to be a rough time on the earth. Everything is going to be in a state of flux, constantly changing. Nothing will stay the same and people will lose any sense of security that they did have about the world. First, they see a type of peace, when one individual rises to the top to take control of the world.

This does not go over well with many, though, who opt to fight against that totalitarian regime that is being set up. War breaks out all over the earth.

Think about the nations that cannot get along *now*. It will only be worse when the Antichrist rises to take his preordained place in the world, as leader *of* the world. Not everyone will go along with the Antichrist's plan...at first.

Think of the problems that face our world in 2010. The Gulf oil leak allowed somewhere between 80,000 and 100,000 barrels into the ocean *daily*. It forced its way out of the manmade well at between 20,000 and 70,000 psi. It was finally contained.

Billions of *barrels* of oil leaked into the ocean, wound up being picked up by the Oceanic current (which moves faster than the currents in the Gulf), and the leaked oil moved across the globe.

We have this problem in the Gulf and the continuing "normal" weather problems like massive tornados that knock homes and towns over and earthquakes that move cities off their foundations, or as in the case of the recent Calexico earthquake, push the bottom edge of California into Mexico by thirty-one inches.

The oil is and will continue to kill wildlife at unprecedented levels, which creates loss of jobs and food. Areas that become uninhabitable because of the oil and destruction will require the relocation of millions of people.

This seems to be just the tip of the iceberg. The United States will become more dependent on foreign oil suppliers, prices will skyrocket, and those who are hurting for jobs and/or money will be at their wit's end. Unable to provide for their household and with the state and local governments incapable of bearing the burdens, who knows what people will do once they realize there is little help.

Scientists have also predicted that within the next few years, we will begin to see solar flares as we have never seen. These may well cause total blackouts throughout the earth, destroying all electronic equipment in a very short time.

Imagine life on the earth instantly reverting to the Stone Age! This could very well be the future scenario that takes place in the not-too-distant future. Tragically, there seems to be little we can do to avoid it. The best we can do is to prepare for some of these upcoming events as best we can.

I am not talking about the madness that went into Y2K preparation, but in many ways, what the future holds *prior* to the beginning of the Tribulation will be far worse. Having food stores on hand with additional resources like water, first-aid supplies, plants, a place to grow fresh vegetables and possibly an emergency source for electricity or a radio that can be hand-cranked to hear the emergency channels and to provide light might be the bare minimum to have on hand. A number of these radios also have USB ports, allowing someone to charge their cell phones!

Why am I advocating this? Simply because though I believe the Rapture will occur *prior* to the start of the Tribulation, we have absolutely no clue *when* the Tribulation will begin. Since we do not know when the Tribulation will start, we have no idea how bad things will become prior to the Rapture.

We *cannot* do what the Millerites did in the mid-1800s, when they sold everything, put on white robes and sat on a hill waiting for Jesus to return! That kind of teaching is absolute nonsense. We are to be working *while* we wait (cf. Luke 19:13; 1 Corinthians 15:58; 1 Thessalonians 5:6; John 9:4; Mark 16:15). Beyond this, many of us authentic Christians may *die* naturally before either the Rapture or the start of the Tribulation.

My sister very unexpectedly died a few years ago, yet she firmly believed that she would be alive for the Rapture. It was obviously not to be, and she is far better off now. We cannot go through this life thinking that we know when God's timetable will kick in, because in most cases, we do not. We should plan for the worst scenario and if the Lord takes us in the Rapture, then someone will break into our home and use what we stored up for our own use but left behind.

Revelation 6:5-6 – The Third Seal
"And when he had opened the third seal, I heard the third beast say, Come and see. And I beheld, and lo a black horse; and he that sat on him had a pair of balances in his hand.

"And I heard a voice in the midst of the four beasts say, A measure of wheat for a penny, and three measures of barley for a penny; and see thou hurt not the oil and the wine."

What John hears and writes down for us is a *terrible* situation. We are talking about *famine* resulting from food shortages throughout the world. This third seal opens and we see a black horse and the rider has a pair of balances. There will be very tough times ahead, with not enough food for people to eat and the danger of a lack of oil and wine as well.

It will cost quite a bit of money to buy just the basics in order to survive. For those who do not have a garden to grow their own food, it will be very tough indeed. Those who *have* gardens may find the need to protect them because of the constant threat of thieves. People will be hungry enough to take whatever they can get. When people get hungry, they are certainly not above stealing.

Wars throughout the world (second rider) give rise to famines. Normally, whenever war occurs (whether local or global), famines, sickness, and death is not that far behind. This is a fact of history that only the completely naïve will attempt to negate.

This third rider brings those very things, on the heels of war. Famines, sickness, and death will occur throughout the world. Notice in most of these judgments, the riders are free to go anywhere on earth? Most of these judgments are not segregated to a specific location on the earth. While some are, most are not, which means that people all over the globe will be impacted by these judgments.

The concept of three measures of barley for a penny, a measure of wheat for a penny, etc., is interesting, but what does it mean? Keathley states, "*The denarius, as a Roman coin, in ancient times was a normal day's wage. In New Testament times this coin would purchase eight quarts of wheat, or eight measures (one measure equals about one quart) or 24 quarts of bar-ley. Wheat was the better grain and barley was normally used only for livestock except in times of scarcity. During the Tribulation, however, one denarius (a full day's wage) will buy only one measure (about one meal) of wheat, or three meals of barley with nothing left. Of course, the larger the family, the worse it will be. But note the words, "do not harm the oil and the wine." These were luxury items which will apparently be unharmed at this point. There will be plenty of luxury items but only the super rich will have them. The average man will spend all he has on the bare essentials.*"[7]

If this is true – and there is little reason to doubt its veracity – the result will be tragic. Again, people who are used to either being able to earn what they need or those who have become used to government handouts will find themselves barely able to survive, if at all. Think of how that will force much of humanity to get what they need any way they can. Of course, this is in the midst of the Tribulation and it is this author's belief that the invisible Church will be gone. Nonetheless, there is no reason to avoid planning for times when things are in short supply.

---

[7] J. Hampton Keathley III *Studies in Revelation* (Biblical Studies Press, 1997), 104

By the way, it is good to point out that certainly some of the imagery John describes *is* allegorical, or figurative. Do I expect an actual white horse and rider to appear on the horizon, or a red one, or a black one? No, these are obviously *symbolic* of something else. They are *literary* devices to give us a picture of the situation as it will exist *during that time*. The symbolism always points to a literal *meaning*.

Winter Walked Through the Valley

People use figurative language all the time during daily discourse. I used to live in upstate New York where the winters could become fierce, with ice, snow, and cold. It was not uncommon to walk out to your car in the morning and have to dig it out. It was also not out of the ordinary to drive to work (once you got your car warmed up) with a bone-jarring ride, because your shock absorbers had not warmed up yet!

Winters could be fun, or terrible. It really depended upon your situation. We might say something like, *"Wow, winter is stomping us this year!"* People understood what that meant. We were *not* saying that winter was actually stomping us with *feet.* No one would take our words in a *literalistic* fashion like that. We were understood to be saying that it was a very *tough* winter. The things that made it tough were the tremendous amount of snowfall, the ice, or the record cold temperatures. All these things together created difficult and even treacherous situations for the average person.

If all a person was going to do was play in the snow, that would be one thing. However, most people still needed to get to work, go to the grocery store, and take care of all the normal routines that needed attention. Snowfall, cold temperatures, and ice made these routines far from normal.

Figurative language is part of every culture. Behind every figurative reference lies the actual meaning, and there is generally only *one* meaning for each figure of speech. If there were more, language would become extremely confusing.

The apostle John is using literary devices here to describe what he is seeing. It may well be that he *saw* a horse and rider, but he also instinctively understood that each rider and horse *represented* something. We all know that pictures are great ways to remember things and they are worth a thousand words. Many of us are also visual learners.

Seeing images which represent something makes it far easier to remember something. Not only that, but also the impact of that image stays with a person at the level of importance by which it was revealed.

Revelation 6:7-8 – The Fourth Seal
"And when he had opened the fourth seal, I heard the voice of the fourth beast say, Come and see. And I looked, and behold a pale horse: and his name that sat on him was Death, and Hell followed with him. And power was given unto them over the fourth part of the earth, to kill with sword, and with hunger, and with death, and with the beasts of the earth."

This fourth seal opens the door to *death* on a pale horse. As a result of the opening of this seal, a fourth of the world's population is killed. Though this rider can seemingly go anywhere on earth, he is allowed to kill only one-fourth of the world's population. Notice also that the rider on the pale horse (Death) is immediately followed by *Hell*. In other words, the people that are killed with the opening of this seal are *unbelievers*. Their lives will be taken from them, and they will be immediately sent to hell for their continued rejection of Jesus Christ. This is not a judgment that will fall on any believers during this part of the Tribulation. It is reserved for unbelievers.

These people die by various means: *sword (war), hunger, death,* and by being killed by the *beasts* of the earth. All of the individuals who die during this judgment will go to *hell,* and Keathley points out that this figure could top 800,000,000! As this is being written, the world's population is 6,697,254,041! One fourth of that is a whopping 16,743,135! That is *huge,* and all from this one judgment.

Dying by war is obvious. This may also include a war against people in general by Antichrist insisting on using cruelty to achieve his ends. Saddam Hussein became known as the Butcher of Bagdad because of his many cruelties. He had no feeling for the people he ruled with an iron fist.

Famines that occur as a result of war will remove many from the planet. Often sickness and diseases follows on the heels of famine. When people cannot get enough to eat, they will eat anything. This lack of food causes their immune systems to weaken severely and death by any number of illnesses will occur.

We are told that people will die by *beasts.* This could be due to the fact that people who become weak through lack of food wind up becoming food for wild beasts. These beasts might find that their own food supply is drying up, so they look elsewhere. The text might also be indicating a resurrected form of Roman coliseum sporting events, where hapless people are tossed into the floor of the coliseum with wild animals that tear them to shreds.

Since we do not know exactly when these judgments will occur, this one may take place *after* the Antichrist has defiled the Temple. When he sits in the Holy of Holies and declares himself god, the Jews will run and hide in the mountains. The Antichrist will now turn his wrath on those he can reach; Christians.

Stopping to consider this, I find it exceptionally ironic that for generations people have wished for and sought a world of love and peace.

There is absolutely nothing wrong with wanting that; however, the world has gone about it the wrong way. Instead of turning to God in repentance, willingly placing themselves under His authority, they have continued to rebel, believing like Nimrod of old that people can do whatever they set their minds to doing.

However, far from a world of peace and love, we see that God has indicated that the coming end of the ages will be rife with hatred, greed, murder, overzealousness for all the wrong things, and a continued disobedience to God. As history winds down, what we will see and experience is far from the love so many like John Lennon have sung about.

Revelation 6:9-11 – The Fifth Seal

"And when he had opened the fifth seal, I saw under the altar the souls of them that were slain for the word of God, and for the testimony which they held: And they cried with a loud voice, saying, How long, O Lord, holy and true, dost thou not judge and avenge our blood on them that dwell on the earth? And white robes were given unto every one of them; and it was said unto them, that they should rest yet for a little season, until their fellowservants also and their brethren, that should be killed as they were, should be fulfilled."

The fifth seal shows us the results of persecution that has become commonplace on the earth. There are untold numbers of martyrs who gave up their lives rather than recant their faith in Jesus Christ. These people remained true to the end, and because of that they are also given white robes, robes that have been cleansed by the precious blood of Jesus Christ.

Notice also that there is a specific number of martyrs that must be killed in order to fulfill that which was preordained by God Himself. Though God allows the devil, the Antichrist, and others to persecute His children, He controls all aspects of this persecution, including the

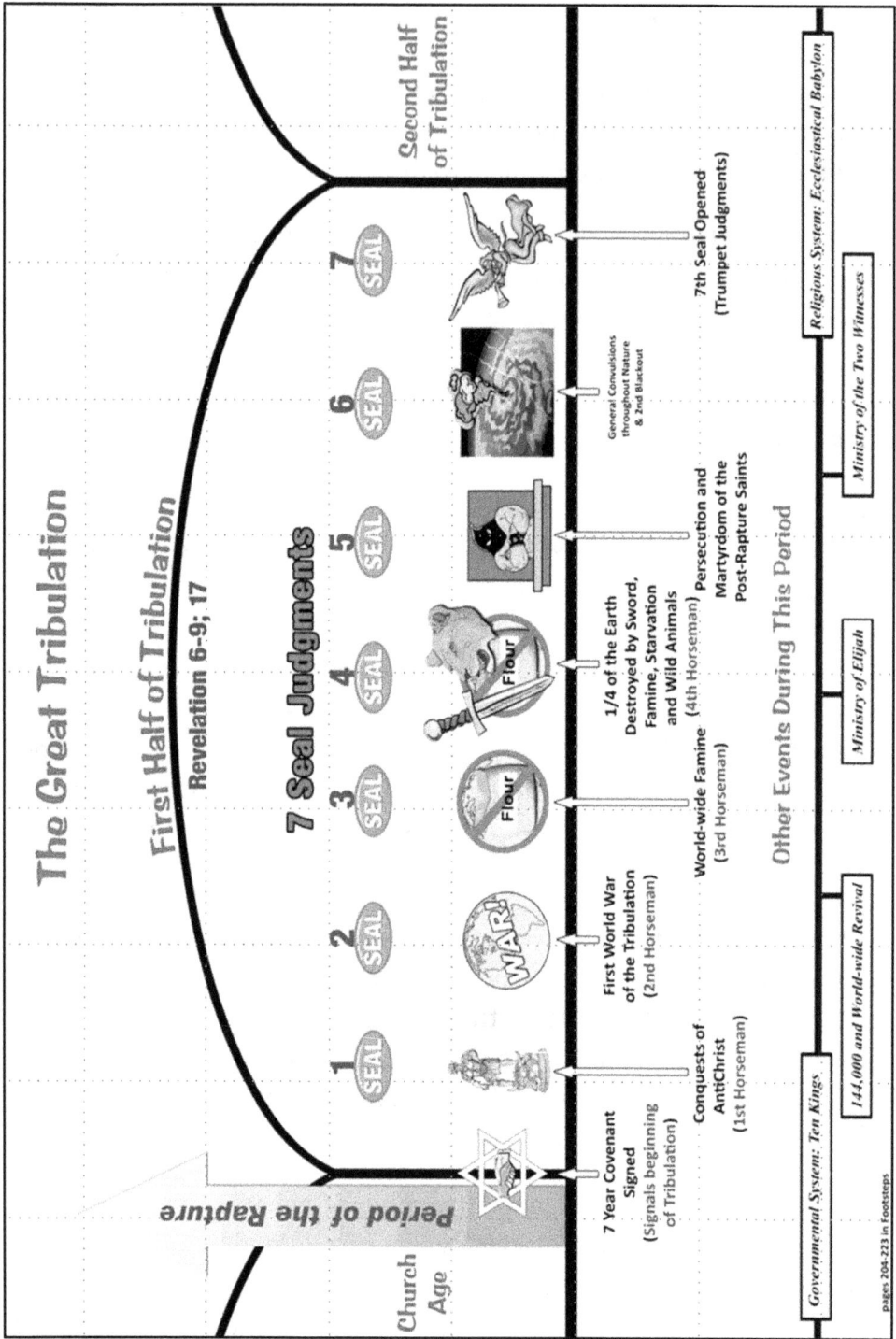

The Great Tribulation

First Half of Tribulation
Revelation 6-9; 17

7 Seal Judgments

| SEAL 1 | SEAL 2 | SEAL 3 | SEAL 4 | SEAL 5 | SEAL 6 | SEAL 7 |

Second Half of Tribulation

Church Age

Period of the Rapture

7 Year Covenant Signed (Signals beginning of Tribulation)

Conquests of AntiChrist (1st Horseman)

First World War of the Tribulation (2nd Horseman)

World-wide Famine (3rd Horseman)

1/4 of the Earth Destroyed by Sword, Famine, Starvation and Wild Animals (4th Horseman)

Persecution and Martyrdom of the Post-Rapture Saints

General Convulsions throughout Nature & 2nd Blackout

7th Seal Opened (Trumpet Judgments)

Other Events During This Period

Governmental System: Ten Kings

Religious System: Ecclesiastical Babylon

144,000 and World-wide Revival

Ministry of Elijah

Ministry of the Two Witnesses

pages 204-223 in Footsteps

actual number of those to be killed. Not one person more or one person less will be killed. This is likely to occur in the *second half* of the Tribulation (cf. Matthew 24:9-14). Things are getting bad for Christians now, but this is only the beginning of the evil that will be perpetrated against authentic Christians during the Tribulation.

John says he sees these martyrs *under* the altar. Keathley points out, *"Only Christ, the true Lamb of God, our Passover, is qualified to be placed on the altar to die for our sins and give access into God's presence. These, however, are under it, under the blood or under the substitutionary death of Christ, and thereby saved and in heaven by the person and work of Jesus Christ."*[8] As often happens (read Foxe's book of Martyrs), people are often inspired to receive Christ based on the death of one of His own. This is also possibly what caused Paul's conversion. He witnessed the death of the very first martyr, Stephen, and the faithfulness of Stephen undoubtedly stayed with him, influencing his own thoughts and ultimately his understanding of the truth about Jesus Christ. Paul understood the Old Testament and benefitted from Stephen's final message.

As Paul (Saul at that time) traveled toward Damascus and met the very Person of Jesus Christ, the death of Stephen may have already prepared him for that meeting.

One of the more interesting things is that these martyred saints, though already in God's presence, are crying out for His justice. *"'Cried out' is the Greek krazo, and means 'to shriek, scream.' This word and the words 'with a loud voice' lay stress on the earnestness of their cry and concern. These saints are in heaven, with no sinful natures and in God's blessed presence. But they are seen crying out for justice. This is not a cry for revenge, but for God's justice and righteousness to prevail on earth against the sin and the atrocities of man in rebellion to God. As in the disciples' prayer, 'Your kingdom come,' they are praying*

---

[8] J. Hampton Keathley III *Studies in Revelation* (Biblical Studies Press, 1997), 107

for the second advent which ushers in God's righteous and just reign on earth."[9]

These martyrs want to know how long it will be before God carries out the sentence against Satan and his minions. They are in God's presence, and as Keathley points out, no longer have sin natures. Because of this, they yearn for God's justice over the situation on earth. They so much want His holiness to reign on earth, as opposed to what they see happening on the earth. Though God's sovereign rule is always in effect, the world is not yet conformed to God's holy character.

It is clear that without the sin nature, God's will is desired that much more. These martyrs, with the sin nature excised from them, want nothing but God's glory to be evidenced throughout the earth and universe! So despicable is evil that those without evil want all evil far from them so that only God's glory will be seen.

Revelation 6:12-17 – The Sixth Seal

"And I beheld when he had opened the sixth seal, and, lo, there was a great earthquake; and the sun became black as sackcloth of hair, and the moon became as blood; And the stars of heaven fell unto the earth, even as a fig tree casteth her untimely figs, when she is shaken of a mighty wind. And the heaven departed as a scroll when it is rolled together; and every mountain and island were moved out of their places. And the kings of the earth, and the great men, and the rich men, and the chief captains, and the mighty men, and every bondman, and every free man, hid themselves in the dens and in the rocks of the mountains; And said to the mountains and rocks, Fall on us, and hide us from the face of him that sitteth on the throne, and from the wrath of the Lamb: For the great day of his wrath is come; and who shall be able to stand?"

---

[9] J. Hampton Keathley III *Studies in Revelation* (Biblical Studies Press, 1997), 107

It is not until the opening of the *sixth* seal that the people on the earth finally begin to admit that these judgments are from the very hand of God. They recognize this as the "*wrath of the Lamb.*" They want the rocks to fall on them in order to be able to hide from His wrath. Of course, this would do no good, since in death they would be brought immediately before Him to face their final judgment.

Can you imagine John's inner reaction to this scene in the verses quoted above? It is difficult to imagine what it looked like to John, though certainly it was terrifying. There is a great deal occurring there:

- *A great earthquake*
- *Sun became black*
- *Moon became as blood*
- *Stars fell from heaven to earth*
- *Heaven separated into parts*
- *Every mountains and island moved out of place*
- *People cry to be hidden from God out of complete fear*

Most people have a difficult time dealing with *one* natural disaster like an earthquake or tornado. To deal with multiple disasters would be completely unnerving. These bring the citizens of earth to the point of wanting to hide from God, or to die (as if either would some-how secure us from God's presence).

Many people today believe in *Annihilationism*, which is the belief that after we die, there is *nothing*. Obviously, this is not the case, and those wishing to die will only hasten their own judgment.

As Keathley and other commentators have pointed out, the first five seals were affected by man's inhumanity to man. Though this is the case, the seals and judgments themselves are *still* from God. This latest seal is God displaying His wrath to those of earth. It is something that even those of earth do not miss. People of all walks of life *fully* recognize it to be from God. Who else could bring such devastation throughout the heavens *and* the earth? No one has to tell the people living on the earth at that future time that God has intervened directly in the affairs of men through the elements of nature. They will *know* it to be the case.

Consider the phrase, "***as a fig tree casteth her untimely figs, when she is shaken of a mighty wind***." Think of it! Picture it! We have all seen or heard of great winds that shake trees until they appear that they will break under their own weight and the pressure from the wind. No leaf remains on a tree with that kind of wind. The idea that the tree is literally *throwing* its leaves to the ground is the picture that comes to mind as we read John's description.

The shaking that causes this to happen is the same shaking that causes the stars to fall from the heavens. Note that not one mountain or island remains in its original place! They are all moved. We have seen only a miniscule fraction of that with recent earthquakes of Haiti and elsewhere. In these cases, not only were cities destroyed, but also in the case of Haiti, the earth's crust was actually *compressed*. Imagine the sight of stars falling from the sky, mountains and islands moving off their original foundations. Everything will be shaken, and the implication is that it all happens at the same time! That is nearly impossible to imagine.

Commentators point out that both Zephaniah and Joel, among other places, describe the Tribulation as being gloom, dark, thick with clouds. It will be a terrible time in human history.

Couple this with the complete blackening of the sun and the moon itself turning red as blood and we gain insight into how terrible and drastic all of this will be for those still living on the earth at that time. There will be *no natural* light. The sun will not shine on the earth or moon. The moon will not reflect the sun's light onto the earth. Instead, it will give off a sickening blood red glimmer.

It is possible that the terrible earthquakes that hit the earth blacken the sun due to the resultant destruction, fires, and whatnot. They may also cause volcanic eruptions such as this modern world has not seen. With all the soot, silt, and rubble in the air from the natural disasters, it would explain why the moon would *appear* as reddish in color. It is also possible that God simply "turns off" the sun for a time.

We have all seen stars falling from the sky. These are commonly termed "shooting stars," and are generally small asteroids or meteorites falling to earth. Seeing one is interesting and often even considered *romantic*. To see a multitude of stars fall to earth is not romantic at all, but quite scary. It would give the impression of the sky actually falling to earth!

Imagine the sky separating like a scroll. Not long ago, a test was done at a laboratory in Norway. Apparently, a high-energy beam was fired into the heavens from *"the United States High Frequency Active Auroral Research Program (HAARP) radar facility in Ramfjordmoen, Norway."*[10] Even though it was done in Norway, it is also reported that the United States was involved (hence the name of the facility). If you stop to consider it, what *possible* problem could a high-energy beam shot into the heavens cause? The photo on the next page is a snapshot taken from the actual video of the event.

According to more than one reporting agency, Norway succeeded in *puncturing* the sky with the 2.3-megawatt short wave signal. That seems weird, doesn't it? How could *anything* puncture the sky, since it appears as though the sky goes on forever and does not have a roof or ceiling? If it actually *did* go on forever, then it would obviously be impossible to puncture it, but it looks as though scientists at the radar facility did in fact punch a hole in the atmosphere. Why? They were searching for inter-dimensional beings or interdimensional life.

---

[10]

http://open.salon.com/blog/norwonk/2010/01/12/norway_unleashed_hell_on_earth

HAARP Experiment

The article in reference states, "*To show how catastrophic for our Planet this massive thermal inversion has been Anthony Nunan, an assistant general manager for risk management at Mitsubishi Corporation in Tokyo, is reporting today that the entire Northern Hemisphere is in winter chaos, with the greatest danger from this unprecedented Global event being the destruction of billions of dollars worth of crops in a World already nearing the end of its ability to feed its self.*"[11]

The ramifications are mindboggling, considering the fact that scientists are so concerned about it. The article goes on to say "*So powerful has this thermal inversion become that reports from the United States are stating that their critical crops of strawberries, oranges, and other fruits and vegetables grown in their Southern States, are being destroyed by record cold temperatures. The US is further reporting record amounts of snowfall in what they are now warning may be their*

---

[11]

http://open.salon.com/blog/norwonk/2010/01/12/norway_unleashed_hell_on_earth

worst winter in 25 years."[12] The article is from January 10, 2010. You will recall that the big question of Global Warming was put to rest due to the unprecedented cold and snow during this past winter. Did this short wave radio signal have anything to do with it? Well, whether it did or did not, it could not have been good.

Now humanity has been able to punch a hole in the atmosphere around the earth. When the sky separates like a scroll, no one will be able to ignore it, and all will understand that it is from God, not man.

The upshot of all of this is that it is God forcing this earth – His Creation – to take notice! He will be ignored no longer. Can someone truly argue that God is not a God of *patience* and *mercy*?

This is where some individuals misinterpret the first five seals. These individuals believe that since these first five seal judgments pit man against man, nation against nation, then it is *man's wrath* (or it is Satan working *through* man) and not the wrath of God. These same folks then believe (based on their assumption) that the Rapture will not occur until near the midpoint of the Tribulation.

Since it should be clear that God is in charge of every judgment that He dishes out on the earth, humankind (and even Satan) are merely *players* or *those on the receiving end* of these judgments that flow from the hand of the Lamb.

Why is it that wars occur? It is because of the rider on the red horse. Why does the death of hundreds of thousands of people happen? It is because of the rider on the pale horse. The specific riders are called forth and *then* the results of their presence take place. The various horses *are* the judgments of God. To say that this is all humankind's doing is to denigrate God's sovereignty.

---

[12]

http://open.salon.com/blog/norwonk/2010/01/12/norway_unleashed_hell_on_earth

The *Lamb* opens each seal. He opens them as He will and the timing of the opening of each seal is in His hands completely. People need to understand that from the very first seal (the rider on the white horse) throughout, this is God's preordained way of gaining absolute and total control of the earth. The Tribulation does not begin with man's judgment of man. It is God's judgment of man beginning with the Antichrist.

For thousands of years – since the fall of our first parents in the Garden of Eden – man has rebelled against God's rule over him. Man has done everything possible to gain his "freedom" from being subject to God's reign in each man's life. It will never happen, even in the afterlife.

The Tribulation begins with God *giving humanity over* to a false messiah, a false Christ. This false Christ will lead multitudes astray. He puffs himself up in order to gain the worship of the masses. God is at the point where He says, "*You have wanted to be rid of me since the beginning. I am now giving you your wish...for a time!*"

From the moment Antichrist steps onto the world's stage He is *overseen* by God's will, yet Antichrist is the first of 21 judgments on the planet. Man continues to reject God, wanting instead someone who will lead them in their own pride and immorality. Just as Israel wanted a human king, so does the world yearn for that one individual who will come to lead people down their chosen path.

It is impossible to say that the first five seals are from man or Satan and God's actual wrath only kicks in with seal number six. This seal is the first time that people are willing to admit that what they are experiencing is *the wrath of God*! They could not see it as clearly prior to this because it was man vs. man. Now, through the elements, it is clearly seen for what it is: God vs. man.

All seals have been opened except the *seventh*. What we will find is that upon opening the seventh seal seven trumpets are found therein, and we will look at each of these when we arrive at chapter eight of Revelation.

Revelation 7 is an interlude, with a number of things occurring in heaven prior to the opening of the seventh seal. Even though these seven seal judgments were terrible, it will only become worse once the seventh seal is opened, revealing the seven trumpet judgments.

As shown by the chart from a few pages back, we are only through the first part of the Tribulation's many judgments. God's wrath has not been fully spent and a great deal more is yet to come.

The beginning of the Tribulation *starts* the process, and it certainly seems to become worse and worse as the Tribulation progresses. After the Antichrist defiles the Temple, things will become far worse, which is why Jesus refers to this part of the Tribulation as the "great tribulation" (cf. Matthew 24).

---- 7 ----

REVELATION 7

C hapter seven of Revelation is an interesting one to say the
least. Part of what makes it interesting is the fact that it *appears* to be a bit of a parenthesis. We are not sure if what is
happening in this chapter happens immediately after chapter six, or
if it refers back (or ahead) to something else entirely.

Again, this is not so unusual, as most people speak like this in normal
conversations. Consider that you are talking to a neighbor, and you
are asking them to watch your house while you are gone with your
family for a seven-day vacation. Your neighbor says he would be

happy to watch your home and then asks where you are going. You tell him that you are going to take a two-day trip up the coast, then return via an inland route.

You continue to let him know the preparations you have made for the trip and may wind up telling your neighbor the things you are going to do, but not in any particular order. You may mention what you will do on Wednesday, and then something jogs your memory, so you then point out the events on *Monday*. This seems to be the case here. The apostle John seems to be giving us a parenthesis, or an *aside*.

However, we must understand that this chapter is in many ways a response to what has occurred with the opening of the sixth seal of chapter six. We read of the tremendously tumultuous turn that has visited the earth and we wonder how anyone could live through it.

Apparently, people *do* live through it, because chapter seven introduces a new scene in which four angels hold back the further judgments to come so that God's chosen can be sealed. The fact that they hold back judgment means that there are people left alive on the earth who will experience that judgment.

Revelation 7:1-3
"And after these things I saw four angels standing on the four corners of the earth, holding the four winds of the earth, that the wind should not blow on the earth, nor on the sea, nor on any tree.

"And I saw another angel ascending from the east, having the seal of the living God: and he cried with a loud voice to the four angels, to whom it was given to hurt the earth and the sea,

"Saying, Hurt not the earth, neither the sea, nor the trees, till we have sealed the servants of our God in their foreheads."

Some commentators believe that the "*winds*" that the angels are holding back are actual *winds*. That may be the case, but it seems more likely that the winds actually represent *judgment*. If so, then it would appear that the angels are preventing a type of judgment from coming to earth *until* God's servants are sealed.

If the winds are actual *winds*, then one must wonder why people need to be sealed *before* the winds can start; unless, of course, these are *hurricane* winds. That does not seem likely because that is not what we read in the text itself. In short, the angels may very well be holding back the winds of *judgment*, which when released will bring terrible things to the earth and to the people living here.

Just as history has repeatedly shown, wherever there is persecution, there is often revival; the same can be said in this chapter. Keathely points out that *"In several places in scripture 'wind' is used as a symbol of divine judgment (Jer. 49:36; Jer. 51:1; 2 Sam. 22:11)."*[13]

While the angels hold back the winds, no judgment takes place on earth. This brief interlude leads to the next set of judgments after the chosen are sealed. It appears as though the winds release what happens *after* the servants of God are sealed. Here is the order in the chapter:

1. *Winds held back*
2. *Servants of God sealed on their foreheads*
3. *A great multitude of martyrs appears in heaven*

Something has happened here. Once the servants of God are sealed, the winds, or judgments, are *released*. The result of this must have something to do with the multitude of martyrs, or there would be no reason to mention them together here. The four angels have all aspects of the globe covered, all "four corners" as it were.

It is possible that the sealing of the 144,000 Jews occurs near the very beginning of the Tribulation. This would make sense, as it is

---

[13] J. Hampton Keathley III *Studies in Revelation* (Biblical Studies Press, 1997), 114

likely that not all Jews will agree with their leadership as they enter into the agreement with Antichrist. These particular Jews may well be wary of Antichrist's intentions and begin seeking God in earnest.

These Jews also may begin looking very closely at the Tanakh (the Old Testament), determining what it says about the Messiah. It may well be that at that time God opens their eyes to the truth found within His Word, just as He did with the thief on the cross, Paul the apostle and countless other individuals. The Holy Spirit does *not* need human beings to make His truth understandable. He simply chooses to *use* human beings in order that we might share in the privilege of introducing people to Jesus Christ.

If these individual Jews become completed Jews, or Messianic Jews, saved by the same shed blood that saves anyone, they may begin their evangelistic efforts almost from the beginning of the Tribulation. We do not truly know when this act by God of sealing 144,000 Jews occurs during the Tribulation.

It is interesting that this appears here, right between chapters six and seven. The upshot is that from the God-ordained efforts of these Jewish evangelists, *multitudes* will become authentic Christians, with most (if not all) laying down their lives as martyrs for Jesus Christ. This is the picture of what we see toward the end of chapter seven, when the innumerable multitude stands before God's throne.

There, clothed in white, they will lay palm branches before the Lord of Glory, as true Messiah and King of all that He has created (cf. Revelation 7:9). Just as the people placed palm branches before the colt upon which Jesus rode into Jerusalem centuries before, these martyrs will do the same in heaven.

What is also to be noted here is that these particular servants are not the ones who die because they are sealed in order that they cannot be killed. The ones who die are those they evangelize. It *seems*, at least at this point, that God keeps these 144,000 safe from harm for the duration of the Tribulation.

"In addition to the physical protection from death, the seal may also point to their protection from the apostasy and deceptions of the beast. It stresses their invulnerability to the beast and the false prophet both physically and spiritually. As the followers of the beast have his mark, so these have the mark of God. Today we are susceptible to certain things, though God may sovereignly protect us, and does, but evidently they will not at all be vulnerable. Further evidence of this is given in 14:1f where these are seen unharmed, standing with the Lamb on Mt. Zion, Jerusalem, and undefiled by the evil of the system of the beast (14:4-5). This passage is a prophetic portrait of the ultimate victory of Christ at the beginning of the Millennium. Ezekiel 9:4-7 undoubtedly provides the OT background for this passage."[14]

Revelation 7:4-8:

"And I heard the number of them which were sealed: and there were sealed an hundred and forty and four thousand of all the tribes of the children of Israel.

"Of the tribe of Juda were sealed twelve thousand. Of the tribe of Reuben were sealed twelve thousand. Of the tribe of Gad were sealed twelve thousand.

"Of the tribe of Aser were sealed twelve thousand. Of the tribe of Nephthalim were sealed twelve thousand. Of the tribe of Manasses were sealed twelve thousand.

"Of the tribe of Simeon were sealed twelve thousand. Of the tribe of Levi were sealed twelve thousand. Of the tribe of Issachar were sealed twelve thousand.

---

[14] J. Hampton Keathley III *Studies in Revelation* (Biblical Studies Press, 1997), 114

"Of the tribe of Zabulon were sealed twelve thousand. Of the tribe of Joseph were sealed twelve thousand. Of the tribe of Benjamin were sealed twelve thousand."

A specific number is provided, which is 144,000. Some commentators say that this number is merely symbolic of something, but should not be taken as a *literal* 144,000. Some believe this number simply represents the invisible Church overall and *not* Israel.

I think that is a difficult position to prove, simply because not only is the exactly number given, but we read that exactly 12,000 are taken from each tribe of Israel. It seems clear enough that God is referencing the nation of *Israel* here. While one might argue that not all of the tribes are listed, that fact does not necessarily prove that it somehow represents the invisible Church. In other instances in the Bible, not all the tribes are mentioned either; however, it is clear that the nation of Israel is being referenced.

It seems to be that God will actually raise up Jewish evangelists to do the job that Israel was *meant* to do when God first created the nation. They will get this chance during the Tribulation period.

Many people believe that Israel is finished, kaput, gone the way of the dinosaur because they rejected Jesus as Messiah. If they want to believe that, they have that right, but it does not seem to square with Scripture.

Israel was created not because God saw the Jewish people and loved them more than anyone else on this planet. He created the nation of Israel because He had a job for them to *accomplish*. That job was to be a light to *all* nations. They were supposed to share their knowledge and understanding of God, as well as His way of salvation (by faith), to everyone around them. Foreigners would come to God *through* the nation of Israel, as she would be the herald of God's salvation. This was the plan.

Instead, Israel succumbed to the *sin* of those nations around them, taking up their practice of worshiping other gods as opposed to teaching those other nation how to worship the one, true God. During the Tribulation period, God will raise up 144,000 Jewish believers to be evangelists to the entire world.

Revelation 7:9 – The Fifth Seal

"After this I beheld, and, lo, a great multitude, which no man could number, of all nations, and kindreds, and people, and tongues, stood before the throne, and before the Lamb, clothed with white robes, and palms in their hands."

Immediately after this act of sealing 144,000 Jewish evangelists, we see a group of people so large that *"no man could number."* Beyond this, these people are from every people, all nations, and all tongues.

Please notice that John has just finished listing a breakdown of the 144,000, showing that 12,000 come from each of the following tribes:

1. Judah
2. Rueben
3. Gad
4. Asher
5. Nephtali
6. Manasses
7. Simeon
8. Levi
9. Issachar
10. Zebulun
11. Joseph
12. Benjamin

Immediately on the heels of this specific information, John then reveals that he sees a crowd of people so large that they could not be numbered by a human being. However, what is even more interesting is the fact that these people are from all nations throughout the world. If this does not prove that the 144,000 are *specifically from the nation of Israel*, then nothing does. If the 144,000 were not officially Jewish, he would not have listed the individual tribes.

There is no way that John would have said, "tribes of the children of Israel" if the 144,000 had not actually been of the nation of Israel, and then followed it by giving an overall account of the fact that heaven will be filled with martyrs from the Tribulation (cf. 7:14).

John distinguishes these martyrs (from the tribes of Israel) as coming from every nation and kindreds. These people are from all nations and various languages. It seems clear God seals 144,000 Jewish individuals (His Remnant), and gives them the job of evangelizing.

In other words, there would be absolutely no reason for John to differentiate between the two groups – the 144,000 sealed and the martyrs – if they were not Jews in the first group and the rest of the world in the second. John clearly notes the difference between these two groups through his delineation of them.

Revelation 7:10-12
"And cried with a loud voice, saying, Salvation to our God which sitteth upon the throne, and unto the Lamb.

"And all the angels stood round about the throne, and about the elders and the four beasts, and fell before the throne on their faces, and worshipped God,

"Saying, Amen: Blessing, and glory, and wisdom, and thanksgiving, and honour, and power, and might, be unto our God for ever and ever. Amen."

In the above verses, we see the reaction of those in heaven as the great multitude referenced in verse 9 appears. There is absolute praise and adoration for God! Note specifically that the Lamb is mentioned here. Without the Lamb there is no salvation. The Lamb has secured salvation, freely giving it to those who believe. In this case, we see a great multitude of people who have been killed *for the sole reason* that they are Christians. Because they are Christians, they do not go along with the program foisted upon the people during the Tribulation. It is because they are Christians that they resist the world, the flesh, and the devil. It is because they resist that they are put to death. Salvation has forced them to make a choice – follow God or the devil – and they gladly followed God to their own deaths.

It is due to salvation that those beings in heaven (not humans) see and understand how great and wonderful God is because He gave Himself in order that human beings might enjoy heaven with Him. This act of selflessness flowed from His love and holiness. Heaven begins to understand the true magnitude of God, His love, and His grace toward those who do not deserve to receive it.

Revelation 7:13
"And one of the elders answered, saying unto me, What are these which are arrayed in white robes? And whence came they?"

Just so that we cannot miss it, so that we know beyond doubt who comprises the great multitude, an elder asks John who he thinks they are, and John does not know. The fact that they are dressed in white robes signifies that they have been completely washed with the blood of Christ.

In this world, though we do not necessarily *feel* it, we are washed in the blood of Christ if we are authentic Christians. We have been cleansed and our sin is *behind* us. We gain this understanding from numerous passages throughout the New Testament, but specifically Ephesians 2 and Romans 1-6.

The blood of Jesus Christ, shed on the cross of death, has cleansed us by faith. In other words, as we come to believe that Jesus is God, that

He died for us never having sinned, and that He rose three days after going into the tomb, we become Christians. That faith that causes us to believe these things about Jesus is what grants us salvation. We do not earn it. We cannot work for it. It is something that is believed, and once believed, God grants that salvation to us.

From the moment we are saved, we are cleansed. Our sin – past, present, and future – is gone because Christ's blood paid for *all* of our sin. We still need to confess sin as we realize it, but the forgiveness from God is there, continually cleansing us.

Though we certainly do not feel cleansed at times in this life, we must learn that we are, by faith. Our sin nature keeps us feeling as though we are still "dirty" and that God turns from us.

The martyrs in heaven are clothed with white robes because not only are they cleansed, but they also are perfectly and forever clean, because they no longer have a sin nature within them. They now exercise Christ's nature perfectly, at all times, never again to even be tempted with sin. It cannot touch or harm them. They are free.

Revelation 7:14-17

"And I said unto him, Sir, thou knowest. And he said to me, These are they which came out of great tribulation, and have washed their robes, and made them white in the blood of the Lamb.

"Therefore are they before the throne of God, and serve him day and night in his temple: and he that sitteth on the throne shall dwell among them.

"They shall hunger no more, neither thirst any more; neither shall the sun light on them, nor any heat.

"For the Lamb which is in the midst of the throne shall feed them, and shall lead them unto living fountains of waters: and God shall wipe away all tears from their eyes."

We learn from the elder that they are the martyrs out of the "great tribulation." This reminds us of what Jesus said in His Olivet Discourse when He spoke of "great tribulation" (cf. Matthew 24, Mark 13, and Luke 21). This "great tribulation" appears to be during the second half of the seven-year Tribulation.

It could very well be that this huge, unnumbered group of people represents *all* the people who emerged from the Tribulation by the time it has ended. We are not really sure. If true, then it would appear as though millions will be martyred for their faith in Jesus during this horrible period just prior to Christ's physical return.

It is also clear that Jesus Christ is the absolute center of everything and from Him flows life abundant. These martyrs will lack nothing forever because Jesus Himself will provide for them in every respect.

8

REVELATION 8

Immediately after we see the sealing of the 144,000 and the martyrs in heaven, we move into Revelation 8. It is here that we pick up where we left off regarding the seals. The parenthesis, or the aside, is over, and we are now back into the action of the Tribulation.

At the beginning of Revelation 8, we see the Lamb opening the seventh seal.

Revelation 8:1
"And when he had opened the seventh seal, there was silence in heaven about the space of half an hour."

The Great Tribulation

First Half of Tribulation

Revelation 6-9; 17

Second Half of Tribulation

7 Seal Judgments

| SEAL 1 | SEAL 2 | SEAL 3 | SEAL 4 | SEAL 5 | SEAL 6 | SEAL 7 |

Church Age

Period of the Rapture

7 Year Covenant Signed (Signals beginning of Tribulation)

Conquests of AntiChrist (1st Horseman)

First World War of the Tribulation (2nd Horseman)

World-wide Famine (3rd Horseman)

1/4 of the Earth Destroyed by Sword, Famine, Starvation and Wild Animals (4th Horseman)

Persecution and Martyrdom of the Post-Rapture Saints

General Convulsions throughout Nature & 2nd Blackout

7th Seal Opened (Trumpet Judgments)

Other Events During This Period

Governmental System: Ten Kings

144,000 and World-wide Revival

Ministry of Elijah

Ministry of the Two Witnesses

Religious System: Ecclesiastical Babylon

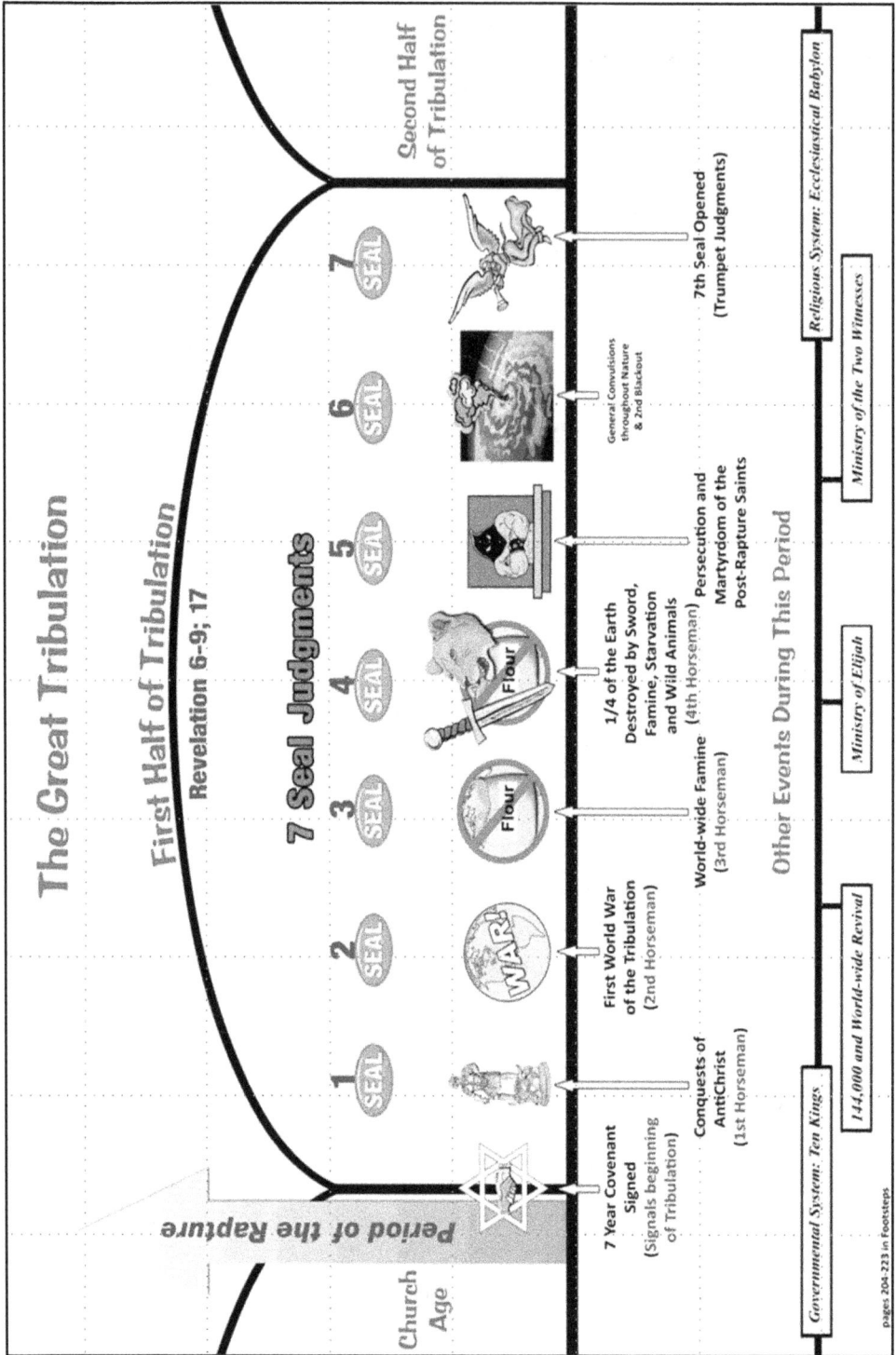

pages 204-223 in Footsteps

The opening of the seventh seal does a couple of things, but the first thing it does is create *silence*. It is like the dark before the storm, or the expectancy just before the orchestra plays. The audience looks intently to the stage covered by a curtain, waiting expectantly. After what seems like an interminable amount of time, the curtain opens, the orchestra plays, and the opera begins.

This silence in heaven is *deafening*. It is designed to get people's attention. All eyes are on the Lamb (and rightly so) and the seventh seal that He just opened. What will happen? John tells us that the silence existed for roughly 30 minutes, or half an hour. In this case also, it is likely that there is nothing symbolic here, other than it being silent in anticipation for what follows. There is no reason to believe that the 30 minutes represents something else. It merely represents thirty minutes of anticipatory silence.

Revelation 8:2

"And I saw the seven angels which stood before God; and to them were given seven trumpets."

The wait is breathtaking and unnerving. Then, seven angels step up to perform their predetermined jobs. Each is given a trumpet. The trumpets are given to these angels under the supervision and direction of the Lamb, God Himself. He is fully in control. No one is able to usurp Him or His sovereignty. This is the recurring theme throughout the book of Revelation as in no other book of the Christian Bible. Jesus is Lord of Lords and King of Kings! He is fully sovereign.

So apparently, the seventh *seal* contained seven *trumpets*. Without the opening of the seventh seal, the trumpet judgments would not have been released. The trumpets are given to the angels and each angel will blow his trumpet at the proper time, releasing more of God's wrath onto the earth and its citizens. However, before the first angel blows his trumpet, there is another brief aside, or parenthesis.

Revelation 8:3-5

"And another angel came and stood at the altar, having a golden censer; and there was given unto him much incense, that he should offer it with the prayers of all saints upon the golden altar which was before the throne.

"And the smoke of the incense, which came with the prayers of the saints, ascended up before God out of the angel's hand.

"And the angel took the censer, and filled it with fire of the altar, and cast it into the earth: and there were voices, and thunderings, and lightnings, and an earthquake."

Here we see another angel stepping out to perform a task. His duty is to combine a large amount of incense along with the prayers of the saints on the golden altar. This altar stands directly before the throne, and in many ways this scene was replicated through the earthly Tabernacle and Temple of Israel. It is impossible to state dogmatically who this particular angel is, as we simply do not know with any real degree of certainty.

If we were to look down on the Tabernacle (and remove the covering to the Holy of Holies) we would see that as the priest came into that area, the first thing he would see would be the Golden Candlestick to his left and the Table of Showbread to his right. Immediately after these items stood the Altar of Incense in the direct center of the room.

The Altar of Incense was literally "in the way" of the entrance to the Holy of Holies. It stood in front of this entrance. For a priest to get to the Holy of Holies, he had to pass by the Altar of Incense. In order to pass by the Altar, he had to make an *offering of blood*. This offering would allow him to move into the Holy of Holies (once each year) to make an offering for Israel's sins. This was accomplished with the sprinkling of blood.

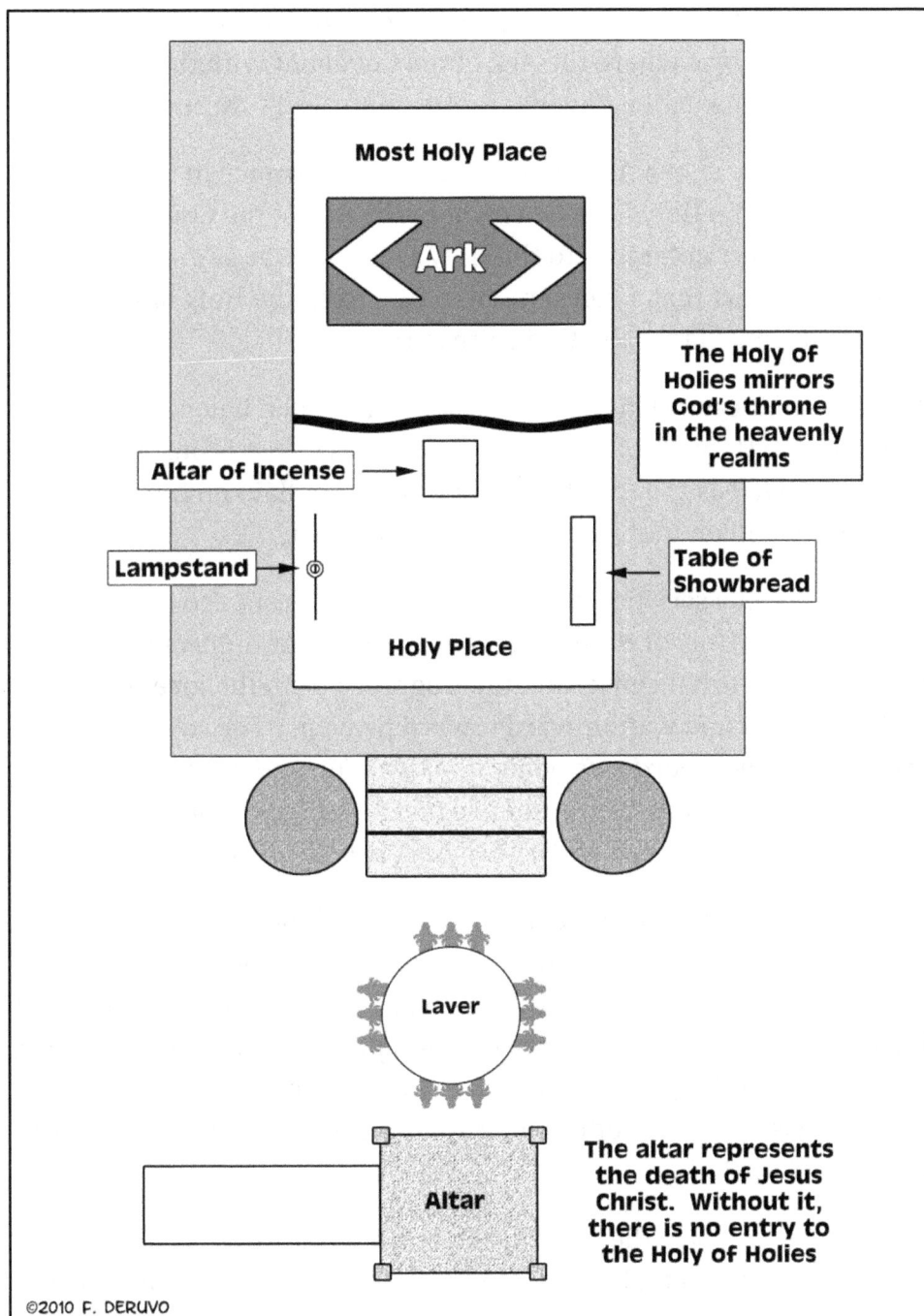

Most Holy Place

Ark

The Holy of Holies mirrors God's throne in the heavenly realms

Altar of Incense →

Lampstand → ⊕

Table of Showbread

Holy Place

Laver

Altar

The altar represents the death of Jesus Christ. Without it, there is no entry to the Holy of Holies

©2010 F. DERUVO

Tabernacle/Temple Design

The earthly Tabernacle was a picture of the Temple in heaven. We see the Altar of Incense standing just before the throne of God. The Holy of Holies was where the Ark of the Covenant with the Mercy Seat sat. The Ark of the Covenant represents God's throne.

In the Tabernacle, the Altar stood before the entrance to the Holy Place. Inside the Holy Place was where the Ark of the Covenant sat. When the priest entered into the Holy Place, he was supposed to be aware of the fact that a veil separated him from the Holy of Holies (aka Most Holy Place) and God's Presence.

The Altar of Incense was inside the Holy Place, just before the entrance to the Holy of Holies. In essence, Jesus Christ is our Altar of Incense as well as the sacrificial Lamb that was slain on the altar *outside* the Holy Place, but also allows entrance to it.

Without Christ's sacrifice, there would be no entrance to the Most Holy Place (or Holy of Holies). It was on this Altar of Incense that the priest would burn incense, and the fragrance from the incense would fill the Temple and waft upward toward heaven. *"The sweet incense ascending heavenward was symbolic of worship and prayer and was a reminder that our prayers must have the character of sweet incense or the mediatorial presence of Christ to be accepted and heard by God."*[15]

Note that the angel takes the incense and combines it with the prayers of the saints. Both are now on the golden altar before God's throne, the incense representing the work of Jesus Christ on behalf of His Bride. The smoke of the prayers mingled with incense rises up before God. God is well aware of every prayer that His saints utter, and because of Christ's efficacious atonement, our prayers are readily received by God.

The angel then takes the *fire* from the altar and throws it toward earth. The fire is actually from the coals that were on the sacrificial

---

[15] J. Hampton Keathley III *Studies in Revelation* (Biblical Studies Press, 1997), 122

altar and used to heat the incense. The coals also represent Christ's sacrifice *and* God's judgment at the same time. This makes sense since Christ experienced God's wrath while on the cross. As the angel throws the fire toward the earth, the immediate reaction is fourfold:

1. *Voices*
2. *Thundering*
3. *Lightnings*
4. *Earthquake*

These are the prelude to what is about to happen on earth, and they speak of God's impending judgment. Obviously, the thunder, the lightning, and the earthquake are *experienced* by people on the earth and are but an indication of further judgment which is to come. The silence got everyone's attention, and now the voices, the thunder peals, the lightning, and the earthquake continue to heighten the suspense leading to what is about to occur.

Revelation 8:6 – Seven Angels

"And the seven angels which had the seven trumpets prepared themselves to sound."

It seems as though this is preparatory for what happens next, but let's recap for a moment. So far, in chapter 8, we have seen these things happen in the following order:

1. *The 7th seal is opened by the Lamb*
2. *30 minutes of silence in heaven*
3. *Seven trumpets given to seven angels*
4. *The altar with the prayers of the saints is mixed with incense*
5. *Fire from the altar is thrown to earth*
6. *Voices, thundering, lightning, earthquake are heard/seen*

Now it is time for the spotlight to highlight the seven angels who hold the seven trumpets. Remember, the seventh seal *contains* these seven trumpets.

Revelation 8:7 – First Trumpet

"The first angel sounded, and there followed hail and fire mingled with blood, and they were cast upon the earth: and the third part of trees was burnt up, and all green grass was burnt up."

This is on the heels of the fire that was thrown to earth by the previous angel. Fire is generally understood to represent judgment and/or purification, so as a precursor to the first angel sounding the first trumpet, *fire* is thrown to the earth in a symbolic gesture of what is to come.

The judgment found within the first trumpet contains:

- *Hail*
- *Fire*
- *Blood*

Numerous commentators believe these three things should be understood allegorically; however, there is nothing in the text that would support the need to interpret allegorically. Consider the ramifications of this mixture hitting the earth. A good portion of the earth would be set ablaze!

Because of the *hail*, *fire*, and *blood*, one-third of the trees and grass throughout the earth are destroyed. Note that human beings are *directly* affected by the hail, fire, and *blood*. There will be deaths (blood) and if that many trees and that much grass is gone (along with agricultural crops), it will affect many things on or around the earth, including animals and people.

There have been any number of documentary-type shows on TV covering individuals who chase after storms and especially tornadoes. What has become increasingly obvious is not only the size and ferocity of many of these storms, but the size and ferocity of the hail that occurs just prior to the full formation of the tornado. In more than one episode, the hail stones have been the size of baseballs and even softballs. They have destroyed car windshields and even hurt and killed people unlucky enough to be caught in the storm. The results of one particular hail storm required several people to be transported to local hospitals for treatment of bloody gashes on their heads and arms.

The first thing it will affect is oxygen. Since green plants take in carbon dioxide and give off oxygen, then there will be *less oxygen* to breathe. Less oxygen means dirtier air, more disease, and even death. So while these three things do not directly affect humanity, they have a direct *effect* on the quality of life for humanity.

The number three is important as far as God is concerned because God is *triune*. During the Tribulation, Satan will also attempt to imitate God by creating his own evil trinity (the "father" is Satan, the "son" is Antichrist, and the "spirit" is the False Prophet). God chooses to obliterate one-third of the grasses and trees that represent part of His nature.

Revelation 8:8-9 – Second Trumpet

"And the second angel sounded, and as it were a great mountain burning with fire was cast into the sea: and the third part of the sea became blood. And the third part of the creatures which were in the sea, and had life, died; and the third part of the ships were destroyed."

A great "mountain" collided with the earth's seas. John states, "*as it were a great mountain.*" That is similar to saying "it was *like* a great mountain." John is not saying it is a mountain, but that it is *like* a great mountain.

This certainly seems to be a very large *asteroid*. Note that it was burning with fire as it goes through earth's atmosphere. This is not unusual at all for asteroids, or comets, or other things that come through the atmosphere. The only thing that is unusual is the apparent size and destructive ability of this particular asteroid. At the same time, scientists have told us that "billions" of years ago, numerous large asteroids have collided with the earth, leaving their imprint.

Interestingly enough, scientists grew very concerned about an asteroid that was headed directly for earth in

The Willamette Meteorite

the not too distant past. The asteroid has been named "2002 NT7"[16] and it is slightly over one mile in width.

Some scientists are saying that this asteroid could hit earth by 2019, while some say it could strike earth as early as 2014[17]. Of course, what is of equal importance is what scientists are saying this asteroid could do if it does strike the earth. *"The heat would set fire to forests and cities, after which dust would fill the atmosphere, obscuring the sun for a month. That in turn would kill plants and animals, so that only creatures that lived underground would have a strong chance of survival."*[18]

---

[16] http://www.independent.co.uk/news/science/milewide-asteroid-heading-towards-earth-poses-greatest-threat-yet-scientists-warn-649383.html
[17] http://www.cnn.com/2003/TECH/space/09/02/asteroid.reut/index.html
[18] http://www.independent.co.uk/news/science/milewide-asteroid-heading-towards-earth-poses-greatest-threat-yet-scientists-warn-649383.html

Fortunately for the earth, that asteroid missed the earth completely, but came too close for the comfort of many scientists. However, others are out there and on their way here.

One of the largest meteorites to hit earth (and remain somewhat intact) is the Willamette Meteorite. This meteor landed in Oregon in the Willamette Valley and is said to weigh roughly 15 tons, or 32,000 pounds.

A number of other large meteorites have impacted the earth, either just above the earth's surface or directly on the earth's surface. Some have caused major damage, including tidal waves.

The Bible says that one day an asteroid (a big one, like a mountain) *will* hit the earth's seas, and by doing so will turn one-third of the sea into blood. It does not say that the sea will become *like* blood (as in figurative language). It says the sea will *become* blood. This can only mean that millions of sea life that lives within salt waters throughout the earth will be destroyed as the huge fiery mountain crashes into the sea. Dead, bloated carcasses of fish, whales, birds and other animal life will empty their blood into the oceans where they die, causing a third of the seas to become blood. Notice also that a *third* of the ships on the sea were also destroyed. This can only be due to a tremendously large *tsunami* that results from the fiery mountain hitting the sea, displacing many tons of water. This trumpet judgment describes *immense* destruction that will visit the earth.

Revelation 8:10-11 – Third Trumpet
"And the third angel sounded, and there fell a great star from heaven, burning as it were a lamp, and it fell upon the third part of the rivers, and upon the fountains of waters; And the name of the star is called Wormwood: and the third part of the waters became wormwood; and many men died of the waters, because they were made bitter."

On the heels of the devastation of the second angel's trumpet judgment, a third angel sounds and this time a great star falls from heaven. This one is burning like a lamp (not that it IS a lamp, but that is burning as IF it were a lamp), likely leaving a trail of fire behind it.

This is most likely a large comet that is so large, it is not destroyed as it enters earth's atmosphere. It lands in fresh waters. The result is the poisoning of these fresh waters. Again, we see that one-third of the fresh waters are made undrinkable, yet many continue to drink from these poisoned waters and die as a result.

Apparently, scientists have learned that *"comet tails do contain an extremely poisonous chemical compound – hydrogen cyanide."*[20] The chemical representation for hydrogen cyanide is HCN. Imagine this chemical mixing with earth's fresh waters. The Arctic Icecap and glaciers represent just over 2% of the earth's water (including salt water). In actuality, that percentage is not a great amount of fresh water when compared with salt water. HCN, when mixed with water, produces hydrocyanic acid, also known as Prussic acid. *"Prussic acid, cyanide, or hydrocyanic acid are all terms relating to the same toxic substance. It is one of the most rapidly acting toxins which affects mammals. Cyanide is a lethal ingredient that has been used in rodent and vermin killers."*[21]

Sometimes, it is relatively easy to just read the words in the Bible and not be impacted by them. It is only when we research what they mean, or what they point to, that we become much more invested with the true meaning of Scripture. In this case, consider a large comet with a long tail striking the fresh water supplies on the earth. This in turn – because of the HCN concentrate in the comet's tail – creates Prussic acid upon mixing with fresh water, which then turns the water into a virtual poison.

---

[20] http://www.space.com/scienceastronomy/astronomy/comet_poison_011012.html
[21] http://www.ag.ndsu.edu/pubs/ansci/livestoc/v1150w.htm

While no poison is a good way to die, dying through this type of poisoning is not pretty. *"Prussic acid is a potent, rapidly acting poison. Signs of prussic acid poisoning can occur within 15 to 20 minutes to a few hours after animals consume the toxic forage. Animals are often found dead. Clinical signs, when noticed, occur in rapid succession. Excitement, rapid pulse, and generalized muscle tremors occur initially, followed by rapid and labored breathing, staggering, and collapse. There may be salivation (drooling), lacrimation (runny eyes) and voiding of urine and feces. The mucous membranes are usually bright pink, and the blood will be a characteristic bright cherry red."*[22]

It is interesting that even though the apostle John would not have known what HCN, or Prussic acid, is, he clearly saw the results of it from the comet hitting the fresh water sources. He also clearly saw the direct connection between that "star" hitting the waters with immediate deaths of people and animals.

What we read in the Bible *might* seem to some to be fairy tales, yet it becomes clear with only a bit of research that there is actual science that backs up the testimony of Scripture. So far, nothing has happened in the book of Revelation that cannot be explained with modern science.

Revelation 8:12 – Fourth Trumpet
"And the fourth angel sounded, and the third part of the sun was smitten, and the third part of the moon, and the third part of the stars; so as the third part of them was darkened, and the day shone not for a third part of it, and the night likewise."

Notice that in each case so far with respect to the trumpets, a portion or one-third of the total is affected. This is true in this case as well. The fourth angel blows his trumpet and a third of the sun was "smitten" so that it was darkened, along with one-third of the stars and

---

[22] http://www.ag.ndsu.edu/pubs/ansci/livestoc/v1150w.htm

one-third of the moon. It appears that the daytime becomes one-third less in the level of light. *"It is interesting that it was on the **fourth day that God created and made visible to the Earth the sun, the moon and the stars**. So now the fourth trumpet judgment is aimed at these heavenly bodies—the gracious provisions of God's common grace (Cf. Matt. 24:29; Luke 21:25)."*[23] (emphasis added)

There are some interesting things happening in our solar system that scientists and astronomers are just now starting to realize. There is a growing belief that something akin to a "death star" is lurking just beyond our solar system that is sending comets to earth. While NASA telescopes cannot yet see it, they are seeing the effects of *something*.[24]

This appears to be a solar eclipse. During a total solar eclipse, the sun is virtually blocked by the moon (from the point of view of people on the earth). During this time, the sun goes dark, the moon darkens, and most of the stars darken as well, though some stars that might not normally be seen are seen and seem to be brighter because of the darkness.

It is also interesting to note that when either a lunar or a solar eclipse happens, most people look up to see the phenomenon. By looking up, either it is meant that they will look through special glasses that protect the eyes or they will look at the reflection of the eclipse, since looking directly at a solar eclipse can cause blindness.

This fourth angel sounds his trumpet and a solar eclipse occurs. This serves to draw the attention of the people on earth, so that they look at the eclipse in some form. The very next verse points out the possible reason why this solar eclipse occurred.

---

[23] J. Hampton Keathley III *Studies in Revelation* (Biblical Studies Press, 1997), 126
[24] http://www.astrobio.net/exclusive/3427/getting-wise-about-nemesis

These are acts of God. Scientists will not be able to explain these phenomena.

Revelation 8:13
"And I beheld, and heard an angel flying through the midst of heaven, saying with a loud voice, Woe, woe, woe, to the inhabiters of the earth by reason of the other voices of the trumpet of the three angels, which are yet to sound!"

Consider this scene. There is a solar eclipse, which apparently causes no damage to the earth or those living on it. Immediately after the eclipse (or possibly *during* the eclipse), an angel flies across the sky. His message is simple: three more trumpets are going to sound and they will bring even more destruction than the first four did!

You have to wonder what the people on earth will be thinking when this event occurs. They will see and/or hear an angel speaking the words we read above in verse 13, and it will undoubtedly be heard by all people in their own language. Will they believe? Will they sense the ominous and immediate future? Will they wonder what is going on and *why*? Some Bible translations say "eagle" instead of angel. If so, God would obviously give this creature the ability to speak!

— 9 —

REVELATION 9

So far we have seen a number of absolutely terrifying judgments hit the earth and the people living on it. Yet they appear to be small if we compare them to what comes next, beginning in chapter nine of Revelation. Imagine, though, living on the earth during these times. It will be scary to say the least. The first woe that the angel (or eagle) spoke of occurs with the fifth trumpet and the second with the sixth trumpet.

These are certainly not going to be pretty. Those who are living on the earth at this time should buckle up!

Revelation 9:1 – Fifth Trumpet, First Woe

"And the fifth angel sounded, and I saw a star fall from heaven unto the earth: and to him was given the key of the bottomless pit."

In this verse, we see another "star" fall from heaven and land on earth. Notice something interesting here, though. This particular star is apparently a *being* of some sort. The previous star we read about was in Revelation 8:10. There the star was described as a great star, which fell from heaven, and it was burning like a lamp. It appears as though that star was *not* a being, but an actual star of sorts. How do we know?

We know from Revelation 9:1, where this particular star is referred to as a masculine pronoun (him). In the previous "star" reference from chapter eight, there is no personal pronoun used at all. John is describing what he sees and he sees a star that falls into the fresh water supplies, turning the water into *poison*.

While it is possible that the star (from Revelation 8) he refers to could be an actual star, it is more likely that, in keeping with a literal interpretation (not literal*istic*), John is describing a comet, though he did not know what else to call it except a star.

In this chapter, John also refers to this phenomenon as a star. This could be because it *appeared* similar to the previous star in chapter eight. However, when the star gets to earth, no destruction results from his "impact" with the earth. Beyond this, this star (him) is given a key and the key is to the bottomless pit.

Of course, students of the Bible disagree as to whether or not this star is an actual star or a being. In spite of any grammatical evidence proffered, people continue to believe that this cannot be a being.

"In the Greek text, 'him' is an intensive, personal pronoun (autos). It is in the dative case and can be masculine (to him) or neuter (to it), but is properly translated 'him' because the context is describing a person.

Some take the pronouns here to refer to the fifth angel, but the nearest subject to the pronoun and the verb is the star."[25] He is later on in verse eleven referred to as *king* of those from the pit. We should also recall that Satan himself is referred to as the morning star (cf. Isaiah 14:12). This being could well be Satan, who fell from heaven to the earth after rebelling against God.

If this star is given a key, then we have *intelligence* here, not an inanimate object. Some commentators believe that this *star* is simply an angel that comes to the earth. Others believe this *star* to be malevolent, or one of the fallen angels. This author believes the *second* option to be more valid because this star "falls" from heaven to earth.

The fact that this individual is given the key to the bottomless pit says something about him as well. Either the only task he is given is to open the pit and then leave, or he is to open the pit because he is somehow *connected* to those within the bottomless pit; these are the only two possibilities.

This second reason is in keeping with one of God's purposes for the Tribulation. *"Also, remember that one of the purposes of the Tribulation is to unmask Satan's true character. The fifth trumpet will begin to do this even more clearly. In the church age, Satan often disguises himself as an angel of light with his servants doing likewise (2 Cor. 11:14-15), but from this point on in the Tribulation, the mask will come off and his true colors will be evident for the whole world to see."*[26]

Revelation 9:2-3

"And he opened the bottomless pit; and there arose a smoke out of the pit, as the smoke of a great furnace; and the sun and the air were darkened by reason of the smoke of the pit. And there came out of the smoke locusts upon the earth: and unto them was given power, as the scorpions of the earth have power."

---

[25] J. Hampton Keathley III *Studies in Revelation* (Biblical Studies Press, 1997), 129
[26] Ibid, 129

The angel's key opens the door to the bottomless pit. This is the same bottomless pit where Satan will be sequestered for the duration of the Millennial Reign of Jesus (1,000 years; Revelation 20:1-6).

As soon as he opens it, smoke so massive and thick comes out that it darkens the sky. The text says, *"the sun and the air were darkened by reason of the smoke."* If we were to take that *literalistically*, we would have to say that the sun was actually darkened by the smoke. However, by taking the verbiage *literally*, we know that what John is saying is that the air became so dark that it *appeared* as if the sun itself also became dark. The sun did not become dark. The sun simply appears to be dark by those on the earth who look up to the sky.

However, that is not the worst of it. The smoke holds a secret, and soon enough, the secret is revealed. Locusts pour out on the earth. These are obviously special locusts. If they were *only* normal, everyday locusts, one would have to wonder why they were in the bottomless pit at all. We have locusts on the earth now that eat their way through fields and crops on a daily basis. They can swarm and leave no grain unaffected by their presence. So are these merely the normal, run of the mill locusts? It really cannot be.

These special locusts were obviously kept in this bottomless pit for a particular reason and because of their *ability*. They are given special power similar to scorpions. Locusts generally do not act like or have the ability to imitate scorpions. Locusts simply eat – and they eat a lot, and they can eat a lot very quickly!

Scorpions, on the other hand, *sting*. The sting of a scorpion is painful and they can kill, depending upon the person they sting. These particular locusts are given that ability to sting people. Again, we must understand that they are *given* this power. It is bestowed on them. By *whom*? It can only come from the Lamb. Either He gives them this power directly, or He allows this angel to give it to them. In any case, the responsibility for their stinging power comes from the

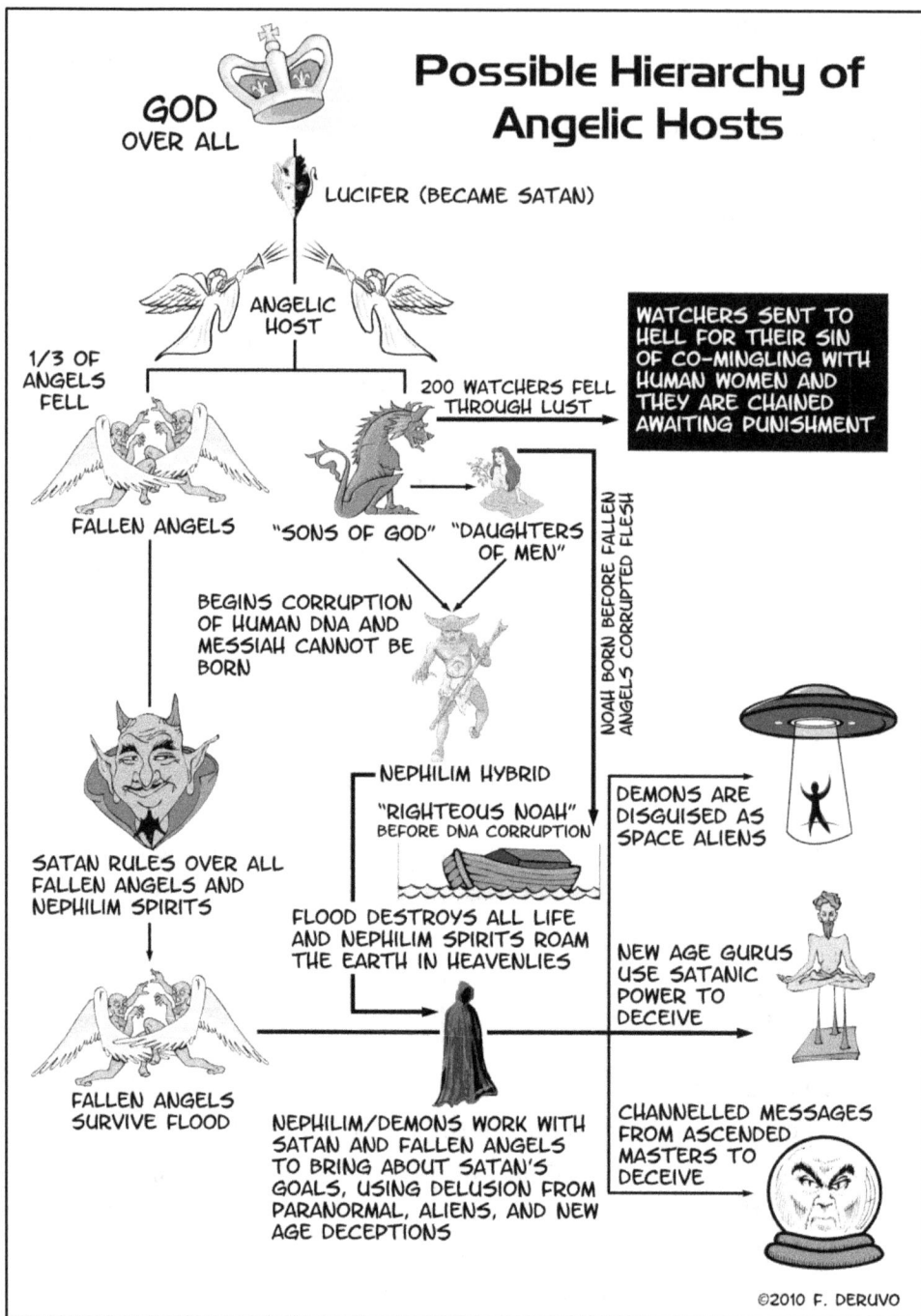

Possible Hierarchy of Angelic Hosts

GOD OVER ALL

LUCIFER (BECAME SATAN)

ANGELIC HOST

1/3 OF ANGELS FELL

WATCHERS SENT TO HELL FOR THEIR SIN OF CO-MINGLING WITH HUMAN WOMEN AND THEY ARE CHAINED AWAITING PUNISHMENT

200 WATCHERS FELL THROUGH LUST

FALLEN ANGELS

"SONS OF GOD"   "DAUGHTERS OF MEN"

NOAH BORN BEFORE FALLEN ANGELS CORRUPTED FLESH

BEGINS CORRUPTION OF HUMAN DNA AND MESSIAH CANNOT BE BORN

SATAN RULES OVER ALL FALLEN ANGELS AND NEPHILIM SPIRITS

NEPHILIM HYBRID

"RIGHTEOUS NOAH" BEFORE DNA CORRUPTION

DEMONS ARE DISGUISED AS SPACE ALIENS

FLOOD DESTROYS ALL LIFE AND NEPHILIM SPIRITS ROAM THE EARTH IN HEAVENLIES

NEW AGE GURUS USE SATANIC POWER TO DECEIVE

FALLEN ANGELS SURVIVE FLOOD

NEPHILIM/DEMONS WORK WITH SATAN AND FALLEN ANGELS TO BRING ABOUT SATAN'S GOALS, USING DELUSION FROM PARANORMAL, ALIENS, AND NEW AGE DECEPTIONS

CHANNELLED MESSAGES FROM ASCENDED MASTERS TO DECEIVE

©2010 F. DERUVO

144

Lamb, which is another indication that this is *God's* wrath at work here and no one else's.

In a previous book, *Demons in Disguise*, a chart was included on the *possible* hierarchy of angels. Included in it are "watchers," who were sentenced to chains in everlasting darkness for the sin they committed against humanity and God (cf. 1 Peter 3:19-20; 2 Peter 2:4; Jude 6). It is possible that some of the *confined* angels are released during the Tribulation.

Revelation 9:4-6
"And it was commanded them that they should not hurt the grass of the earth, neither any green thing, neither any tree; but only those men which have not the seal of God in their foreheads. And to them it was given that they should not kill them, but that they should be tormented five months: and their torment was as the torment of a scorpion, when he striketh a man. And in those days shall men seek death, and shall not find it; and shall desire to die, and death shall flee from them."

This is interesting. Note that they are given specific instructions. Again, by whom? In the absence of a particular commander, we can rightly assume that it is God who charges them in this regard. These locusts are not allowed to hurt the grass or any green thing like trees. These locusts have one specific duty, and that is to hurt those who are not sealed of God on their foreheads. They must relegate their stinging ability to those who up to this point have rejected God.

Notice that they were not only given strict limitations on what they could hurt, but also for *how long* they could do it. For five months, they are allowed to torment the people of the earth who do not have the seal of God on them.

Most scorpions on planet earth have a moderate level of toxicity. The pain from the sting can be immense, but is not considered to be a serious health threat. Imagine being stung by a wasp. That is painful enough. Now imagine being stung by wasps for *five months!*

These particular locusts are obviously more than simple locusts, because a locust by itself would not know the difference between green grasses, trees, and human beings. It would especially not know the difference between human beings that had the seal of God and those that did not.

These are unique creatures and they are likely *demons*, whom John calls locusts because of what they look like and because of what they do. They sting and no one dies. In fact, the last verse in the quoted section states that though people will *want* to die, death will not come to them. Can you imagine that? People will be in such pain that they will seek death – possibly even through suicide – and they will not die! God is angry, and He wants the world to know He is angry with them for the centuries that He has been ignored, denigrated, and blasphemed. This is God's time to pour out His wrath onto the world, and He is doing just that.

Revelation 9:7-11

"And the shapes of the locusts were like unto horses prepared unto battle; and on their heads were as it were crowns like gold, and their faces were as the faces of men.

"And they had hair as the hair of women, and their teeth were as the teeth of lions.

"And they had breastplates, as it were breastplates of iron; and the sound of their wings was as the sound of chariots of many horses running to battle.

"And they had tails like unto scorpions, and there were stings in their tails: and their power was to hurt men five months.

"And they had a king over them, which is the angel of the bottom-less pit, whose name in the Hebrew tongue is Abaddon, but in the Greek tongue hath his name Apollyon."

The verses just quoted explain to us what John saw. Remember, he was looking at these creatures from his perspective and described them from that vantage point. What we see is a weird mix of things.

Are these creatures actually *creatures*? Could they be war machines? First, because they are given special instructions to not hurt grass or trees, but only those who do not have the seal of God, it seems likely that we can rule out machines of any type. Of course, some will disagree with that and that is fine. There is no need to argue about it.

What do we see here in these verses? We need to try to grasp a mental picture of these creatures and then go from there.

- *Their bodies are shaped like horses*
- *They wore crowns of gold*
- *Their faces were men's faces, or human faces*
- *They all had long hair*
- *Teeth similar to lions' teeth*
- *They wore breastplates of iron*
- *Powerful wings*
- *Tails like scorpion tails able to sting*

This creates an interesting picture to say the least. Could there actually be creatures that looked as John described? Certainly, a creature like this would look very weird to us if we had never seen one before. This is what makes the area of Crypto zoology so difficult for many to accept, simply because the creatures that people have allegedly seen are such that we cannot *categorize*. People say they have seen Tera-torns (birds that have an allegedly very large wingspan of well over 25 feet), or Chubacabra, or Mothman, or any number of other freakish creatures. We have no way to classify or categorize them.

The "Locust" of Revelation 9?

Many sci-fi and fantasy movies recently have portrayed Centaurs, Fawns, giants, ogres, and others with a great deal of realism. They are no longer difficult for us to imagine.

With respect to Revelation 9, we need to remember that these creatures came from the bottomless pit. If they came from the bottomless pit, they would have been *placed* there and that would have happened because of something they *did* that God did not like. "*In Scripture locusts are associated with divine wrath (Ex. 10:12-20). This is why they are called locusts. But unlike the locusts of history who attack*

148

vegetation, these are commanded not to hurt the grass, etc.; their purpose will be to hurt men."[27] They will attack all but the 144,000.

The crude illustration included on the previous page simply shows a visual *possibility* of what the creature looks like that John described. We will not know for sure until it is actually released onto the earth from the bottomless pit.

It is helpful to remember the words of Jude regarding fallen angels:

"And the angels which kept not their first estate, but left their own habitation, he hath reserved in everlasting chains under darkness unto the judgment of the great day" (Jude 1:6).

Apparently, these particular angels did something so horrendous that God simply placed them in chains in total darkness ("under darkness") until the Day of Judgment. What was it that they did? No one knows for sure, and there have been many guesses. After having studied the issue for some time, this author is content to say that somehow, some way, these angels co-habited with human women. We read about this in Genesis 6:2.

"That the sons of God saw the daughters of men that they were fair; and they took them wives of all which they chose."

It was immediately *after* this occurred that we read the words, *"And the LORD said, My spirit shall not always strive with man, for that he also is flesh:* **yet his days shall be an hundred and twenty years**" (emphasis added).

Why did God decide at that point that men would have 120 years to live and that's it? What happened? Some believe "sons of God" refers to the line of Seth, while others believe it to be referring to angels who later fell. If the latter, then this would explain why God did what

---

[27] J. Hampton Keathley III *Studies in Revelation* (Biblical Studies Press, 1997), 131-132

He did, because He originally made everything to come forth after its kind (cf. Genesis 1).

In other words, God specifically made it so that only *like begets like.* Horses would give birth to horses. Dogs would give birth to dogs. People would give birth to people, etc.

Unfortunately, it appears that angels *may have* deliberately over-stepped their bounds here by finding some way to "procreate" with human women. If so, the result would have been what we read in Genesis 6:4. *"There were giants in the earth in those days; and also after that, when the sons of God came in unto the daughters of men, and they bare children to them, the same became mighty men which were of old, men of renown."*

Here is the order of how things went:

1. *Sons of God saw human women and made wives out of them*
2. *God decides that man has only 120 years left on earth*
3. *Giants are born to the women who "married" these sons of God*

Could it be that not only did God so decide to limit the remaining time on earth before man would be destroyed (through the Flood), but He also sentenced the angels who perpetrated this offense to the dungeons of blackness and in chains? It seems possible.

Are these the same beings in the bottomless pit? It is doubtful. The beings in the bottomless pit seem to be a conglomeration of beings all rolled up into one being. Because they are so strange looking to us, we find it difficult to believe they are anything but actual crea-tures, or types of machinery.

Let's go back to the sons of God for a moment. Admittedly, it is diffi-cult to think about angels finding some way to procreate with human women, isn't it? How could that have physically happened? No one really knows. People also defer to Christ when He said that the angels in heaven are neither married nor given in marriage (cf. Matthew 22:30). To these folks, this means they have no ability to procreate. However, this is not necessarily what that text means. It *could* simply mean that the role God defined for an angel does *not* include being married, though they might be physically capable of intercourse.

Whenever we see angels in the Bible who take on some type of human form, they always appear as *men*. If this is so, then it is quite possible that all angels in heaven are of the male gender. It does not necessarily mean that the angels are *genderless* when Christ says they do not marry. They simply do not marry because it is possible that all angels are masculine.

However, let us say that they *cannot* procreate. Would this stop them from finding a way to intermingle with human women? Remember, these beings obviously *lusted* after women ("*the daughters of men that they were fair*"), so women were a feast for the eyes, in that even these angels (if that is what they were) found themselves wanting them physically. Even if they could not physically procreate, could they do something else? Could they take DNA from the women and combine it with their own to create a *hybrid* creature that we come up against in Genesis 6:4 and elsewhere?

If so, this would adequately explain where the likes of Goliath and those like him came from and how they got into this world. Was Goliath merely a fluke? His four brothers were taller than he was (cf. 2 Samuel 21:16-22). If the sons of God were the fallen line of Seth, that would *not* explain the proliferation of gigantic men on the earth – and by the way, we have no record of giant *women* from the Bible.

The point is that if somehow these *were* angels and these angels left their first estate by finding a way to procreate with human women, this would obviously go against God's ordered creation where everything came after *its kind*. If so, this is the first record of someone tinkering with human DNA to create something else entirely.

So what does this have to do with the locusts from the bottomless pit? The offspring from this illicit union of angels with human women created *something*, and that something was not fully human. It was partially angelic, albeit fallen, and partially human. Because the human genome was *changed* through the intermingling of these angelic beings with women, there is an excellent chance that these beings did not have spirits as pure human beings have spirits.

However, because they are part angel, they would still live forever in the spiritual realm. In addition, because they are angelic, like the angels who fell they would have no chance of redemption, since salvation was provided for human beings *only*. These hybrid creatures were not fully human but only partially human, and did not qualify for the redemptive process.

It is very possible that if these fallen angels *did* co-habitate with human women by tinkering with their human DNA, they could have done the same thing with animals. In fact, there is reason to believe that many of the myths and lore we have down through the ages of Nymphs, Satyrs, Fawns, Centaurs, etc., may have their origins in this very process. It is possible that these creatures *did* exist prior to the Flood that destroyed everything except Noah, his family and the animals that God *specifically* brought to him to save.

If these creatures were created the same way – by doctoring or mixing *their* DNA with DNA from *other* creatures – it would explain how we got the locusts that fly out of the bottomless pit. They could very easily be something that fallen angels "made" from various strains of DNA. Yes, it sounds fantastic, but we really have no idea what angels are capable of doing.

Another possibility is that they were created this way by God. Prior to falling (if they are part of the group of angels that fell and were not created *by* the fallen angels), they may have looked similar, but the fall made them more evil looking. After all, do we really know what *all* spiritual beings look like? From the descriptions that the Bible presents of a number of beings, they are strange (to us) to say the least.

Certainly, they know far more than the most intelligent person on this planet does, but far less than what God knows. That still leaves a great deal of room for *super* intelligence. Angels could have been the ones who introduced iron, or magic, or fire, or any number of things to the human race – we just do not know.

If the reader is uncomfortable with this theory, that is fine. It is extended as one *possibility*. This author fully believes that the creatures that come out of the bottomless pit are just that – creatures kept there, away from humanity until the appointed time of their usefulness.

Please note also that these locusts have an *actual king*, though they themselves also wear crowns. The angel's name is Abaddon, or Apollyon, and he is the *king of the bottomless pit*. This is very likely Satan, who "fell to earth" and was given the key to unlock the pit so that the locusts could exit. Given their marching orders, they are ready to do battle for five months against humans *not* sealed with God's seal. Notice also that they are not allowed to kill anyone. Machines would not be able to make this distinction. Just as Satan was limited in his approach to Job in the Old Testament, these creatures receive the same type of limiting commands.

Revelation 9:12
"One woe is past; and, behold, there come two woes more hereafter."

The locusts – *whatever* they are – represent the first of three woes. Though this one seems terrible enough, the two coming are nothing to sneeze at.

A *woe* is tremendous grief, which often calls for cries of deep sorrow. What these locusts do to people for five months certainly causes a good deal of grief, terror, and sorrow. The fact that people will *want* to die but be unable to find death simply adds to the terror.

Sixth Trumpet, Second Woe – Revelation 9:13-15
"And the sixth angel sounded, and I heard a voice from the four horns of the golden altar which is before God, Saying to the sixth angel which had the trumpet, Loose the four angels which are bound in the great river Euphrates. And the four angels were loosed, which were prepared for an hour, and a day, and a month, and a year, for to slay the third part of men."

We have now moved on to the sixth angel who sounds his trumpet. Once he does, John hears a voice from the four horns of the golden altar. Whether the actual altar here speaks or a voice from the direction of the altar is not clear. It is interesting to realize that the four horns speak to the sixth angel saying that the four angels bound at the great river Euphrates should be *released*. Do you notice how everything connected with these judgments and God's throne is very much like a *pageant*? Now whether or not the actual horns speak or it us a being near the four horns of the altar is not really the main point. The point is found in what is *said*, which is to release the four *fallen* angels, and only *fallen* angels would be *bound*.

The angels were prepared specifically for that time, and their job is to kill one third of humanity. The language is very specific here, indicating that those four angels are to be released at a precise hour, of a firm day, of a specific month, and of a certain year. It is difficult to argue the specificity away here by looking at the text allegorically.

If the altar is actually speaking, we need to realize that this particular altar is the same one that hears the prayers of God's people. It represents mercy to those who are saved, yet in this instance, it is calling for death on those who are not saved.

Prior to this, we read of instances in which one-third of the water or vegetation was destroyed. We also know that many individuals have died because of the previous seals and trumpets. This is the first time when a specific number of human beings – one-third – will die as a direct result of one of the judgments of God.

Consider it. Over *22 million* people will be gone from the face of the earth! It is difficult to imagine such a number. Yet men's hearts remain hardened, unwilling to submit to God's authority.

Revelation 9:16-19

"And the number of the army of the horsemen were two hundred thousand thousand: and I heard the number of them.

"And thus I saw the horses in the vision, and them that sat on them, having breastplates of fire, and of jacinth, and brimstone: and the heads of the horses were as the heads of lions; and out of their mouths issued fire and smoke and brimstone.

"By these three was the third part of men killed, by the fire, and by the smoke, and by the

Two Hundred Million Horsemen

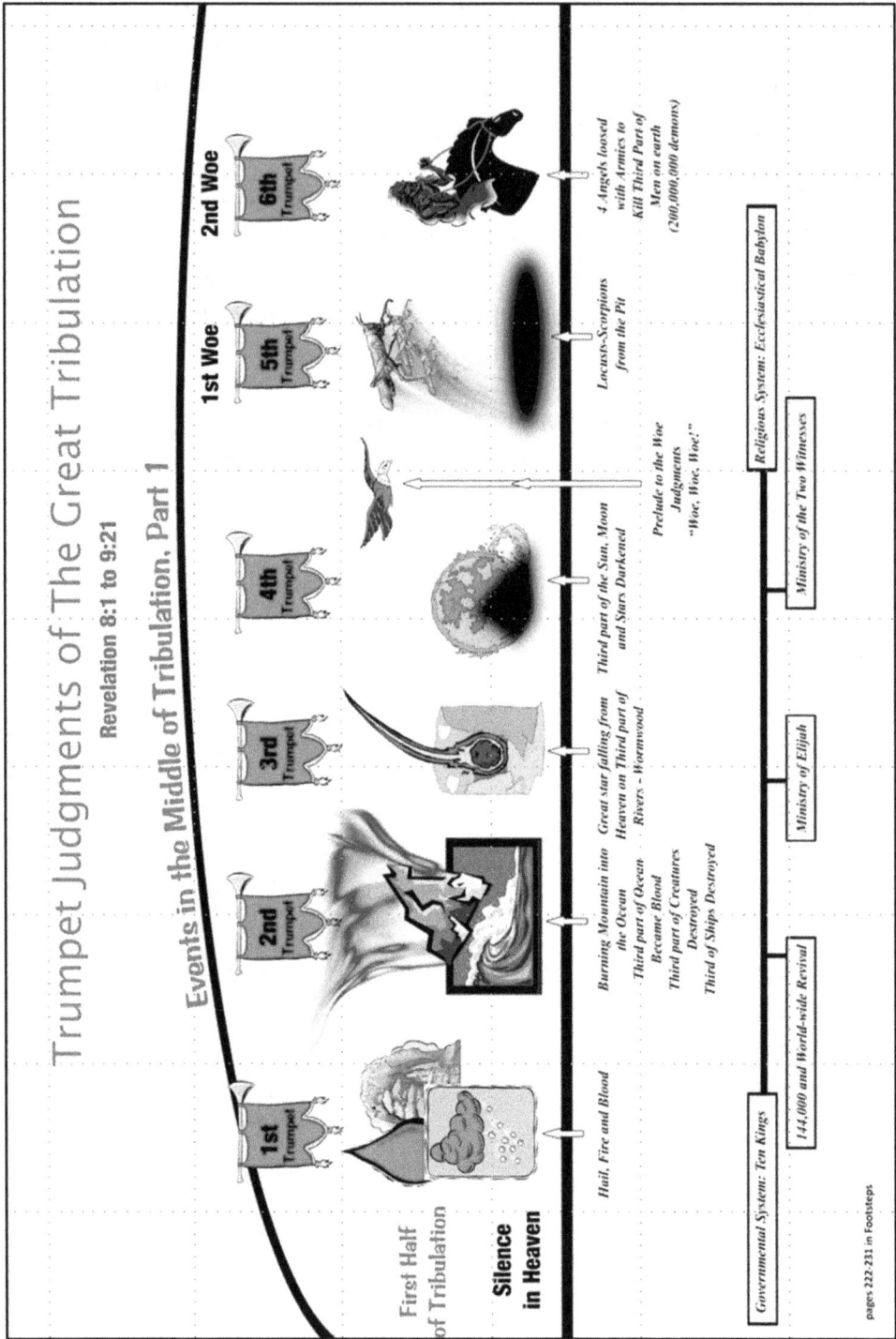

Trumpet Judgments of The Great Tribulation

Revelation 8:1 to 9:21

Events in the Middle of Tribulation, Part 1

1st Trumpet	2nd Trumpet	3rd Trumpet	4th Trumpet	1st Woe 5th Trumpet	2nd Woe 6th Trumpet

First Half of Tribulation

Silence in Heaven

Hail, Fire and Blood

Burning Mountain into the Ocean
Third part of Ocean Became Blood
Third part of Creatures Destroyed
Third of Ships Destroyed

Great star falling from Heaven on Third part of Rivers – Wormwood

Third part of the Sun, Moon and Stars Darkened

Prelude to the Woe Judgments "Woe, Woe, Woe!"

Locusts-Scorpions from the Pit

4 Angels loosed with Armies to Kill Third Part of Men on earth (200,000,000 demons)

Governmental System: Ten Kings		Religious System: Ecclesiastical Babylon

| 144,000 and World-wide Revival | Ministry of Elijah | Ministry of the Two Witnesses |

pages 222-231 in Footsteps

brimstone, which issued out of their mouths.

"For their power is in their mouth, and in their tails: for their tails were like unto serpents, and had heads, and with them they do hurt."

With the release of the four angels, we immediately see a large army of *two hundred million* soldiers (200,000,000). John tells us he *heard* the specific number. Many have tried to put an identity to these forces, claiming that they represent the armies of China. Others try to associate them with modern day weaponry that John was unable to describe adequately. However, it is probably best to look at them as *supernatural* beings, like the locusts. The description of these beings, though different from the locusts, is nevertheless shocking:

- *Breastplates of highly polished metals and jewels*
- *The heads of the horses were like lions*
- *They spit fire and smoke and brimstone from their mouths*
- *Their tails were like snakes with heads*

Verse 19 tells us that the power of these beings was in both their tails and their mouths. Fire, smoke, and brimstone issue from their mouths, while it appears that through their tails, serpents bite to kill.

These are also weird-looking creatures, which certainly seems to suggest a supernatural origin. The Bible does not really describe too many supernatural beings for us. We are left to imagine. It is possible that we would not be able to picture them (or believe it) if they were described to us in detail. We have nothing in our world that resembles many of these creatures.

These beings ride on horses, but the focal point is the rider. These riders are protected with breastplates of fire, jacinth, and brimstone. Brimstone is often a name associated with sulfur. Jacinth can be either a reddish jewel or a reddish/purple flower. In either case, it is probably either that John is telling us the *color* of the breastplate, or that it is made out of jacinth jewels. If this *is* the case, it would also explain the look of *fire* to it because of the reflective properties of the red jacinth.

In any case, if we are to understand this literally, these supernatural creatures are fearsome to behold. Imagine a creature running toward you that looked like a horse, yet had a head like a lion. It wore protective breastplates and could spit fire and brimstone at you. Beyond this, even if it was in front of you, it still had the power to kill because of the serpent-like tail with a head. They are obviously creatures that will be taken seriously when released onto the earth and will kill one-third of all humanity.

The total number so far is at least one-half of the world's population that has been decimated. There is more to come.

As of the middle of 2010, the world's population was 6,829,600,000. One-third of that is *22,765,333*. That is a large amount of dead people! These creatures obviously do their job, and they do it well.

The real tragedy here is the reaction the remaining people of the world have on all of this mayhem and death. We see the results in the next few verses, which close chapter nine.

Revelation 9:20-21
"And the rest of the men which were not killed by these plagues yet repented not of the works of their hands, that they should not worship devils, and idols of gold, and silver, and brass, and stone, and of wood: which neither can see, nor hear, nor walk:

"Neither repented they of their murders, nor of their sorceries, nor of their fornication, nor of their thefts."

The world has just experienced the death of *millions* of people worldwide from supernatural demons. You would *think* that the remaining people would look at that tragic statistic and realize that they needed to get their lives right before God. Unfortunately, this is *not* the case.

In spite of the fact that those alive have witnessed all the plagues, beginning with the first seal and going through this most current sixth trumpet, there is *no repentance*. Not only do people continue to worship idols, but also continue *killing* each other, performing occult magick, fornicating one with another, and stealing! These people do not *get it*. Human life will mean *nothing*, as it will be extremely easy to take another life. Hearts will be incredibly hardened.

Of course, God needs to open their eyes to the truth, but people are also responsible to *want* their eyes open to the truth. This is why God can and does hold individuals responsible for their actions. The thief on the cross *saw the truth*, and because he saw it, he embraced it. The people here in the ninth chapter of Revelation know what is happening, but stubbornly refuse to embrace that truth. Knowing that these plagues are judgments from God (cf. Revelation 6:17), they continue to deny that He is God, preferring instead to live life as they have done.

The text tells us that they continued to worship the things their hands made. Those things consisted of gold, silver, brass, stone, and wood. Is John talking about *actual* idols here? He could very well be, but he might also be including *more* than idols.

The Emergent Church has its idols. More and more, leaders within the Emergent Church are embracing aspects of Roman Catholicism, which has too many idols to number. If they are not venerating a statue of Jesus or the Virgin Mary, they are rubbing their prayer beads during the Rosary.

Besides the obvious idols, though, people have other things they consider to be idols. Cars, houses, clothes, swimming pools, pool tables, land, gold, jewelry, or anything else that people tend to long for can be idolatrous.

In spite of all the judgments that have been poured out onto humanity, people continue their lives with no changes. Life goes on. It is noteworthy here to point out that Satan lives to deceive. The leaders within the Emergent Church are a perfect example of this deception that they are peddling. They *firmly* believe that they are correct, that the broad way is the way to eternal life, and that the narrow way is the way to hell.

Those people go by the way they *feel* through their own intellectual discourse with others who agree with them. It is like one huge self-congratulatory party they have, each patting the other on the back with their latest book. Their books are filled with tripe and falsehoods, the kind of falsehoods that only come from hell itself. The author of those falsehoods is Satan and his minions.

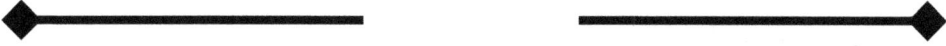

REVELATION 10

We left chapter nine with the world having experienced *one-third* of a population loss – in addition to the previous one-fourth population loss – and in spite of this, no one repents. That leaves roughly **7,588,444** people remaining on the earth and they do not seek God! No one felt the need to change his or her direction in life. So secure in their life of falsehoods had they become that no amount of judgments God sent their way would move them from their position. The last judgment in chapter nine was the sixth trumpet that released the four angels bound at the Euphrates

River. The 200 million soldiers follow this, which ultimately kill one-third of the populace on earth.

As we enter chapter ten, our attention is again directed toward what God is doing as we watch a new scene unfold. This scene does not unfold with another judgment. Instead, there is another *interlude* between judgments.

Revelation 10:1
"And I saw another mighty angel come down from heaven, clothed with a cloud: and a rainbow was upon his head, and his face was as it were the sun, and his feet as pillars of fire."

This particular angel is different from some of the others we have seen so far, yet he appears to be another angel, due to the use of the word "another." This one is classified as a *"mighty angel"* and is *"clothed with a cloud."* There is a *"rainbow upon his head"* and a brightness that rivals the sun exuding from his face. His feet are as if they are pillars of fire. Notice the angel *"comes down"* as opposed to *"fell from."* Everything points to the fact that this angel is *not* a fallen angel. If we did not know better, we might think this is Jesus Himself. Numerous commentators believe this to be the case.

However, it is doubtful that this angel *is* Jesus, simply because he is only identified as (another) "angel," though a mighty one at that. This mighty angel is unlike the *Angel of the LORD* in the Old Testament (cf. Genesis 16:7-14; 22:11-15; 31:11-13; Exodus 3:2-4, et al). While this angel's appearance is *similar* to Jesus' at times, there are differences.

This particular angel could very well be Michael the Archangel, who is described as *"one of the chief princes"* in Daniel 10, or he could be another angel similar in rank to Michael. The truth is that we simply do not know, because this angel is not given a name. Gabriel is also described in that chapter of Daniel, and is in many ways similar to this angel in this tenth chapter of Revelation. *"His body also was like the beryl, and his face as the appearance of lightning, and his eyes as lamps of fire, and his arms and his feet like in colour to polished brass, and the voice of his words like the voice of a multitude"* (Daniel 10:5-6).

The fact that this angel's face is as the sun may mean that he reflects the glory of God, as did Moses when he came down from the mountain after being in God's presence (cf. Exodus 34:29; Matthew 17:2). The angel's feet are like pillars of fire, which of course can mean many things. This can be representative of the fact that he possesses great strength in his feet. Nothing stops him from going where the Lord would have him go. It also may simply be a part of the way the angel was created.

The rainbow around his head makes us think of the Noahic Covenant and God's promise never to destroy the human race again using a global flood. God's covenant *remains* and His promises will not be broken, certainly not by Him, nor by anyone else.

Revelation 10:2
"And he had in his hand a little book open: and he set his right foot upon the sea, and his left foot on the earth."

Once the angel touches the earth, he sets his right foot upon the sea and his left foot on the earth. He is obviously a very large angel, being able to set one foot on ground and one on the sea. He holds an open book. Unfortunately, we do not learn what this book is or what it represents, as we are not told here in Revelation or anywhere else in the Bible .

"In contrast to the seven-sealed book in Christ's hand (Rev. 5), this is a little book and it is open. "Open" is in the perfect passive to show the book had already been opened. It was an open book, which may indicated that it contained Old and New Testament prophecies of the com-

ing events, though the exact contents of this little book are not revealed in this chapter. The point is this book had been opened prior to this chapter, unlike the seven-sealed book that had its contents revealed gradually, seal by seal in the progression of the book of Revelation."[28]

Commentators have disagreed over what this book is, and it is really anyone's educated guess. It could be the scroll that the Lamb took in chapter five or something else entirely. In any case, though we do not know what it *is* – other than being a little book – we *do* know what it *does*, as we learn in the next verses.

Revelation 10:3-4
"And cried with a loud voice, as when a lion roareth: and when he had cried, seven thunders uttered their voices. And when the seven thunders had uttered their voices, I was about to write: and I heard a voice from heaven saying unto me, Seal up those things which the seven thunders uttered, and write them not."

Before we learn more about the book the mighty angel holds, he cries with a loud voice. In response, seven thunders utter their voices. This are not merely the same type of thundering that one would hear during a rainstorm, because these thundering voices apparently *say* something. In fact, John was about to write down what he heard, but was stopped by a voice from heaven. This voice from heaven is most likely the Lord's voice. The thundering represents impending judgment.

John is told that he must not write down what he heard. Of course, because he was not allowed to write down what he heard, we all would like to know what it was that he heard. Sorry, it is off limits until such a time as the Lord has preordained to release that information. To even put any type of guess to the content of the seven

---

[28] J. Hampton Keathley III *Studies in Revelation* (Biblical Studies Press, 1997), 140

thundering would be foolish and a grand waste of time, as no clue is provided.

"From the nature of the passage, or context, this apparently deals with God's judgments and purposes for these things, but the details are sealed."[29] The best we can determine is that it is something extremely important (as is anything the Lord says), and it is not to be known until the appointed time. We need to leave it there and trust God.

Revelation 10:5-7

"And the angel which I saw stand upon the sea and upon the earth lifted up his hand to heaven,

"And sware by him that liveth for ever and ever, who created heaven, and the things that therein are, and the earth, and the things that therein are, and the sea, and the things which are therein, that there should be time no longer:

"But in the days of the voice of the seventh angel, when he shall begin to sound, the mystery of God should be finished, as he hath declared to his servants the prophets."

Our attention now returns to the mighty angel straddling the land and the sea. He raises his hand to heaven and swears an oath. Notice that he swears by *"him that liveth forever and ever, who created heaven..."* The mighty angel includes everything that *Jesus* is here and we can read about these creative attributes in Colossians 1.

The angel finishes his oath by stating that the time has come to complete the *"mystery."* One can only assume that the remaining plagues and judgments of the Tribulation will happen in quick succession for the remaining three and a half years left of this terrible time on earth.

---

[29] J. Hampton Keathley III *Studies in Revelation* (Biblical Studies Press, 1997), 140

The mighty angel points toward the coming trumpet sound of the seventh angel. When the seventh angel sounds his trumpet, we are then on the *downside* of the Great Tribulation. The last pieces of the puzzle will begin to fall into place.

So far, up to this point in Revelation we have been involved in an interlude. Between the last judgment – the *sixth* trumpet – and the coming *seventh* trumpet, this bit of pageantry is taking place in heaven.

This seems like a good time to point out something about which some students of the Bible and commentators have disagreed. In going through the book of Revelation, not everything is *chronological* in nature. This will become evident in chapter eleven of Revelation. Every so often, there seems to be a break in the activity of judgment. We either are then privy to a *summation* of events, a view *backwards*, or even a view *ahead*.

Because of this, it is common to hear people argue that for such and such an event to take place, there just does not seem to be enough *time* for it to happen. They use this as a means of proving their own point about something, such as the Marriage Supper of the Lamb and the resurrection. We will get into that soon.

The problem, of course, is that where God and heaven are concerned, *time* is not a factor at all. Where *earth* is concerned, this is obviously the case, but not where God or the eternal realm is concerned, which is why it is called the *eternal* realm, because it is not *governed* by time.

God and the realm in which He officially resides (though He is also everywhere at once) is not hampered or affected by the passage of time. It makes no difference, so when people argue about the lack of time, or there not being enough time for things to happen, they seem to be forgetting that eternity is not affected by time. As this issue comes up in future chapters, we will remind our readers.

The mystery that the mighty angel speaks of is not meant as a *puzzle*. A puzzle means someone does not know the answer and must figure it out. In using the term "mystery," God is merely saying that He has *kept* some of the information to Himself, only to be revealed when it is the appointed time.

For instance, the words that the seven thundering spoke are a mystery to us because they are *unknown*. They are, of course, completely known to God Himself. We cannot figure them out. He needs to reveal them to us.

The same is true with the mystery the mighty angel refers to here. It is a mystery from *humanity's* perspective, but certainly not God's. He has kept the times and seasons from us so that we would not be able to pinpoint when things will occur in the future.

However, when we get to the "in-between" time of trumpet six and trumpet seven, God is letting us know through the mighty angel that this mystery will culminate soon. Everything will be fulfilled in real time. It will come to completion, and there is to be no doubt about that.

God's mercy has kept things at bay for quite some time. People may disagree that His mercy has done that, but the truth remains that without His mercy, this world would not have lasted as long as it has lasted.

The mighty angel prepares us for the opening of the seventh trumpet, which also releases the *final seven* judgments, the *bowl* judgments. These last seven judgments will happen in succession and will bring all things related to the Tribulation and the Great Tribulation to its preordained conclusion.

Even though the first part of the Tribulation (3 ½ years) was replete with a variety of judgments directly from the Lamb, there were also periods of respite, or interludes. Some of them almost seemed to be deliberately drawn out.

We also note that the Antichrist has been relatively quiet during this first half of the Tribulation. In some ways, it is almost as if he has been *non-existent,* except for when he first came onto the scene with the opening of the first seal and the white horse.

Once the seventh trumpet sounds, however, almost immediately we see Antichrist come to the fore with a real crowd pleaser. However, prior to this, has the Antichrist truly been quiet, doing nothing? No, he has not. We will see this in the book of Daniel. What he *has* been doing is preparing himself for the assault he plans to make on the world and ultimately on Jesus Christ at His second return.

According to Daniel, the Antichrist has been clawing his way up to the top of the totem pole, even killing to do so. This serves to get the notice of those other leaders around him who are part of the 10-Kingdom world government, and it also serves to take out two individuals who threatened to overcome him, or at least give him a fight.

Revelation 10:8-11

"And the voice which I heard from heaven spake unto me again, and said, Go and take the little book which is open in the hand of the angel which standeth upon the sea and upon the earth. And I went unto the angel, and said unto him, Give me the little book. And he said unto me, Take it, and eat it up; and it shall make thy belly bitter, but it shall be in thy mouth sweet as honey. And I took the little book out of the angel's hand, and ate it up; and it was in my mouth sweet as honey: and as soon as I had eaten it, my belly was bitter. And he said unto me, Thou must prophesy again before many peoples, and nations, and tongues, and kings."

John is told to ask for the little book and when he receives it from the angel he is told to eat it and warned that it will taste sweet, but will leave his stomach bitter. This is the way it is with prophecy. The *end result* of it is often sweet, yet between then and now it can be very bitter.

Do not let anyone tell you that studying prophecy is a waste of time. It is only a waste of time if studying it does not provide a greater impetus for *evangelism*. Authentic Christians must always be about the Father's business, and that involves the *Great Commission*. We cannot go through this life looking forward to living with Jesus in heaven if we could care less about those around us who might be on a different path altogether. In fact, a Christian who thinks like that should stop and verify his own Christianity. If he has no real thought or sadness when it comes to the lost of this world, then he is either not a Christian, or an extremely immature one.

John was told that he would prophecy before many people of various languages and nations, as well as kings. Even though a prisoner on the Isle of Patmos, the book of Revelation would make the rounds, and here in 2010 it is nearly in every corner of the world. The message of the book speaks to people, warning them of coming calamity, telling them that it is not too late to turn to Jesus. Notice that the book affects John. So should God's Word affect all authentic Christians *before* they move out in obedience.

The sadness is when people *reject* the message of our Savior and Lord. It is when they believe that they do not need to heed Him, nor do they need His salvation, that the Holy Spirit is grieved. To reject Christ is to call Him a liar. Rejecting Him until death is the unpardonable sin, which results in an eternal separation from Him. For those who chose in this life to consistently reject the identity of Jesus as well as the truth of His message, they have opted to remain separate from him now. They will continue to be separated from Him after they die, for all eternity.

The Good News of Jesus Christ along with His coming Kingdom provides great hope and joy for all those who are His and who await His return. Those that consistently reject Him and His message create bitterness for themselves and tragic sadness for authentic Christians because of their refusal to believe Jesus Christ.

11

REVELATION 11

Chapter 11 begins with John being given a reed, and he is told to measure the Temple area, but to leave out the outer court. The reason he is told to leave out the outer court is because that area will continue to be trampled by the Gentiles until the appointed time of 42 months. Forty-two months is equal to 1,260 days, and each half of the Tribulation/Great Tribulation lasts for 1,260 days, totaling seven years. Remember, this is based on a calendar year of 360 days, not 365 days. Chapter 11 is another pause.

Revelation 11:1-2

"And there was given me a reed like unto a rod: and the angel stood, saying, Rise, and measure the temple of God, and the altar, and them that worship therein. But the court which is without the temple leave out, and measure it not; for it is given unto the Gentiles: and the holy city shall they tread under foot forty and two months."

This particular section of Revelation is greatly debated. It all boils down to how people interpret this section, though. Many prefer to allegorize or spiritualize the text. Yet there is nothing within the text or context that tells us to do that. People have a very difficult time accepting the fact that there will be another Temple. John is definitely told to measure it, and he is specifically told only to measure the areas called the Holy Place and the Holy of Holies.

A reed would make a great measuring stick, because as a bamboo-like material, taken right from the Nile River (or similar), these reeds are strong and fairly straight. Inherently, they make a good tool for measuring.

A couple of things we need to realize here is that this last kingdom – first mentioned in Daniel as well as other books of the Old Testament, and now in Revelation – is the last Gentile empire prior to the return of Jesus Christ. Because this is a Gentile empire, it is obviously led by a Gentile. This proves that the Antichrist will be/is Gentile in ethnicity, not Jewish as some believe.

The fact that a Gentile will lead this last empire, which will ultimately revolt against Jesus Christ as He returns to earth, does not surprise me. In fact, I think it is very interesting that a Gentile will be the one who solves the problem of the Middle East.

It would also not surprise me to find that the coming man of sin (the Antichrist) who leads this final empire and rebellion will be Muslim.

Some may balk at that, because the natural inclination is to claim that Jewish leaders would never trust or be willing to work with a Muslim individual to settle the peace problem in the Middle East.

However, it should be noted that there is currently such a man now. Adnan Oktar (who goes by the pen name *Harun Yahya*) is an Islamic Creationist and anti-Zionist. He is also considered to be a brilliant intellectual who has millions of copies of his 225 (yes, that is two hundred, twenty-five) books in print. In spite of the fact that he is anti-Zionist, he also believes that Christians, Muslims, and Jews can and should work together to rebuild the third Temple on the Temple Mount.

Not long ago, Oktar met with three representatives from the recently revived Jewish Sanhedrin to find ways to make the Temple a reality. Though there are controversies surrounding Oktar, he is prolific, charming, and brilliant. He is also a Muslim that endeavors to work with Jewish leaders to make the third Temple a reality.

Jewish leaders who have met with him have little to no difficulty believing him to be sincere. Please note that I am not indicating that Oktar is the coming Antichrist. I am merely stating that it is not unheard of for Jewish leaders to be willing to work with a devout Muslim in order to bring about what they perceive as the necessity of a third Temple.

Oktar presents his message as something that benefits Christians, Jews, and Muslims. Those of us who understand what the Bible says know that this will never happen. In the meantime, he has met with and continues to meet with many Jews from Israel to bring forth what he considers the common goal of the three main religions around the globe.

While many violent Muslims around the world seek to destroy Jews and Israel, Oktar takes a different and perhaps unique approach.

Here is his statement concerning the "people of the book" from one of his sites:

"There are two varieties of Zionism today. The first of these is the Zionist conception of the devout Jewish people, who wish to live in peace and security in Israel alongside Muslims, seeking peace and wishing to worship in the lands of their forefathers and engage in business. In that sense, Muslims support Zionism. We would fully back the devout Jewish people living in peace and security in their own lands, remembering Allah [God], worshiping in their synagogues and engaging in science and trade in their own land.

The Zionist belief held by a devout Jew and based on the Torah does not in any way conflict with the Qur'an. The Jews' living in that region is indicated in the Qur'an, in which it is revealed that Allah [God] has settled the Children of Israel on it:

Remember when Moses said to his people, "My people! Remember Allah's [God's] blessing to you when He appointed prophets among you and appointed kings for you, and gave you what He had not given to anyone else in all the worlds! My people! Enter the Holy Land which Allah [God] has ordained for you. Do not turn back in your tracks and so become transformed into losers." (Surat al-Ma'ida: 20-21)

"It is the "irreligious, godless Zionism" that we as Muslims condemn and regard as a threat. These godless Zionists, who do not defend the existence and oneness of Allah [God], but, on the contrary, encourage a Darwinist, materialist perspective and thus engage in irreligious propaganda, are also a threat to devout Jews. Godless Zionism is today engaged in a struggle against peace, security and moral virtue, and constantly produces strife and chaos and the shedding of blood. Muslims and devout Jews must join forces to oppose this godless Zionism and encourage belief in Allah [God]."[30]

---

[30] http://www.unionoffaiths.com/statementtojews.html

As stated, it would *not* surprise me to learn that the coming future Antichrist is to be a Gentile individual of *Muslim* persuasion. We have seen that Jewish leaders are not opposed to working with a Muslim who approached them with *respect* and appeared to have *their* interests at heart. At the same time, it is very likely that a Muslim leader is the *only* type of person that *violent* Muslims would be willing to hear and obey.

Of course, time will tell, so I am not making predictions, but simply educated guesses based on God's Word and what I see in the world today.

It should be clear from this alone that man is always trying to do what he thinks God wants, but by man's energy and ideas. God fully rejects the areas outside the Holy Place and Holy of Holies because these are said to be trampled by the Gentiles. This is what will occur during the second half of the Tribulation.

Remember, Antichrist enters into a seven-year covenant (one "week" according to Daniel 9:27) with Israel. In the middle of the "week," or three and a half years into it, he breaks the covenant and desecrates the Temple by proclaiming himself to be God. This, of course, does not sit well with Jews, who run for their own safety.

It is likely that many Muslims at this time will applaud and cheer this move by Antichrist. It may also be that prior to making a pact or covenant with Israel, secret talks might have taken place assuring Muslims that though the Jewish Temple will be rebuilt, the Antichrist himself (thought to be Islam's Mahdi) will turn it into a mosque for Islam. If Muslim nations could be given such a promise, then it stands to reason why they might go along with his plan of covenanting with Israel at all.

Islamic nations will simply lay low for the first part of the Tribulation until Antichrist desecrates the Temple. Then they will exult in joy, joining their "savior" in his conquest of the earth! To this author, this is a real possibility that bears consideration. From the middle of the Tribulation to the end, for the remaining forty-two months, Antichrist and Gentiles will trample God's Temple. In the end, Jesus Himself will *reclaim* it.

Revelation 11:3-8

"And I will give power unto my two witnesses, and they shall prophesy a thousand two hundred and threescore days, clothed in sackcloth.

"These are the two olive trees, and the two candlesticks standing before the God of the earth.

"And if any man will hurt them, fire proceedeth out of their mouth, and devoureth their enemies: and if any man will hurt them, he must in this manner be killed.

"These have power to shut heaven, that it rain not in the days of their prophecy: and have power over waters to turn them to blood, and to smite the earth with all plagues, as often as they will.

"And when they shall have finished their testimony, the beast that ascendeth out of the bottomless pit shall make war against them, and shall overcome them, and kill them.

"And their dead bodies shall lie in the street of the great city, which spiritually is called Sodom and Egypt, where also our Lord was crucified."

Immediately after John measures the Temple area, God points out two people who will be witnesses for Him during this second half of the Tribulation. Notice God says that He will give "power" to His two witnesses. Why? It is because of their particular ministry and their need to protect themselves.

The two witnesses enjoy God's power and provision and are able to do the following:

- *Shoot fire out of their mouths to kill anyone who attempts to harm them*
- *Shut heaven so that there will be no rain*
- *Turn water to blood*
- *Bring numerous plagues to the earth whenever they want*

That is some power. They will be able to kill anyone who attempts to hurt them and will do so by being a human flamethrower. I would imagine that it would only take one or two people to become an example of this type of death to keep everyone else away from them.

Beyond this, they will be able to control the rain, as well as the content of the water, and to create plagues whenever they feel like it. People on the earth will certainly fear them. They will undoubtedly marvel at their ability as well.

Do we know who these individuals are here? As you can see, we are not told their identity, which of course has made people debate their identity for years. People believe these witnesses could be Elijah and Moses, because of the similar miracles that these two witnesses will do.

Can we know for certain? I do not believe we can know. While it is fine to make educated guesses, it is not good to be dogmatic about the identities of these individuals. Interestingly enough, there is at least one person on the Internet who claims to be one of the witnesses mentioned in the text. His name is Ronald Weinland and he hails from Herbert W. Armstrong's cult, Worldwide Church of God.

Weinland believes he is one of these two witnesses, and not long ago revealed on his website the identity of the other witness. *"[N]ow is the time to publicly reveal the name of the second end-time witness. It is my wife Laura. We are a family through whom God will be working to bring an end to this age and setting the stage (and much more) for the age to follow. Many will mock and ridicule, but as we go forward, this time God will place fear in those who mock Him and His servants. Power has been given to make this so."*[31]

Weinland also believes that we are *now* in the midst of the Tribulation. He states, *"We are at the very end-time for man's self-rule on earth. The Seventh Seal has been opened and now the First Trumpet has been blown."*[32] He originally made the above two statements on April 18, 2008 and then repeated them on his blog on December 13, 2008.

Could Weinland be one of the witnesses? Not if we take Scripture literally, as it should be taken. Weinland has gone to great lengths to "reveal" the message of the seven thunderings, and has also developed a timeline for the events of the end times, including the Tribulation. If we are to understand Revelation as has been outlined in this book, then it is clear that Weinland *cannot* be one of the witnesses at all. He has actually prophesied *incorrect* things, which makes him a *false prophet*, if this author's understanding of Revelation is correct.

It seems apparent that the Tribulation cannot begin without the Antichrist signing a covenant with Israel that leads to temporary peace in the Middle East. Has this taken place yet? Not to this author's knowledge. If it has not taken place yet, then the Tribulation could not have actually begun, much less the Seventh Seal!

Weinland is woefully incorrect. He is deceived and deceiving those who listen to him and believe him. This is tragic; however, he is unwilling to listen to anyone who does not believe he is who he says he is with respect to the two witnesses. The fact that he believes his wife to be the other witness is equally absurd, but also *convenient*.

---

[31] http://ronaldweinland.com/index.php?paged=2
[32] Ibid

The two witnesses here in Revelation 11 will have God's power, which will work mightily in and through them. They are witnesses *for* God to the lost of this world.

Is God merciful? He is absolutely merciful! These two witnesses are not raised up for the purpose of *killing* people or sending *plagues*. They are raised up to be God's *witnesses*. Their job is to *evangelize* the world at this point in the Tribulation. They can kill *as needed* and send plagues *as needed*, but that is not their main purpose.

Consider the fact that even amidst all the turmoil that God sends to earth's rebellious people, He *continues* to call people to Him. At this point in the Tribulation, He does so through these two witnesses.

Why then do these witnesses have the power they have if their job is to primarily witness? It is safe to say that people will want them out of the way and *dead*! People do not want to hear about Jesus Christ anymore. Try to evangelize someone and see what happens. You may well be ridiculed or accused of spreading intolerance or even *hatred*. It is because authentic Christians know that there is only one way to God, and that is through Jesus Christ!

The world believes that Jesus is only *one* path among *many* (if they believe in Jesus at all). There is a great deal of antagonism toward Christians and Christianity today, and that is due solely to *Satan's* hatred of God and His children. Because God lives within us through the Presence of the Holy Spirit, authentic Christians come under attack. Satan hates God and he hates authentic believers.

During the Tribulation period, people will be so antagonistic to Christians that they will kill them just as easily as look at them. The two witnesses are another way of revealing God's power to the world. God *could* simply protect them, allowing nothing to harm them. It is obvious, though, that God wants these two men to have power to kill and inflict fear in those who reject Him. This again is His mercy at work! For those who see the witnesses, hear their preaching, and see the mighty deeds they are capable of doing, people will either be drawn to them or be repelled by them. Most will be *repelled*.

During this period during the ministry of the witnesses, nothing will be able to hurt them. Only when God's timing arrives will they be killed, and they will be killed by the *Antichrist*. He is the one who comes up out of the pit. They will witness for 1,260 days, as it states in verse one. That equals 42 months, or 3 ½ years! Again, we must base this on God's prophetic year, not our calendar. His is 360 days long.

The beast – *Antichrist* – will gain an initial victory over these two troublesome prophets! When he does, the world will literally rejoice at his victory and their deaths! The term "beast" in Revelation can mean the system created by the beast or the beast himself, and that is only determined based on the context of the particular passage.

After the two witnesses are killed, their bodies are refused burial. People prefer to see them lying in the street, dead. This will give the people confidence, knowing that their deaths were not merely a dream or wishful thinking. They are gone!

Scripture says that their bodies will lie in the street for three days, in the "*great city, which spiritually is called Sodom and Egypt, where also our Lord was crucified.*" The Lord was crucified just barely outside of the Temple walls of the city of *Jerusalem*. Notice here it is referred to as Sodom and Egypt.

The main reason it is referred to as Sodom is due to the "fornication" that takes place within the rebuilt Temple. God has always viewed idolatry as a form of fornication. Israel, the wife of God the Father, was found many times to have strayed, following foreign gods. When this occurred, they were guilty of spiritual *adultery*. Fornication is between two people who are not married. When a married partner enters into an illicit affair with someone other than his or her spouse, it is called *adultery*.

Sodom was noted for its *fornication*, *adultery*, *lasciviousness*, and its *homosexuality*. They remained unrepentant to the end, when God rained fire and brimstone down on them from heaven.

Jerusalem will literally become a city of harlotry during the Tribulation. As we consider the Middle East now, we see orthodox Jews who are intent upon rebuilding the Temple. The Temple Institute of Jerusalem has completed nearly all the furnishings for the Temple, including the clothing for the priests.

Outside of Jericho, a full scale Temple is being erected in order to train priests for when the actual Temple is built on the Temple Mount in Jerusalem. The problem is that God will honor *none* of it. To Him, this coming rebuilt Temple is anathema, nothing more than *idolatry*.

Israel has rejected her Messiah, and Jesus promised that He would not return until Israel begged Him to do so. The coming Temple will be desecrated and eventually destroyed when Jesus returns. Jerusalem and its leaders turned their backs on Jesus, the true Messiah. For that, God calls Jerusalem "Sodom" and "Egypt." *"In Scripture, 'Egypt' stands for the world, and 'Sodom' for the flesh. The point is the great city is dominated by the world system, by the flesh, and by Satan through the beast. The city has spiritually become totally reprobate along with the rest of the world."*[33]

Revelation 11:9-10
"And they of the people and kindreds and tongues and nations shall see their dead bodies three days and an half, and shall not suffer their dead bodies to be put in graves. And they that dwell upon the earth shall rejoice over them, and make merry, and shall

---

[33] J. Hampton Keathley III *Studies in Revelation* (Biblical Studies Press, 1997), 149

send gifts one to another; because these two prophets tormented them that dwelt on the earth."

What a marvelous time of celebration the world will enjoy because of the deaths of the two witnesses! Such a time of feasting and merriment has not been seen in the world for the longest of times. The Antichrist is the man of the hour, the hero, the 'divine son' who overcame the two witnesses. These witnesses were nothing but a thorn in the world's sides and now they are *gone!*

Note the use of the word "tormented." This is the way the world will see these two individuals. They will be viewed as tormentors of the worst kind, the religious kind. The very presence of the two witnesses will prick people's consciences, convicting them of their sin and rebelliousness.

People will not want to be reminded of how evil and rotten they are, and in that sense, the testimony of the two witnesses will rub the world the wrong way. People will become so fed up with them that they will want them dead; however, they are afraid to attempt to kill them because of the fire that shoots out of their mouths! They have to do their best to put up with the presence of the witnesses while trying to ignore them.

When Antichrist kills the witnesses (only as God allows), the entire world celebrates! What they could not do, the Antichrist did! Truly, he must be the Messiah, the final Mahdi! The people on earth are so happy that they send each other gifts to celebrate the occasion! It appears that this celebrating is done over a period of days, not just a brief moment or an hour in time.

One commentator notes that this may well be during the actual Christmas season. It is possible, but there is really nothing in the text that promotes that idea, except for the fact that the celebration of Christmas is nearly global.

Revelation 11:11-12

"And after three days and a half the spirit of life from God entered into them, and they stood upon their feet; and great fear fell upon them which saw them.

"And they heard a great voice from heaven saying unto them, Come up hither. And they ascended up to heaven in a cloud; and their enemies beheld them."

After three and a half days, the witnesses come back to life! Obviously, for the bodies to be lying in the street for that length of time under the heat of the sun and the elements undoubtedly means that the bodies began to decay from the moment of death. By the time we get to three days later, the bodies likely smell and have begun to rot.

At this point, no one can say that the witnesses were not really dead! They were dead, and the condition of their corpses proves it. At this point, though, God pulls another miracle by raising these men from the dead for all the world to see!

Consider the fact that what happens across the world from where you live can be witnessed in seconds or minutes because of technology. The proliferation of cameras in cell phones and security cameras along with everything else has made sharing news faster and easier. What happens in any part of the world is quickly seen in every other part of the world. We cannot escape it.

When the witnesses rise from the dead, we can be assured that someone with a video camera will catch the event digitally. In a matter of moments at the longest, it will be posted to any number of Web sites throughout the world. There will also likely be news crews covering the deaths of the witnesses, drawing the news out for as long as possible. Because of this they will be right there when God calls these men back to life.

Every eye will have the opportunity to see what is taking place in Jerusalem. People will see it even if they are not in Jerusalem. It will shock the world.

Many people today do not believe in God. They readily and arrogantly admit it. They believe God to be antiquated, out of date, a remnant of the Dark Ages. Modern man is far above such outmoded curiosities. I have talked to many atheists who come across as being supremely arrogant. They believe they have arrived at the real truth, and Christians especially continue to believe in fables and myths. These people view authentic Christians pitifully. With a big sigh, they wish we could get to the place where they are, a place that has truly freed them from the bondage of religious mythology.

This type of thinking precludes any acceptance of the supernatural in personal form. These people laugh at miracles, including the virgin birth or the resurrection of Jesus from the dead. I have long thought that even if Noah's Ark could be pulled from its resting place in one piece, to the atheist it would prove nothing, except that there is a large boat that was stuck inside a glacier. How do we know it's Noah's? Could it have merely been a hand built dwelling place for a large colony of people, and from that, a fable came to be?

If God showed Himself to the entire world now, telling everyone exactly what they must do to be saved and that Jesus Christ is the only way, people would scoff. It's some type of holographic joke, they would argue, and certainly nothing to take literally. Pshaw...their arrogance ridicules such things as impossible.

Not long ago, what appears to be encrusted chariot wheels, horse bridles, bits, and skeletons of horses and humans were found at the bottom of the Red Sea. While we have photos of these things, Egypt was very quick to shut down any and all expeditions that purposed to raise these items to the surface.

Nonetheless, word was out. Not a few atheists, while admitting that *something* could be there, certainly needed more proof than one or two chariot wheels before they were willing to believe that Moses led a large company of people out of Egypt, after which they were chased by Pharaoh and his armies. Though the Israelites were able to cross the Red Sea on dry ground, the water engulfed the Egyptians, destroying them in their tracks. Can you hear the atheists as they harumphed and snorted arrogantly?

While the two witnesses will rise from the dead right before the entire world, after being dead for days, the world reacts only in fear, never taking it to the desired end: repentance. The sense of the Scripture here is that these dead men stand erect very quickly! They do not slowly get up. They arise with purpose! That freaks everyone out, as I am sure you agree that it would. The fear that engulfs the world and especially those who are near the scene could very well cause people to lose control of their bowels! Yet in spite of this, there is no repentance. They experience no desire for change within, but only fear.

So this event draws a crowd – a fearful one at that – and all wait expectantly for what might happen next. The people are in shock, yet they are also curious. What will happen?

The two witnesses are called from heaven to "come up." Since the voice says "come," the voice must be above the earth, or in heaven. The voice does not say "go up," but "come up," a huge difference. This is God, calling His witnesses from heaven, to heaven.

The two witnesses immediately take off upward for heaven, ascending in a cloud. This cloud reminds us of the Shekinah Glory evidenced in the Old Testament when God was present. It should also remind us of Jesus ascending into heaven and being received into a cloud. At that point, the disciples on the ground could no longer see

Him and two angels stood by to bring the men back to earth (cf. Acts 1), so to speak.

Revelation 11:13

"And the same hour was there a great earthquake, and the tenth part of the city fell, and in the earthquake were slain of men seven thousand: and the remnant were affrighted, and gave glory to the God of heaven."

Every time Israel rejected God in the Old Testament, God sent some form of judgment their way. If they rejected a prophet, a judge, or ultimately Jesus Himself, judgment came, and it often came quickly. This is no different here. The two witnesses are ultimately rejected by the world, killed by the Antichrist, and their dead bodies treated sacrilegiously. After God restores their lives and calls them up to Him, He then sends judgment in the form of a great earthquake.

God takes His two witnesses out of the earth with an event that will not soon be forgotten by the world. The two witnesses did not merely *disappear* or fade away as they were lying there on the streets, dead. God *first* returned life to them, then He did something else that demanded attention; He brought them up to heaven out of sight of those on the earth.

After three and a half years of ministry, the witnesses are killed, then left to decay for three and a half days (one day for each year of ministry?); then they are raised to life and ascend into heaven. Now, since these events will be recorded by any number of cameras, both professional and consumer, how will they be disputed? The visible evidence is overwhelming.

As a reaction to the way God's two witnesses were treated by the world and killed by Antichrist, God sends a mega-earthquake as judgment. The text tells us that the earthquake was so powerful that one-tenth of the city was destroyed and seven thousand men were killed. This is a large number of people for one earthquake to take in death.

The most important part of this text is that the *remnant* became frightened and glorified God. The New American Standard Bible does not say "remnant," but simply says "the rest." However, the idea is the same since the verse is obviously referring to Jerusalem ("the city fell") here. That would be the only city that God is dealing with now because that is where the two witnesses had their ministry, and it is where Antichrist desecrated the rebuilt Temple and likely where he moved his headquarters to for quicker access to the city.

It is clear that the city is Jerusalem, so then the people referred to here are those living in Jerusalem at the time the earthquake strikes. Those who did not die give glory to God. This will be the group of Jewish people who become saved during the Tribulation. These will recognize God's hand in judgment and turn their praise and adoration to Him because of His sovereignty.

Revelation 11:14
"The second woe is past; and, behold, the third woe cometh quickly."

The earthquake was the second woe. It was extremely destructive not only to structures, but to people. Seven thousand people die during that event! Now for those who believe that the numbers in the book of Revelation are simply symbolic of something else, they should really reconsider their position. These numbers are very specific, and for that reason alone they should be taken as literal amounts.

Revelation 11:15-17
"And the seventh angel sounded; and there were great voices in heaven, saying, The kingdoms of this world are become the kingdoms of our Lord, and of his Christ; and he shall reign for ever and

ever. And the four and twenty elders, which sat before God on their seats, fell upon their faces, and worshipped God, Saying, We give thee thanks, O LORD God Almighty, which art, and wast, and art to come; because thou hast taken to thee thy great power, and hast reigned."

Immediately following the announcement that the second woe has occurred, we are told that the third woe will come quickly on its heels. This brings us to the seventh angel, who sounds his trumpet.

The blowing of the trumpet by the seventh angel brings an announcement that tells the entire world that the kingdoms of the world are now officially the kingdoms of God the Father and Jesus Christ, God the Son. Because the kingdoms of this world have now fully and finally become God's (again, after falling into the wrong hands with the sin of Adam and Eve), we are told that He will reign forever and ever.

This statement does *not* mean that God has *not* reigned while the kingdoms of this world were in the hands of Satan. God has never ceased to reign. His sovereignty has always remained safely intact. However, Satan gained *control* of this world and the air above it through the fall of Adam and Eve. This control extended to this planet in its entirety, under the careful, watchful, and sovereign eye of Almighty God.

The twenty-four elders of heaven take time out to literally fall before God in Christ, worshiping Him and thanking Him because of who He is and for His character. They also thank Him because of His power, and it is through that power that He reigns, taking all control away from Satan and his minions.

What we shall see is that as it started, so it shall end. By this, it is meant that Satan tempted Adam and Eve from *without*. In other words, when he tempted them to disbelieve God, he could not use any part of the earth because he had no claim on it. He used the body of the serpent because the serpent was *willing* to be used in such a way, which is why God cursed the serpent. The serpent was *not* Satan, but Satan used the serpent for his purposes.

Once our first parents fell through sin, Satan gained immediate access to this world. He successfully wrested control of it from Adam and to himself. In order for that control to be taken from Satan, it would have to be done *legally*. This Jesus did throughout His entire earthly life, culminating in His death and resurrection. This is what numbered Satan's days to be in control of this earth and the air above it. The kingdoms of the earth fell under Satan's control.

Just as Adam and Eve were to rule over the earth, controlling all aspects of it, this is what Satan now does because control and rule changed hands to Satan. During the Millennial Reign of Jesus, Satan is cast in the bottomless pit during that time of 1,000 years.

When Satan is released for a time, he will once again be given the opportunity to draw people away from God. Even though very limited in what he can use for his purposes, he will nonetheless be successful to some degree. We will have more to say about this later.

With this seventh trumpet, God takes back full control of everything that Satan *did* control. Satan literally has nothing except the people on the earth who already follow him, along with the Antichrist and False Prophet.

Revelation 11:18-19
"And the nations were angry, and thy wrath is come, and the time of the dead, that they should be judged, and that thou shouldest give reward unto thy servants the prophets, and to the saints, and them that fear thy name, small and great; and shouldest destroy them which destroy the earth. And the temple of God was opened in heaven, and there was seen in his temple the ark of his testa-

ment: and there were lightnings, and voices, andthunderings, and an earthquake, and great hail."

Wow, the previous scene was taking place in heaven, with the praise for, adoration of, and declaration to God. In contrast, the scene on earth is quite different.

Notice that the reaction to God's judgment is one of *anger*. The text states, "the nations were angry." The nations were *angry*? What do the nations have to be angry about? Very simply, the people of these nations have *finally* realized that God's wrath is here and His wrath is great. They also know that the time of judgment is here.

Now when the Bible says "is here," it could mean any number of things. In this case, it means that it is a <u>sure thing</u>. There is no escaping it, no matter what excuse they give or how they would like to deny it. God's judgment is coming and no one will be spared.

There are four groups of people in this coming judgment:

1. *The dead*
2. *The servants (prophets) of God*
3. *The saints*
4. *Those that fear His Name, great and small*

Groups 2, 3, and 4 are really part of the same group, the people who have God's salvation. The dead refer to those who are dead without Christ, those who have died without salvation. In other words, these judgments are coming with surety, as clear as the sun in the sky when it is shining.

The first group will be destroyed, because they have destroyed the earth. By that, it is meant that due to their rebellious nature, they have destroyed the very order that God created. Doing what they wanted to do constantly, these people preferred their own (evil) desires to God's holiness and righteousness.

In these days, and those leading up to the return of Jesus Christ, men are becoming experts at following their own will and their own desires.

Solomon had something to say about this type of person in Proverbs 10. *"Treasures of wickedness profit nothing: but righteousness delivereth from death. The LORD will not suffer the soul of the righteous to famish: but he casteth away the substance of the wicked. He becometh poor that dealeth with a slack hand: but the hand of the diligent maketh rich. He that gathereth in summer is a wise son: but he that sleepeth in harvest is a son that causeth shame. Blessings are upon the head of the just: but violence covereth the mouth of the wicked.*

The memory of the just is blessed: but the name of the wicked shall rot. The wise in heart will receive commandments: but a prating fool shall fall. He that walketh uprightly walketh surely: but he that perverteth his ways shall be known" (Proverbs 10:2-9).

These are the dead, those who do not know Jesus Christ because they have never entered into a relationship with Him. They make all kinds of noise, they believe they are correct in what they think and attest to, but they are dead. They have no spiritual life, nor do they have spiritual insight. They will die and will ultimately be cast from God's presence in paradise to suffer His wrath eternally in the Lake of Fire.

Conversely, those who know Christ, who are born of the Holy Spirit, and who have entered into a genuine relationship with Jesus Christ will gain the final victory. The righteous are delivered from death to spend eternity with Christ in paradise.

From the reaction of the nations, we immediately see the inside of God's Temple. It is a harrowing sight for those who will be cast from His presence for all eternity. The heavenly Temple opens (which sits perfectly juxtaposed against the desecrated Temple on earth), and we see the Ark of His testament. This is the testimony of His right-eous Law, and all that represents God's holiness. With it, we see *"lightnings, and voices, and thunderings, and an earthquake, and great hail."* God's presence is meant to be felt at this point, as people will quake with fear.

Hebrews 10:31 tells us that it is a terrifying thing to fall into the hands of *the* (not "a") living God, and rightly so! His presence will cause men to become so weak-kneed that they will not be able to stand. All the haughty, arrogant atheists who have spent their lives presupposing that God does not exist, and causing others to believe it as well, will *see* the reality of God and His awesome presence, from which they will not be able to escape. Is there a worse fate?

12

REVELATION 12

Chapter 11 ends with judgment and moves us right into chapter 12, which seems to be a sort of interlude. It is a summary of the entire salvation event, starting with the birth of Israel.

Let's take a look at the text.

Revelation 12:1-4

"And there appeared a great wonder in heaven; a woman clothed with the sun, and the moon under her feet, and upon her head a crown of twelve stars: And she being with child cried, travailing in

birth, and pained to be delivered. And there appeared another wonder in heaven; and behold a great red dragon, having seven heads and ten horns, and seven crowns upon his heads. And his tail drew the third part of the stars of heaven, and did cast them to the earth: and the dragon stood before the woman which was ready to be delivered, for to devour her child as soon as it was born."

These first few verses are really providing a very brief summary of the *purpose* for Israel, the Messiah that came *from* Israel, and Satan's role in all of this. John describes the woman as a great wonder. The woman is:

- *Clothed with the sun*
- *The moon is under her feet*
- *She wears a crown of twelve stars*
- *She is ready to give birth*

The woman who is clothed with the sun, with the moon under her feet, can be none other than the nation of Israel. We need only go back to the book of Genesis for confirmation of this in the life of Joseph, starting in chapter thirty-seven.

"And he dreamed yet another dream, and told it his brethren, and said, Behold, I have dreamed a dream more; and, behold, the sun and the moon and the eleven stars made obeisance to me.

"And he told it to his father, and to his brethren: and his father rebuked him, and said unto him, What is this dream that thou hast dreamed? Shall I and thy mother and thy brethren indeed come to bow down ourselves to thee to the earth?

"And his brethren envied him; but his father observed the saying" (Genesis 37:9-11).

Joseph was obviously chosen by God for some great purpose, and to prepare him for it God allowed Joseph to use and even brag about the gift he had of interpreting dreams.

At this point, Joseph was 17 years old, and his brothers did not like him at all. To them, he was a goody-two-shoe, loved much by their father, who showered Joseph with love and gifts. It was clear to the brothers that Joseph was the favorite.

On top of this, Joseph seemed to have an insight into the dream world, or at least stated he did. Every one of his dreams so far were about how his brothers would serve him. The text just quoted is a different dream in which he includes the fact that "*the sun and the moon and the eleven stars made obeisance to me.*"

We can stop at that point and simply start making educated guesses as to what Joseph means, but we do not have to, as the interpretation of this dream is made clear for us by Joseph's father. When Joseph told his father the dream, his father Jacob replied, "*Shall I and thy mother and thy brethren indeed come to bow down ourselves to thee to the earth?*" In effect, Jacob understood that the sun represented him (Jacob), while the moon represented Jacob's wife, Joseph's mother. The eleven stars represented Joseph's eleven brothers.

Notice when Jacob provides that interpretation (apparently, Joseph was not the only one who could interpret dreams), neither God, nor Joseph, nor anyone else corrects him, so we can assume that Jacob's interpretation is correct.

Here again is what we have:

- *The Sun = Joseph's father*
- *The Moon = Joseph's mother*
- *The eleven stars = Joseph's eleven brothers*

Revelation 12 - The Woman

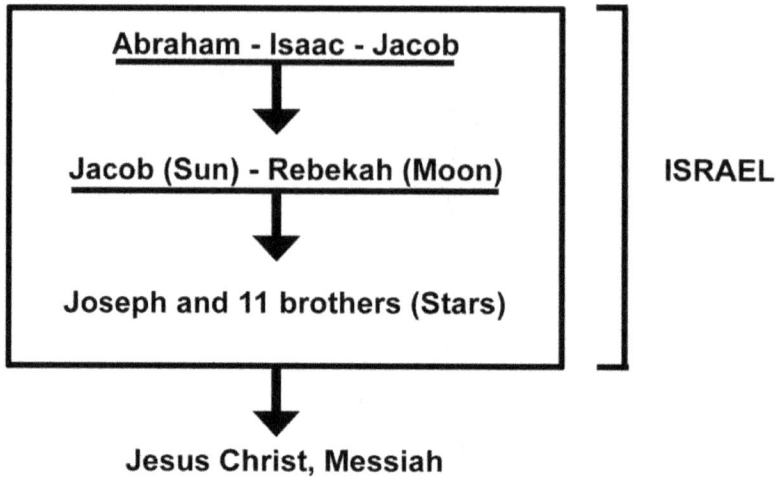

```
┌─────────────────────────────────────┐  ┐
│   Abraham - Isaac - Jacob            │  │
│              ↓                       │  │
│   Jacob (Sun) - Rebekah (Moon)       │  │  ISRAEL
│              ↓                       │  │
│   Joseph and 11 brothers (Stars)     │  │
└─────────────────────────────────────┘  ┘
              ↓
      Jesus Christ, Messiah
```

For the record, the eleven brothers and Joseph become the Patriarchs of the nation of Israel. Abraham, Isaac, and Jacob were the root of Israel, with the twelve brothers (the Patriarchs) being the foundation, and from them, Israel was born. From Israel, the Messiah came.

So it is clear from the Genesis passage alone that this reference to a woman clothed with the sun, and the moon at her feet, wearing a crown of twelve stars, represents the parts of the nation of Israel. The child is Jesus and the Dragon is Satan, as John points out in verse 9 of chapter 12.

The Dragon represents himself through the main empires spoken of in Daniel 7. *"After this I saw in the night visions, and behold a fourth beast, dreadful and terrible, and strong exceedingly; and it had great iron teeth: it devoured and brake in pieces, and stamped the residue with the feet of it: and it was diverse from all the beasts that were before it; and it had ten horns"* (Daniel 7:7).

Regarding the Dragon, Keathley points out, *"That the red dragon is called "great" points to the magnitude of Satan's power and activity in* the world. *"Red" emphasizes his murderous and blood thirsty character and behavior throughout history (cf. John 8:44). "Dragon" pictures his ferocious and intensely cruel nature. "Having seven heads and ten horns" relates him to the ten nation confederation of the revived Roman empire, the system of the beast (13:1). "Seven diadems" speaks of his ruling power, but also usurped power and authority which he has and will have especially in the last days. Satan is really a dragon, a hideous beast. Today he often appears as an angel of light; he masks his true identity, but in the Tribula-tion he will be seen for what he really is."*[34]

Satan as the Dragon sweeps one-third of the heavenly stars from heaven. It should be clear that these stars represent angels, since the Dragon we know to represent Satan. There is no possible reason why Satan would waste his time taking literal stars out of the heavens. These stars are the angels who fell, enamored by Satan's might, intelligence, and deception. Notice the text states that he took the stars and *threw* them down to earth. The idea here is that he deceived these angelic beings and by deception made them follow in his steps of rebellion. He controlled their rebellious thinking and because of it, was the reason they fell. The angels who fell are still culpable, however, because it was ultimately their decision to *believe* Satan that caused their fall.

After he throws these angels to earth, he attempts to snatch the child as the woman gives birth.

Revelation 12:5-6
"And she brought forth a man child, who was to rule all nations with a rod of iron: and her child was caught up unto God, and to his throne. And the woman fled into the wilderness, where she hath a place prepared of God, that they should feed her there a thousand two hundred and threescore days."

---

[34] J. Hampton Keathley III *Studies in Revelation* (Biblical Studies Press, 1997), 156

The woman gives birth to a man child, Jesus the Messiah. He is to rule all nations with a rod of iron. This is exactly what He will do during the Millennial reign after the Tribulation ends (cf. Revelation 19:15).

Jesus is born, lives, dies, is resurrected, and ascends to the Father's throne in heaven. The events between His birth and ascension are implied here. The devil was completely unsuccessful at every attempt to thwart Jesus, either by making Him sin, or by having him killed by Herod, or others.

Jesus gave up His life willingly when the time for it was right. No one, including Satan, controlled him. Of course, since Satan was unsuccessful in snatching and devouring Jesus, with Jesus always remaining apart from all of Satan's attempts to overcome Him, Satan attempted to turn his attention to Israel. Even this did not work, because Israel fled into the wilderness and was protected by God for 1,260 days, or 42 months, or 3 ½ years, which represents the second part of the Tribulation.

As an aside here, because people do not see seven years specifically spelled out in the book of Revelation they come to the conclusion that the Tribulation is only 3 ½ years in length, not a full "week," or seven years, as stated in the book of Daniel. This is simply not true.

We know that the very first seal of the rider on the white horse takes place, and with the breaking of that seal, the Antichrist appears on the earth. According to Daniel 9:27, Antichrist enters into a covenant with Israel for a period of seven years. This *starts* the Tribulation. Even though Antichrist is relatively quiet or in the background to some degree during the first part of the Tribulation, it does not mean that the Tribulation has *not* begun. It has absolutely begun, and the events from the first seal through the seventh and the first trumpet through the seventh all take place *before* this point in time when Israel flees into the wilderness. We know that she will be in the wilderness for 1,260 days, or 3 ½ years. If Israel (or the Remnant of Israel for the Last Days) flees into the wilderness, then obviously things have taken place *before* and *leading up to* this point.

Everything that takes place before this point is the first half of the Tribulation. Here in Revelation 12, when we see the failure of Satan to gain the victory over Israel and Jesus, the woman flees into the wilderness for safety.

Revelation 12 is a very truncated version of the events that have and will take place in the world regarding Israel, Jesus, and the future Tribulation period. Revelation 12 leaves out all the details between the birth of Christ to His ascension. Since we know these other events occurred in between His birth and ascension (from other portions of Scripture), then it is also clear (or should be) that major events were left out of the history of Israel, both past and future.

Revelation 12:7-9

"And there was war in heaven: Michael and his angels fought against the dragon; and the dragon fought and his angels, And prevailed not; neither was their place found any more in heaven. And the great dragon was cast out, that old serpent, called the Devil, and Satan, which deceiveth the whole world: he was cast out into the earth, and his angels were cast out with him."

In a previous section (Revelation 12:1-4), we read briefly of Satan (the Dragon) taking one-third of the angelic host and throwing them to earth. There is more detail given to us in these three verses. We see that an actual war took place, with Satan and his angels vs. Michael and his angels. This obviously means that Michael oversees multitudes of angels, as does Satan.

The text informs us that in spite of the ferocity of the war, Satan and his angels lost the battle and were cast out from heaven. These three verses specifically connect the "Dragon" with "Satan." Notice Satan's job is to deceive the entire world. Whether that's his job or desire, we can know that both go hand in hand and it is what he excels at doing.

In this text, we see that all of these beings were cast out of heaven and to earth. What this means is that though *"neither was their place found any more in heaven,"* Satan continued up to this point in the Tribulation to have *access* to God's throne. From this point forward neither he nor his minions have access any longer.

I was teaching this in a Sunday morning Bible class and a couple of individuals became upset when I told them that Satan continues to have access to God. They were incredulous and could not help but ask why Satan would be able to have access, since he was kicked out of heaven already.

The answer is that having *access* does not equal having a *place in* heaven. It is most likely that this passage describes the time after Satan fell and was able to convince, through deception, multitudes of angels to join him in rebellion.

We know that Satan fell and with him followed many angels, who became fallen angels just as Satan himself had fallen through his disobedience and pride. However, just because his position to which God had originally created him was eliminated, it does not mean that God would not expect him (and even *demand* him) to report to Him on occasion.

We see this very thing in the book of Job. *"Now there was a day when the sons of God came to present themselves before the LORD, and Satan came also among them. And the LORD said unto Satan, Whence comest thou? Then Satan answered the LORD, and said, From going to and fro in the earth, and from walking up and down in it"* (Job 1:6-7). The fact that Satan would report to God does not surprise me in the least for a number of reasons. First, having to report to God in front of God's very throne would be galling to Satan. Remember, this was the same throne that Satan said he would rise *above* (Isaiah 14:13). Second, the very fact that Satan reported to God meant he continued to be under God's direction and full sovereignty, whether he liked it or not. Third, the fact that he reported *with* other angels (sons of God) also reminded him that he was a created being as these other angels were, and there was no forgetting it.

Originally, though Satan was kicked out of heaven with those angels who chose to follow him, it does not imply that he was never able to go back into it to stand before God's throne and give a reckoning of himself before God. This was mandatory, and this falling out of heaven simply tells us that in spite of Satan's promises found in Isaiah 14:13-14, none will come true. Isaiah 14:15 states instead, "*Yet thou shalt be brought down to hell, to the sides of the pit.*" This is God's promise to Satan and it *will* come to pass.

This section of the text in Revelation 12 refers to the fact that though Satan and his followers still had access to heaven, it is at this point in the Tribulation that even *access* to heaven is now denied. As Satan's place in heaven was previously eliminated, now access to it is also eliminated. The next time he stands before God's throne, it will be to receive his judgment.

Revelation 12:10-12
"And I heard a loud voice saying in heaven, Now is come salvation, and strength, and the kingdom of our God, and the power of his Christ: for the accuser of our brethren is cast down, which accused them before our God day and night.

"And they overcame him by the blood of the Lamb, and by the word of their testimony; and they loved not their lives unto the death. Therefore rejoice, ye heavens, and ye that dwell in them. Woe to the inhabitants of the earth and of the sea! For the devil is

*come down unto you, having great wrath, because he knoweth
that he hath but a short time."*

Because access to heaven is with finality denied to Satan and his angels, we now hear a loud voice that proclaims, "*Now is come salvation...*" In other words, the time for Satan's judgment and for God to
make all things right is *at hand.* The return of Jesus Christ to earth, to
institute His Millennial Kingdom, is very close to happening.

Of course, the other thing to note here is that because Satan is denied
access to heaven, he can no longer accuse Christians any longer before God's throne. He knows that this part of his game is over and he
can no longer waste God's time with accusations and words that have
no basis or merit. It is doubtful that John is exaggerating here when
he says that Satan accuses the brethren "day and night." In eternity,
time does not exist. The idea that John wants us to recognize is that
Satan *continuously* accuses us before God. At this point in the Tribulation, he will no longer be able to do that. "*The angelic conflict and
the slandering accusations of Satan that God has allowed throughout
history to demonstrate His divine essence, especially His holiness, will
at this point be just about over.*"[35]

The individuals who "overcame" (with finality) are those who relied
on the efficacy of Christ's blood atonement. This is the basis for their
testimony, and they were willing to give up their lives because of
their love and devotion to Jesus Christ. "*Here we see the attitude
which overcomes Satan. In this statement, we see two vital attitudes of
faith that give the capacity to serve the Lord regardless of what Satan
might throw at us. First, there is the perspective of eternity that sees
this life as a vapor, a training ground, and a preparation for eternity (1
Pet. 1:17 2:12). But this leads to a second attitude of faith, self sacrifice
even unto death, for this life is not the end, it is only the beginning. Obviously then, lying at the foundation of such attitudes of faith is more*

---

[35] J. Hampton Keathley III *Studies in Revelation* (Biblical Studies Press, 1997), 160

Bible doctrine—the doctrine of death or dying, the doctrine of our eternal hope and our inheritance, an inheritance that is untouched by death, unstained by evil and unimpaired by time (1 Pet. 1:3-5; Matt. 6:19-21; 2 Cor. 4:16 18; 5:10)."[36]

The text tells those in heaven to rejoice because Satan, the accuser, can darken its doorway no longer! Heaven can now be cleansed from his evil and malicious presence. However, those on earth will soon be on the receiving end of his hatred and wrath! Why is Satan so angry? Simply because he knows his time is *short.* God is not mocked at all. What he allows, He allows for a purpose. Everything He said He would bring to pass, He *will* bring to pass!

Satan knows that he has very little time to achieve anything, and his energy is directed toward hating those who belong to Jesus. On those, he will expend his anger.

Revelation 12:13-17

"And when the dragon saw that he was cast unto the earth, he persecuted the woman which brought forth the man child.

"And to the woman were given two wings of a great eagle, that she might fly into the wilderness, into her place, where she is nourished for a time, and times, and half a time, from the face of the serpent.

"And the serpent cast out of his mouth water as a flood after the woman, that he might cause her to be carried away of the flood.

"And the earth helped the woman, and the earth opened her mouth, and swallowed up the flood which the dragon cast out of his mouth.

---

[36] J. Hampton Keathley III *Studies in Revelation* (Biblical Studies Press, 1997), 161

"And the dragon was wroth with the woman, and went to make war with the remnant of her seed, which keep the commandments of God, and have the testimony of Jesus Christ."

Notice the first thing that Satan attempts to do when he realizes he has lost a war, resulting in his inability to gain entrance to heaven any longer, is to persecute the *"woman which brought forth the man child."* We have only two choices here: 1) we can take the text as literally meant, in which case the woman here is Israel (since Jesus came from the nation of Israel), or 2) we can allegorize the text, finding a way to make it refer to the Church. The problem with this latter option is that there is no reason to allegorize anything. The woman is either symbolic of Israel or not. If not, then those who believe it does not refer to Israel have a difficult job ahead of them to prove that. As such, it is better to take the text as it seems to be meant, that the woman who gave birth to the man child means Israel, from which Jesus came from the tribe of Judah.

The next verse speaks of giving the woman two wings of an eagle, allowing her to fly into the wilderness. Since we know that the woman is not a literal woman, but merely a symbolic woman (representing Israel), then she could not literally have actual eagle wings allowing her to literally fly. That is an unnecessary interpretation. *"This is based on two Old Testament passages, Exodus 19:4 and Deuteronomy 32:11-12, where God's protection and deliverance of Israel is likened to an eagle who carried her to safety from the clutches of Egypt. So likewise, God will work to deliver Israel from the clutches of Satan. Matthew 24:16 refers to this same flight where Christ exhorts those in Judea to flee to the mountains when they see the abomination of desolation take place in the city of Jerusalem."*[37]

The clear meaning is that Israel is able to flee as fast as possible to a place in the wilderness God has set aside. Here, God Himself will pro-

---

[37] J. Hampton Keathley III *Studies in Revelation* (Biblical Studies Press, 1997), 162

tect and sustain her, either directly, or through other people living near that same area. Israel will remain there for a time, times, and half a time. This is reminiscent of the book of Daniel, chapter nine. This refers to the three and one-half years remaining of the Tribulation. It appears, then, that this event occurs at the *midpoint* of the Tribulation.

Of course, not all of Jewish people living in Israel will be saved here, but only the Remnant. We see this in many sections of the Old Testament, but specifically in Zechariah. *"Zechariah 13:8 reminds us of a sobering truth; two thirds of the nation of Israel in the land will perish. Evidently many will ignore the warning of Matthew 24:16 and refuse to flee. These will be put to death."*[38] Two-thirds will die. This is indicative of another Jewish holocaust that will occur in the future, during the second half of the Tribulation.

Verse 15 speaks of Satan throwing water like a flood after the woman. Again, we must realize that the woman here is not really a woman, but is Israel. Therefore the flood that is spoken of in verse 15 likely refers to an *army* of people that Satan prods into chasing after these Jewish people who are fleeing from him. This certainly should remind us of Pharaoh's attempt to hunt down the Israelites that he originally (and finally) allowed to leave the land.

The next verse points to the fact that earth itself comes to the aid of the woman, Israel. This could occur any number of ways, but since the land of Israel is a land of many terrains, with caves and valleys, it is possible that the land will hide them from her persecutors, or Israel's persecutors will be swallowed via small earthquakes, or both.

Verse 17 is scary in its implications. *"And the dragon was wroth with the woman, and went to make war with the remnant of her seed, which keep the commandments of God, and have the testimony of Jesus*

---

[38] J. Hampton Keathley III *Studies in Revelation* (Biblical Studies Press, 1997), 162

Christ." Because Satan is unsuccessful in overcoming Israelites who flee into the wilderness, he turns his attention to those he *can* get to, and he does so with a vengeance. No Christian at this point is safe, either Jew or Gentile, throughout the rest of the world.

It is at this point that we move into Revelation 13 and see more of the Beast, his world system, and his attempt to raise himself higher than God. By far, this leads into the worst period of time in the entire history of humankind.

◆──────── 13 ────────◆

REVELATION 13

Revelation 13:1-10

"And I stood upon the sand of the sea, and saw a beast rise up out of the sea, having seven heads and ten horns, and upon his horns ten crowns, and upon his heads the name of blasphemy.

"And the beast which I saw was like unto a leopard, and his feet were as the feet of a bear, and his mouth as the mouth of a lion: and the dragon gave him his power, and his seat, and great authority.

"And I saw one of his heads as it were wounded to death; and his deadly wound was healed: and all the world wondered after the beast.

"And they worshipped the dragon which gave power unto the beast: and they worshipped the beast, saying, Who is like unto the beast? Who is able to make war with him?

"And there was given unto him a mouth speaking great things and blasphemies; and power was given unto him to continue forty and two months.

"And he opened his mouth in blasphemy against God, to blaspheme his name, and his tabernacle, and them that dwell in heaven.

"And it was given unto him to make war with the saints, and to overcome them: and power was given him over all kindreds, and tongues, and nations.

"And all that dwell upon the earth shall worship him, whose names are not written in the book of life of the Lamb slain from the foundation of the world.

"If any man have an ear, let him hear.

"He that leadeth into captivity shall go into captivity: he that killeth with the sword must be killed with the sword. Here is the patience and the faith of the saints."

For those familiar with the scenarios revealed in the book of Daniel, these first ten verses of Revelation 13 remind us specifically of Daniel 2:42, 44; 7:7, 8, 20; 8:25; 11:36; and 9:27. In the first verse, the KJV makes it sound as if John is referring to himself ("And I stood..."), though a number of other versions indicate that the dragon is standing on the seashore waiting for his beast to rise from the sea.

The Times of the Gentiles, Order of Ruling Empires and Antichrist Stage

As can be seen from the timeline below, each section of prophetic Scripture is covered by a number of Scripture passages. In some cases, more detail is provided. For example, Daniel 7 provides more detail on the passage from Daniel 2, etc. In other cases, only one or two aspects of prophecy is covered by one passage as in the Revelation 13 passage, which focuses entirely on the Fourth Empire.

Legend:
- Daniel 2:31-45
- Daniel 7:1-28
- Revelation 13:1-10
- Revelation 17:7-14
- Times of the Gentiles

RAPTURE PERIOD
Rapture will take place somewhere during this time period leading up to the beginning of the Tribulation

2nd Coming of Messiah (Ends Great Tribulation)

Messianic Kingdom — 1,000 Year Reign
- Daniel 2:31-45
- Daniel 7:1-28

Daniel 7:1-28 - Four Visions and the Four Beasts

| Eagle-winged Lion-like (Babylon) | Bear-like w/3 ribs in mouth (Medo-Persia) | Leopard-like Fast growth (Hellenistic) | Diverse w/Ten Horns Eleventh Horn arises (United/Rome) |

Daniel 2:31-45 - Five-Part Statue of Nebuchadnezzar's Dream

| Head of Gold (Babylon) | Breast & Arms of Silver (Medo-Persia) | Belly & Thighs of Brass (Hellenistic) | Legs of Iron (United/Rome) |

Revelation 17:7-14 - First Five Heads

| Tarquin Kings 753-510 B.C. | The Counsulors 510-494 B.C. | Plebeians 494-390 B.C. | Republicans 390-59 B.C. | Triumvirate 59-27 B.C. |

Revelation 17:7-14 - Sixth Head to Seventh Head
Sixth "head" Present in 27 B.C. - Includes first four stages of 4th Empire into Tribulation with the Seventh Head

Daniel 7:1-28

Daniel 2:31-45 — Ten Toes (Ten Division)

TRIBULATION

Developmental Prelude to 4th Empire

1st Empire	2nd Empire	3rd Empire	4th Empire Stage 1	Stage 2	Stage 3	Stage 4	Stage 5
Babylon	Medo-Persia	Hellenistic	United (Rome)	Two Division	One World Gov't	Ten Division	Absolute Imperialism
909	539 / 536	331 / 323	1453	1914 / 1948 / 1967 / 2008			

United Stage | Four Division Stage — Daniel 7:1-28

Christ crucified

586 B.C. Solomonic Temple Destroyed

Two Division: East-West Balance of Power

One World Gov't

Ten Division: Ten Horns (Ten Kings)

Absolute Imperialism (Antichrist Stage)
Beast of Revelation 13:1-10
*Seventh Head/Eleventh Horn, then 8th Horn
"Parenthesis" ends here →

Times of the Gentiles BEGINS in 586 B.C.

Continues until Times of the Gentiles is fulfilled (Luke 21:24)

Times of the Gentiles ENDS

"Parenthesis" begins with the Crucifixion - God has temporarily set Israel aside to call from the Gentiles a people for His Name (Acts 15; Romans 9-11, also cf. Daniel 9) Three events are between the 69th week and the 70th week of Daniel: 1) Messiah's death, 2) Destruction of Jerusalem (A.D. 70) and 3) Continuing wars (over control of Jerusalem) to the end

*From Revelation 17, we read that the term "seven" refers to the heads, while the term "eight" refers to the horns. The Antichrist is of the SEVEN HEADS because the heads are chronological and sequential, coming one after the other in past to future history, with the Antichrist the last to appear.

He is also an EIGHTH. The Ten Horns represent the Ten Kingdoms that come out of the One World Government (the 4th stage of the 4th Empire of Imperialism). These kings are contemporary and rule together. When the Antichrist begins to take control, he uproots (kills) three of the ten horns. SEVEN remain throughout the remainder of the Tribulation with the Antichrist becoming the EIGHTH contemporary king, ruling over the other SEVEN who have submitted to his authority.

Daniel 2 - God's Revelation for Israel

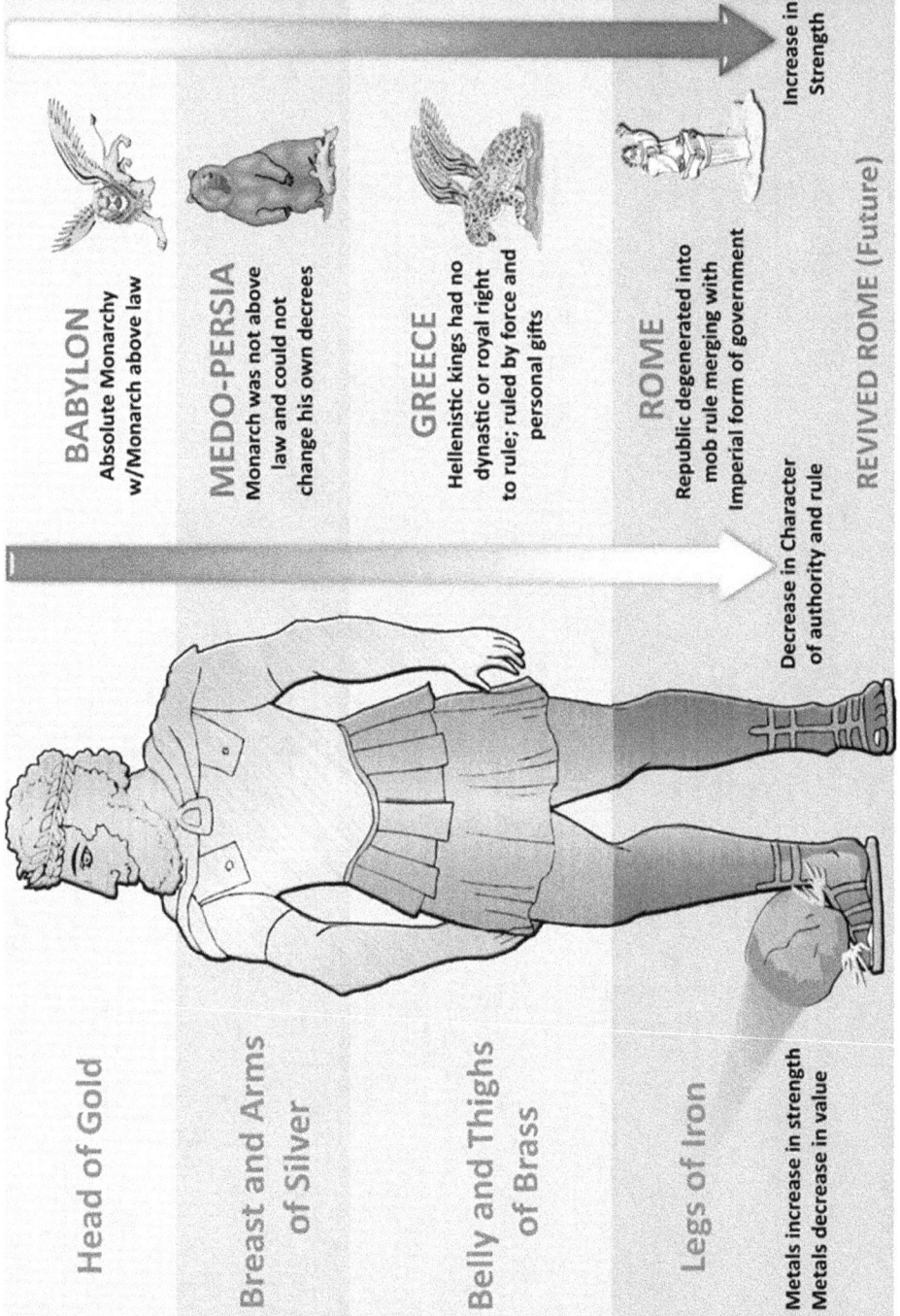

Increase in Strength

BABYLON
Absolute Monarchy
w/Monarch above law

MEDO-PERSIA
Monarch was not above
law and could not
change his own decrees

GREECE
Hellenistic kings had no
dynastic or royal right
to rule; ruled by force and
personal gifts

ROME
Republic degenerated into
mob rule merging with
Imperial form of government

Decrease in Character
of authority and rule

REVIVED ROME (Future)

Head of Gold

Breast and Arms
of Silver

Belly and Thighs
of Brass

Legs of Iron

Metals increase in strength
Metals decrease in value

Times of the Gentiles (A)
Daniel 2:31-45

1st Gentile Empire
Head of Gold
BABYLON
Jerusalem and Solomonic Temple Destroyed
Israel taken captive to Babylon

586 B.C.   606 to 536 B.C.
Ruler: Nebuchadnezzar
Lion-like Beast w/Eagle's Wings
pages 20-24 in Footsteps

2nd Gentile Empire
Arms/Breast of Silver
MEDO-PERSIAN

539 to 331 B.C.
Rulers: Darius/Cyrus
Bear-like Beast Devouring Flesh yet Lopsided

3rd Gentile Empire
Belly/Thighs of Bronze
HELLENISTIC

331 to 323 B.C.
Ruler: Alexander the Great
Leopard-like Beast w/Four Wings

To 0 B.C. and Christ's Birth

Alexander's Empire Dividing Among Four Commanders After His Death
- Ptolemy
  - Egypt
  - Palestine
  - Arabia Petrea
- Seleucus
  - Syria
  - Babylonia
  - India
- Cassander
  - Macedonia
  - Greece
- Lysimachus
  - Thrace
  - Bithynia

Many older manuscripts state *"he* stood," which obviously refers then to the Dragon. The reality is that the difference means little if anything. The point is that John sees this beast as indicated in the second part of the first verse, or the second sentence (depending upon the translation).

The beast that rises out of the sea is likely referring to the Gentile nations of the world. *"The 'sand of the sea' undoubtedly portrays the many people who make up the nations, the number of whom is as the sand of the sea (Rev. 20:8). Standing on 'the sand of the sea,' suggests Satan's position as the usurper of the earth and its many peoples and of his power over them. Remember that Isaiah likens the nations to a roaring and restless sea that cannot be quiet and whose waters (their humanistic way of life and political agitation) can only churn up refuse and mud; a fitting picture of the products of a world without peace with God. They have no peace because they have rejected the true Prince of Peace and will turn to their own solutions to life and to the antichrist as their means to world peace, but in reality, this will be not much more than a self-centered pursuit for comfort and personal affluence (cf. Isa. 17:12-13; 57:20-21; Rev. 17:1, 15)."*[39]

This beast has *seven heads* and *ten horns.* On his horns sit ten crowns and on his head the name of blasphemy. Revelation 17 details just exactly what this blasphemy is that John sees. Once John finishes describing this beast, another beast appears, beginning in verse 11. By the way, as a bit of an aside here, the Antichrist will be the *eleventh* horn that grows from the ten. After killing three "horns," he will become the *eighth.* More on that later.

We have included a detailed chart on the previous page that breaks down Daniel 2 and 7, along with Revelation 13 and 17. We apologize that the type is small, but that is one reason we like to publish this size book, because it allows us to keep our charts (and text) larger.

---

[39] J. Hampton Keathley III *Studies in Revelation* (Biblical Studies Press, 1997), 166

Be that as it may, in some cases, like this one, the reader will possibly need to pull out the old magnifying glass.

At any rate, as you can see, included in the previous charts are explanations of the beasts from Daniel 2 and 7, along with explanations of the beasts in Revelation 13 and 17. At first glance it appears rather complex, but once the reader becomes familiar with all the information that is there, it will make more sense.

We know at this point that the Dragon (Satan) is extremely angry. He wants to find a way to persecute Israel, and he also intends to bring his own promises to fruition, specifically with respect to being worshipped. Whoever is motivating him directly gives him power. We know that it is the Dragon, as stated in the second part of verse 2 ("...*and the dragon gave him his power, and his seat, and great authority*").

John comes back to this beast in Revelation 17:9-10, where he explains the meaning of the seven heads. *"'The seven heads are seven mountains on which the woman sits and they are seven kings...' The seven heads are seven mountains and seven kings. Some see this as a reference first to the seven hill city of Rome, and then to seven dynasties or rulers of the old Roman empire, as kings, consuls, dictators, decemvirs, military tribunes and emperors, or as seven successive emperors of Imperial Rome, as Nero (A.D. 54 68), Galba (A.D. 68), Otho (A.D. 69), Vitellius (A.D. 69), Vespasian (A.D. 69 79), Titus (A.D. 79 81), and Domitian (A.D. 81 91) under whom great persecution of the church occurred. So it would thus refer to the city and to those who ruled in Rome. Quite clearly the beast is not only a kingdom or an empire, but also a man (cf. 2 Thess. 2:8 9; Dan. 9:27; 11:36; 7:24 25)."*[40]

This is difficult to pin down. We know the terminology is symbolic. John tells us that the seven heads are seven mountains upon which

---

[40] J. Hampton Keathley III *Studies in Revelation* (Biblical Studies Press, 1997), 168

Times of the Gentiles (B)
Daniel 2:31-45
Developmental Prelude to the Fourth Gentile Empire
Previous Forms of Roman Government

THE 1ST HEAD

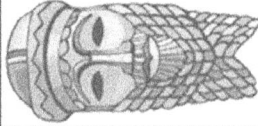

The Tarquin Kings

*753 - 510 B.C.

THE 2ND HEAD

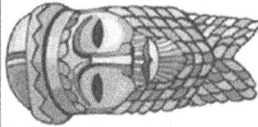

The Counsulors

*510 - 494 B.C.

THE 3RD HEAD

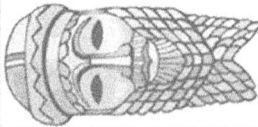

The Plebians
or Dictators

*494 - 390 B.C.

THE 4TH HEAD

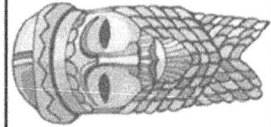

The Republicans
or Decimvers
(Oligarchy of Ten)

*390 - 59 B.C.

THE 5TH HEAD

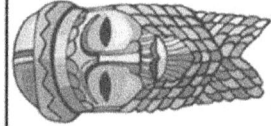

The Triumvirate

*59 B.C. – 27 A.D.

*dates are approximate

pages 24-25 in Footsteps

214

Times of the Gentiles (C)
Daniel 7:1-28

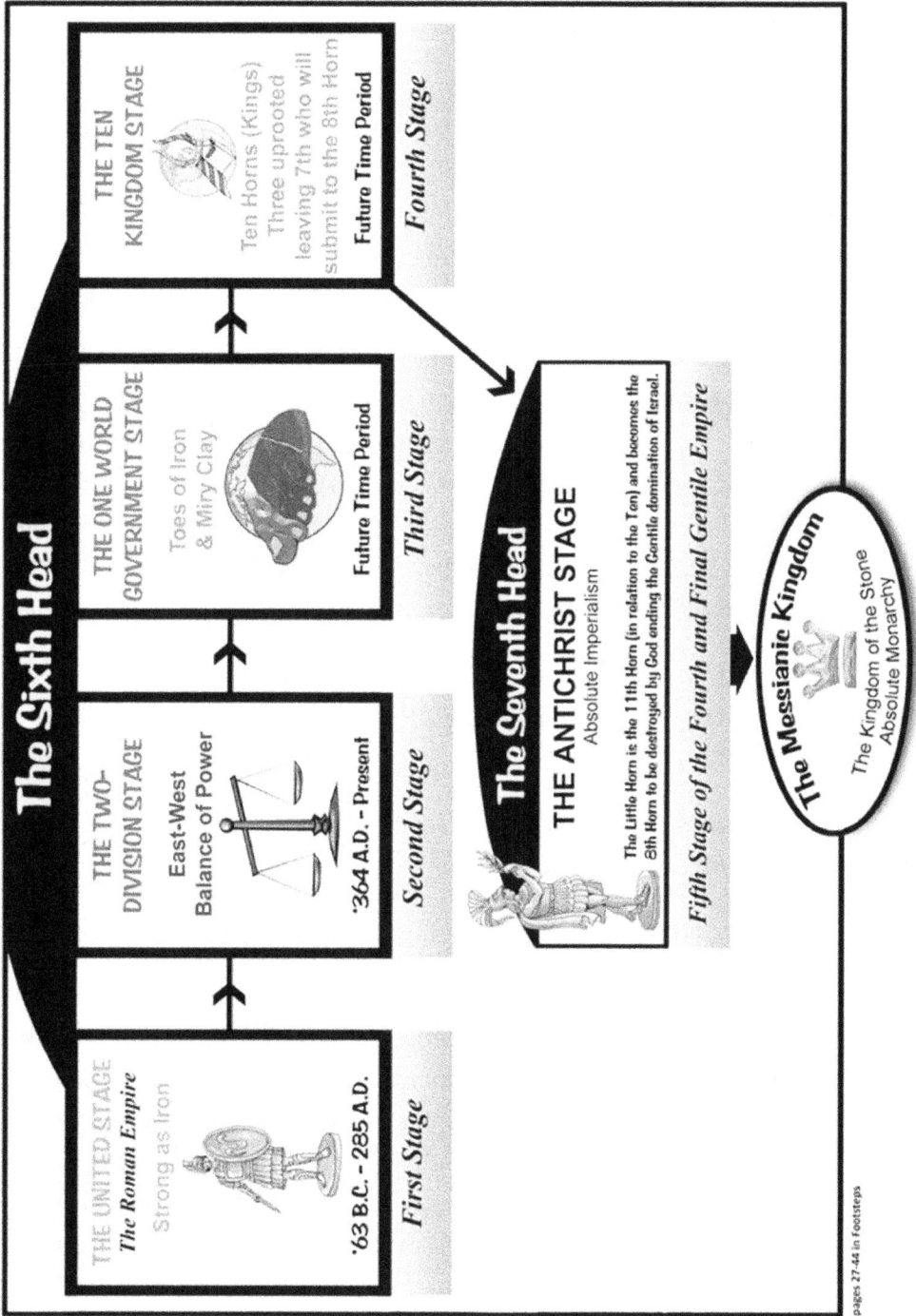

The Sixth Head

THE UNITED STAGE
The Roman Empire
Strong as Iron
'63 B.C. – 285 A.D.
First Stage

THE TWO-DIVISION STAGE
East-West
Balance of Power
'364 A.D. – Present
Second Stage

THE ONE WORLD GOVERNMENT STAGE
Toes of Iron
& Miry Clay
Future Time Period
Third Stage

THE TEN KINGDOM STAGE
Ten Horns (Kings)
Three uprooted
leaving 7th who will
submit to the 8th Horn
Future Time Period
Fourth Stage

The Seventh Head

THE ANTICHRIST STAGE
Absolute Imperialism

The Little Horn is the 11th Horn (in relation to the Ten) and becomes the 8th Horn to be destroyed by God ending the Gentile domination of Israel.

Fifth Stage of the Fourth and Final Gentile Empire

The Messianic Kingdom
The Kingdom of the Stone
Absolute Monarchy

pages 27-44 in Footsteps

215

the woman sits. There are also seven kings associated with the mountains. Commentators vary in their opinion. Dr. Arnold G. Fruchtenbaum offers an opinion that makes a good deal of sense; however, even in that, it is difficult to be dogmatic about it. In the end, we cannot be 100% sure.

The previous two charts are based on information found in Fruchtenbaum's book *Footsteps of the Messiah*. His take on this section of Revelation is interesting and seems to fit the pieces together.

Keathley offers what he believes to be a best scenario, stating, "*another and I believe a better interpretation of the seven heads is that the seven heads represent seven phases of Gentile powers or nations which find their culmination in the beast. The ten horns look at the future history of the beast and the seven heads, the past history. The seven heads are mountains, seven successive historic Gentile kingdoms, who are represented by seven kings or rulers. This is supported by the following:*

"*(1) Revelation 17:10 tells us the seven mountains are kings. This could indicate that the mountains are symbolical for the kingdoms these seven kings represent.*

"*(2) Rome is known as the city of seven hills, but the hills of Rome are not mountains.*

"*(3) The term mountain is commonly used in Scripture as an image of a kingdom (Psalm 30:7; Isaiah 2:3; Dan. 2:35, 45; Jer. 51:5).*

"*(4) But more importantly, chapter 17 deals with the harlot system of Babylon which goes all the way back to the time of Nimrod and all these Gentile world powers have been her lovers and supporters, not Rome alone (cf. 17:1 2, 15). It is more likely that the seven mountains refer to seven successive Gentile kingdoms which go way back, far beyond Rome.*"[41] Keathley believes the mountains reference the kingdoms

---

[41] J. Hampton Keathley III *Studies in Revelation* (Biblical Studies Press, 1997), 168

leading up to Rome that had something to do with Israel as well. So for him, the kingdoms are *Egypt, Assyria, Babylon, Medo-Persia, Greece,* and *Rome.*

Based on this then, Keathley breaks it down thusly: "*What about the seventh head? Revelation 17:10 explains the seventh head. It is really a future kingdom though it has historical roots in the sixth kingdom. Revelation 17:10 says, "five are fallen." These five are Egypt, Assyria, Babylon, Persia and Greece. "One is," which is the sixth, the Roman empire of John's day. "And the other is not yet come," this is the revived Roman empire, the ten nation confederation or the ten horns under the leader-ship of the white horse rider in the first half of the Tribulation.*"[42]

In the third verse, John notes that one of the beast's heads is wounded to the point of death. However, the head miraculously heals, and because of this, everyone "wonders" or marvels after the beast. People have long debated this description. What does it mean? Is John talking about an actual person, or is he referencing one of the empires that a head of the beast represents?

We learn in the text that John references seven mountains, which likely refer to seven specific kingdoms, as already pointed out. However, John also tells us that these "heads" also point to seven *kings* (cf. Revelation 17:10). If this is so, then it could very well mean that a *type* of empire is resurrected during the Tribulation. We will discuss more on that when we get into Revelation 17. In the previous charts, we can see how Fruchtenbaum sees these heads, with the sixth head made up of four individual parts. These lead into the seventh head; Antichrist and his empire or kingdom.

If they also represent specific *kings*, then the one who receives a fatal blow and is resurrected probably refers to Antichrist. We know from

---

[42] J. Hampton Keathley III *Studies in Revelation* (Biblical Studies Press, 1997), 168

Revelation 17 that this is referring to the seventh head, which *is* Antichrist.

Though commentators disagree on whether it is the empire, the king, or both that are resurrected, in this author's mind, it is impossible to have one without the other. Antichrist is the king of the seventh head, therefore without him the *kingdom* does not exist.

Theoretically, why would the people of the world marvel after an *empire* or *kingdom*? In order for that to occur, the resurrected kingdom would need to be filled with grandeur and splendor, something that everyone found extremely attractive. Beyond this, people would also have to be very much aware of history to know that this seventh head is a resurrected form of a kingdom like it that existed centuries prior.

If we compare that with the idea that it is the Antichrist who dies and is resurrected, the entire concept becomes much more plausible. We immediately see that if someone died and then rose again, and billions of people witnessed it, it would be a remarkable event to be sure. If this did (or does) occur, then people would certainly marvel after the beast (Antichrist) because of his power to heal himself and his ability to resurrect himself.

The other thing to consider, though, is that many today do not believe in the resurrection of Jesus Christ. Some go so far as to say that He did not even really exist. If someone in the 21st or 22nd century was able to *appear* to do what Jesus is said to have done (die and resurrect), there is a great possibility that people would be convinced that this Antichrist was, in fact, the Messiah.

Verse 4 clarifies for us that the beast here likely refers to an empire *and* an actual person. *"And they worshipped the dragon which gave power unto the beast: and they worshipped the beast, saying, Who is like unto the beast? Who is able to make war with him?"* Here John notes that because of the seemingly fatal wound from which the Antichrist rose from the "dead," the people worshiped the Dragon (Satan). Satan *finally* gets what he has desired for centuries! He is worshipped. The people also worship the beast and they wonder, "*who is like unto the beast?*" and "*who can make war with him?*" He is seen as matchless in *character* and *power*. People will follow him in amazement, never having seen anything like the beast before! The beast here is specifically referenced with the word *him* indicating that he is indeed a person. He is the king of the final human empire, and because it is so closely associated with the Antichrist, the empire is also called *the beast*.

We all know of the power of numerous dictators throughout the history of the world. Closest to this day and age is Adolph Hitler, who gained control of an entire nation. They became so brainwashed that they were able to do anything Hitler wanted, seeing it as morally *right*. Millions of people died under Hitler. His desire to obliterate all Jews is known throughout the world, except by those who prefer to bury their heads in the sand, or to simply deny that the holocaust occurred at all.

Antichrist will be the consummate dictator, so charming, so intelligent, so remarkable that it will be nearly impossible *not* to fall in line behind him. Because he will *seem* to have died and risen again, the people will gladly follow his rule, doing whatever he tells people to do. Those who do not will be eradicated.

Recently, I was watching a documentary about Saddam Hussein, who became known as the Butcher of Bagdad. The documentary followed his rise to the top of the pile politically. One of the things Hussein learned quickly was that by treating people terribly through persecution, beatings, imprisonments, and even death, the entire population could be controlled. That of course is nothing new at all, yet Hussein seemed to excel at it.

I recall one chilling scene when he had just become *the* leader of his country. He had called for a huge gathering of the top people in the military and the government. He rose to give a speech and calmly stated that there were traitors in the midst. He then just as calmly began announcing their names one by one, telling them to report to the back of the large auditorium.

As each person's name was called, you could see him slowly get up and, with a worried expression, resolutely walk to the back of the auditorium, where they were taken outside. In short order, they were all shot for treason. There was no such thing as a trial. It was Hussein's word against theirs, and the only thing that Hussein was interested in was *creating fear*. It is likely that none of the men singled out were guilty of anything except being part of that government and being in that room when their names were called.

After the last condemned man walked out of the arena, there was deafening silence. Hussein took his seat and lit an expensive Cuban cigar, simply sitting there with what appeared to be a slight smirk on his face. Then, one man began chanting, "*Long live Saddam! Long live Saddam!*" with the volume and intensity of a man who realized that he could just as easily have heard his name called.

Within seconds, the entire hall erupted in praise of "king" Saddam, as he continued to sit in his chair, on the stage, smoking a cigar. There was no reaction apart from that.

When dictators rise to power, they usually find that keeping people in fear is the best way to control the people. No dictator worth his salt is going spend time *loving* or *caring for* the people. No, that will not do. That is a sign of weakness. Better to keep them in fear, always wondering what you are going to do.

Even with Hitler, though the German people adored him, they were obviously afraid of him as well. To be seen as not following the Fueh-rer would likely mean instant death.

The coming man of sin, the beast, the Antichrist, will *seem* to care for the people. His power will eclipse the worst dictator this world has ever seen. People will willingly follow him wherever he leads, and unfortunately, most will follow him straight into the Lake of Fire!

As to the actual death and resurrection of the Antichrist, the question is asked whether it will be real or not. Judging from Satan's ability, we know he has the power to take life, but there is nothing in Scrip-ture that indicates he can *give* life. Either God will allow Satan this one time to bring someone back from the dead (doubtful), or Satan will make this "death" look extremely real (probable), so then he is not actually raising anyone from the dead.

Since Satan is often known for his deceptions, this is probably one of them, on a grand scale. If he is capable of convincing people that he is Jesus Christ (or Archangel Michael, etc.), he can certainly pull off a stunt that makes it appear as though the Antichrist has actually died and been resurrected. In either case, the death and resurrection of Antichrist will appear to be the real thing, causing people to dedicate their lives to him, following him wherever he leads.

Immediately after Antichrist has managed to ensnare the world into following him like the Pied Piper, we read the following in verses 5 and 6: "*And there was given unto him a mouth speaking great things and blasphemies; and power was given unto him to continue forty and two months. And he opened his mouth in blasphemy against God, to blaspheme his name, and his tabernacle, and them that dwell in heav-en.*"

Once he has the world's attention and adoration, he wastes no time in offering blasphemies to God Almighty. Verse five states, "*And there was given unto him a mouth speaking great things and blasphe-mies; and power was given unto him to continue forty and two months."* Satan is the motivator, the puppet master, who literally grants Antichrist power and his seat of authority. This is what Satan offered to Jesus Christ during His wilderness temptation (cf. Matthew 4), but Jesus refused without hesitation. Here, Antichrist is offered the same deal and accepts the offer.

Satan instills Antichrist with the ability to spout all manner of blas-phemies against Almighty God. However, God allows Antichrist to continue for forty-two months, until the end of the Tribulation. It will be at this point that Jesus Christ returns physically, destroying Antichrist with one breath.

What will Antichrist say? What will he claim? What type of blas-phemies are we speaking of here? In short, he will say anything he can say that pokes fun of, denigrates, castigates, or impugns the holy character of God. He will raise himself up above God, likely asking who can go against him (Antichrist), and who is like him (Antichrist), echoing the sentiments of the people.

He may laugh with sordid glee, presupposing that he is greater than God is and will prove it to the people of earth. He will puff himself up any way he can so that all on the earth will come to believe that Anti-christ is the greatest being that ever lived and is truly the messiah and Mahdi.

Can you hear him standing there at a podium wondering aloud (with a mocking tone), *"where is this God people speak of? I have yet to see Him."* He may say what Elijah said when he confronted the prophets of Baal (cf. 1 Kings 18). This was where Elijah poked fun at the god of the prophets, wondering why he had not responded to their yelling and their cutting themselves. Elijah even egged them on to yell loud-er because maybe Baal was preoccupied or was out of earshot.

I can see this taking place with Antichrist. Remember, God is purposefully quiet at this point, allowing Antichrist to brag and to do what he needs to do so that God's purposes will be fulfilled. Because God is quiet and does not take Antichrist out with a lightning bolt (and also because Antichrist appeared to die and rise again), the people of the world will be won over by this handsome, charming, intellectual and intelligent man, the leader of the world. He will be the consummate con artist, making all other con artists look like children in a sandbox.

He could also well attempt to call God "out" from His perceived hiding place. Satan wants nothing more than to defeat God, something he will never even come close to achieving. At this point in the Tribulation, Satan's anger will know no bounds. The blasphemies of the Antichrist may well be from Satan's own lips, doing all he can to draw God out into the open. If this is the case, it is ridiculous for Satan to even consider. He will be like a child who has thrown tantrum after tantrum, only to be completely ignored by his parents. Nothing he does will draw them out and cause an eyebrow to raise. Yet he will persist, because he has nothing else left.

Revelation 13:7-9

"And it was given unto him to make war with the saints, and to overcome them: and power was given him over all kindreds, and tongues, and nations.

"And all that dwell upon the earth shall worship him, whose names are not written in the book of life of the Lamb slain from the foundation of the world. If any man have an ear, let him hear."

In the three verses above, we see two contrasting ideas. Verse 7 informs us that power was *given* to him to make war with the saints and to overcome them. In other words, those who are Christians (or who will *become* Christians), will be the Antichrist's main target. Satan's hatred of believers will know no bounds at this point and he will be *allowed* to come against the saints in the Tribulation period and kill them.

Opposite of this is the idea that everyone else who lives on the earth will worship him. The people who do this are those whose names were not written in the book of life from the foundation of the world.

Many people have a problem with the concept of election. They do not want to entertain the idea that God would simply pick some for salvation while bypassing others. To them, it does not appear *loving* or *holy*. In short, it does not seem to be in keeping with God's character. That is because we are fallen human beings who are trying to figure this out so that our finite minds can understand it. That is impossible.

It seems clear from this passage that before the earth was created, God had names written in the Lamb's book of life. This is interesting for a number of reasons. First, it tells us that God did the choosing, though some will undoubtedly look at that verse and add to it by stating, "*God looked down the annals of future time, saw those who would receive Him, and those are the names He wrote down in the book of life.*" The text does not state that at all. It states that the names were already written down previously. The assumption is that God chose those who would be saved. Nothing in the verse implies that man had any part of this process. God did it all. God even seems to emphasize this with the words "*he that hath an ear, let him hear.*" MacArthur rightly points out that the second part of the phrase "*what the Spirit says to the churches" is missing.*" The reason is that God is not merely talking to the churches here, but to the world. All are invited to receive salvation, but not all will receive it.

It is also very possible that the Church is no longer on the earth, having been *Raptured* prior to the start of the Tribulation. Since we know that Jesus spoke to the various churches through John in the beginning of the book of Revelation, it seems odd now that He would also cease to include them if they were still on the earth. If this is so, then it does *not* mean that anyone who becomes a Christian after the Church is gone must become a Christian with a completely different method.

What this means is that the Church is one particular entity, just as Israel is one particular entity. Those who become Christians during the Tribulation period will be every bit as saved as those of the Church or the Remnant of Israel who turn to Christ. These individuals will simply *not* be part of the Church, Christ's Bride.

Revelation 13:10
"He that leadeth into captivity shall go into captivity: he that killeth with the sword must be killed with the sword. Here is the patience and the faith of the saints."

This verse informs us that the Christians during this time *will* be patient, and many will be executed for their faith. It is also an encouragement by Jesus that though death will come, the victory of eternal life will be sweet. Death and any pain associated with it cannot compare to the eternal beauty of heaven.

While some Christians will be tossed into prison ("captivity"), many more will die through execution. Note also that the text specifically says the sword will be used in death. It is interesting to realize that in countries where Islam thrives, people are often killed by having their heads cut off.

This was a favored way of executing people under the reign of Saddam Hussein, though not the only mode he used. The Antichrist will be worse than any dictator the world has ever seen. Fully empowered (and even possessed) by Satan, the Antichrist will be the most intelligent, cunning, and charming dictator this world will have ever seen. He will come as a peacemaker, but with an agenda that causes the death of all those who do not join him.

Revelation 13:11-12

"And I beheld another beast coming up out of the earth; and he had two horns like a lamb, and he spake as a dragon.

"And he exerciseth all the power of the first beast before him, and causeth the earth and them which dwell therein to worship the first beast, whose deadly wound was healed."

As if one beast fully controlled by Satan is not enough, we see another one. Unlike our first beast who came out of the sea (normally referring to Gentile nations), this beast comes up out of the earth. The earth here could likely mean the lower parts of the earth, or the abyss, since it is normally seen as being "under" the earth.

Though this beast is similar in nature to the first beast, his role is completely different. Many have pointed out that when this beast makes his appearance, the false trinity will be complete; the Dragon, the Antichrist, and the False Prophet. Together they vie for their own way and worship. The second beast's job is to promote the first beast, to cause people to worship him. Notice also that this second beast has the same power as the first beast. This is because both beasts are fully empowered by Satan.

The fact that this second beast arrives on the scene with two small horns (like a lamb), but speaks as a dragon is very significant. Jesus spoke of this type of individual when He stated, *"Beware of false prophets, which come to you in sheep's clothing, but inwardly they are ravening wolves"* (Matthew 7:15). All those who came before this beast were types, or typical of what the second beast would be one thousand fold. This beast only *appears* as a lamb but will be *empowered* by the Dragon (Satan). His words ensnare the gullible into believing that all of his lies are the total truth.

John reminds us here that the first beast had a wound that was fatal, and came back from the dead. This is the job of the second beast, to remind people that the first beast is worthy to be worshiped because he died and rose again. The second beast (aka the False Prophet, cf. Revelation 16:13; 19:20; 20:10) ensures that the people do not forget this, and he is even given power to perform what appear to be mighty miracles. These will further cause people to wonder with amazement.

The False Prophet has the power to cause everyone to worship the first beast, either through coercion or through miraculous works.

Revelation 13:13-14
"And he doeth great wonders, so that he maketh fire come down from heaven on the earth in the sight of men,

"And deceiveth them that dwell on the earth by the means of those miracles which he had power to do in the sight of the beast; saying to them that dwell on the earth, that they should make an image to the beast, which had the wound by a sword, and did live."

The False Prophet is given tremendous power, causing those on earth to believe that this must be God in the flesh! He causes it to rain fire. This will remind people of the two witnesses and their ability to destroy with fire from their mouths. At this point, the witnesses may or may not already be on the scene. If they are not yet on the scene, then when the two witnesses shoot fire out of their mouths, people may simply think it is an effort on the part of the two witnesses to imitate the False Prophet.

If the two witnesses have already been on the scene and struck people dead with fire from their mouths, they will likely marvel even more at the False Prophet who, rather than shoot fire out of his mouth, was able to call fire down from heaven! The idea that John is trying to get across is that the False Prophet will use one miraculous sign after another to deceive people into thinking he is the real deal, and if he is the real deal, then so is the first beast, who *must* be worshipped! *"Whatever this will be, it is clearly designed to counterfeit the miraculous works of God, either that of Elijah in 1 Kings 18:38 or that of the two witnesses in Revelation 11:5 (cf. also 2 Kings 1:10 15; Lev. 10:1 2). Some have suggested that this could be a reference to fire from heaven to imitate that which occurred at Pentecost (Acts 2:3) and could be a reference to pseudo-charismatic gifts to create a counterfeit religious community whose allegiance is to antichrist.*

"Whatever it is, it is a prominent sign and shows the kind of power Satan will display through his puppets, the beast and the false prophet."[43]

Miracles are not always of God. In fact, it is logical to assume that with the death of the last apostle, the sign gifts died out. This does not mean that God does not heal anymore, because He does, as His will dictates. Nevertheless, to hear many tell it, the sign gifts are just as active today as they were during Christ's day, or Paul's. This is in spite of the fact that the signs were given as a means of proving Christ's deity, or the fact that God had called certain individuals to be apostles. The miracles confirmed that they had God's stamp of approval on them.

Think of the miracles that Kathryn Kuhlman, Oral Roberts, Benny Hinn, Robert Tilton, Jim Bakker, and many others have claimed or been credited with *performing*. In each case, it appeared to be nothing more than a performance. There was no credible indication that there actually was a miracle.

People can and are too often taken in by miracles, or what appear to be miracles. In the course of this century and the previous century, many have stepped forward to claim that they have seen the apparition of the Virgin Mary. Probably one of the most famous is connect-

---

[43] J. Hampton Keathley III *Studies in Revelation* (Biblical Studies Press, 1997), 179

ed with Fatima, Portugal. Three children allegedly saw the Virgin Mary, and it is to them that she allegedly gave three secrets, which were later revealed.

On one particular occasion, the Virgin Mary promised that she would provide an undeniable sign that would offer proof that what she was saying would happen during her last visitation. She did not say what the miracle was, but on the appointed day – October 13, 1917 – over 70,000 people gathered to witness what they believed would be the promised miracle.

What took place has become known as the Miracle of the Sun. It was during this day that the sun is said to have "*appeared to change colors and to rotate like a fire wheel. Then it seemed as though the sun would crash down to earth. For some the sun appeared to fall from the sky before retreating, for others it zig-zagged. The phenomenon is claimed to have been witnessed by most people in the crowd as well as people many miles away.*"[44] Not all in attendance saw the phenomenon. Some saw colors, or the zigzag, while some saw nothing at all.

Was it real? If Satan has the ability to control the weather (as he did in the book of Job), then he can easily create a situation in which a huge number of people witness a mass hallucination. No scientist registered anything unusual about the sun that day. Had the sun really moved as it did, it would have caused major polar disruptions here on earth (unless God was the one who did the moving of the sun). Though there are a few pictures of the crowds during the event, there are no known photos of the sun that day.

Miracles (or supernatural phenomenon) have been performed by Satan and his underlings. We know this from Pharaoh's sorcerers or wizards as well as other portions of Scripture. They were able to duplicate everything that Moses did, with the one exception of the

---

[44] http://en.wikipedia.org/wiki/Our_Lady_of_F%C3%A1tima

snake. When Moses told Aaron to drop his staff to the ground, it became a snake. The court wizards did the same and their staffs turned to snakes. However, Aaron's staff, as a snake, devoured the other snakes (cf. Exodus 7).

We learn something else here about the wound of the first beast. John tells us that it was a wound of the *sword*. John could mean an actual sword or a wound received in battle, since the sword often means warfare in Scripture.

Revelation 13:15

"And he had power to give life unto the image of the beast, that the image of the beast should both speak, and cause that as many as would not worship the image of the beast should be killed."

Now this is interesting. It appears as though the False Prophet will actually be able to animate an image of the beast. Whether a statue or painting or something else entirely, we do not know. Whatever it is, we know that it is not a living being, yet the False Prophet makes it appear as though it is alive. He is able to make this image speak, and people are given the ultimatum that everyone should worship him (the first beast) or die.

This reminds us of Nebuchadnezzar, who built an image to himself and whenever the music sounded, people were supposed to stop what they were doing and worship the image that Nebuchadnezzar had constructed. Those who refused would be executed (cf. Daniel 3).

Of course, the huge difference between Nebuchadnezzar's image and the image of the Antichrist is that the Antichrist's image will be so real and so lifelike that the wonder of it will cause people to believe that the image *is* the Antichrist. The fact that this image will actually speak will amaze. This will be far more revolutionary than any figure or shape controlled by animatronics! It will appear as life itself is operating from within the image of the Antichrist.

Revelation 13:16-18

"And he causeth all, both small and great, rich and poor, free and bond, to receive a mark in their right hand, or in their foreheads:

"And that no man might buy or sell, save he that had the mark, or the name of the beast, or the number of his name. Here is wisdom. Let him that hath understanding count the number of the beast: for it is the number of a man; and his number is Six hundred threescore and six."

This particular text has been the cause of great debate for centuries. The bottom line is that no one knows exactly what this mark refers to or exactly what it means.

Verse 16 is clear that the False Prophet goes beyond Nebuchadnezzar in making people take a mark that in some way represents the first beast, or Antichrist. Those who refuse to do so will not be able to buy or sell.

Over the decades, people have said that this mark is an economy without cash and that people will need to have some form of credit card to use since cash would no longer be accepted. Others have stated that it is the UPC symbol since it has the numbers 6, 6, and 6 built into it (which is true, it does). Still others believe that the number of the beast is somehow connected to an implant that is surgically placed just under the skin. This implant will contain all of the financial information of each individual, and without it neither selling nor buying can occur.

Some commentators believe that this number of his name references something to do with the Hebrew version of the Antichrist's name. This is because Hebrew letters also reference a number, not just a letter.

Recently, I read of one idea that indicated the possibility of the mark being accepted by people under the pretense of it being an *antidote* for a new virus that would kill within days. Without the antidote, no one would have a chance to survive. Of course, people would clamor for it, especially if the virus was intentionally released to the public without the public knowing.

Once the antidote was injected, with it was a new strain of DNA that would literally change every human's DNA into something that could only be described as a human hybrid. In this way, since people would no longer be *only* human, salvation would be impossible, much like the fallen angels and the Nephilim created from mixing angelic DNA with human DNA.

Whatever the case turns out to be, it will obviously become clear during that period of the Tribulation. Only the people living during that time will need to know to be aware of the mark. Until then we can only guess, and there seems to be no shortage of guessing all around.

The False Prophet will deliberately set this system up so that finding and killing those who refuse to worship the beast (Antichrist) will be fairly easy.

As an aside, let me repeat that I am a firm believer in the PreTrib Rapture. I believe that the Church will be taken out of the picture completely prior to the opening of the First Seal, when God's wrath begins to pour out onto the earth. Having said that, I would also like to state without equivocation that if I am wrong in my understanding of Scripture, then I am wrong. Unlike some who believe that not only am I wrong, but I am wrong because I am fully deceived, I believe that if the PreTrib Rapture does *not* occur as I believe it will, then if I am alive at the start of the Tribulation, it is obvious that I will go through at least part of it. Eventually, I like millions of others will be killed for refusing to accept the mark of the beast.

I want readers to know that I do not find this fact horrifying. In fact, if the Lord were to choose to send to me to a part of the world *now* where I might easily be persecuted or be called on to die for my faith, so be it. Christ Himself said that there is no greater love that someone could have for another than he who is willing to lay down his life.

Jesus Christ gave His life *for me*. While I hate the thought of any pain (especially if it is drawn out) prior to my death, I am confident that the Lord will *keep me* from denying Him, and that my death will fully glorify Him.

Death is merely the pathway to paradise. It is nothing to shrink from at all. In fact, if we are living the Christian life authentically, then we should be longing for that day. Those who do not are most probably too enamored with the things of this earth.

Along these lines, I also believe it is important to take precautions, by storing foodstuffs, water, electronic devices that do not require batteries (hand crank), and other things as well. If possible, Christians should *grow* as much of their food as they can. Why should we do this if the PreTrib Rapture is going to occur prior to the Tribulation? Simply because we do not know how *bad* it will get on earth *before* the PreTrib Rapture occurs! Why be stupid about it?

We are already in the process of adding supplies, including emergency food that will last three to six months. Water is the most important thing, and aside from our bathtubs, which could be cleaned and used to store water for our use, we have an eight hundred gallon above ground pool in our backyard that remains clean and free of debris. Do I really want to drink pool water? No, but if it will keep me alive, then I will do so. It is my suggestion that each Christian make a plan, because we really do not when the world economy will collapse. We are not privy to knowing how scarce food might become (or how expensive!) as time marches onward. To whimsically ignore the signs and take no thought of survival or how to care for your family during the coming times of crisis is completely irresponsible. Prophezine.com is a place on the 'Net that offers many practical suggestions on how to turn your home into a place that is fully prepared for what is coming and what the Christian may experience. Are you aware that you can grow potatoes in a garbage can? These folks have a DVD filled with articles on preparing for the coming rough times, and it is available for a nominal price.

Do you have a hand crank emergency radio? We do, and it has a built-in flashlight and a USB port, allowing you to recharge your cell phone. It is capable of receiving the major emergency networks to keep abreast of what is happening in the world. Things like this are not *fear mongering*. They are practical and will do a world of good when things get rough.

We cannot prepare for every eventuality and God will certainly protect us, but He also expects us to act wisely. He is not going to fill your refrigerator with food. That is up to you to do by going to the grocery store yourself. He will provide the job and/or money that you will need to shop for groceries.

Christians need to be smart, making the most of opportunities. This should not only be for evangelistic opportunities. It should also include protecting and caring for your family.

Obviously, this passage in Revelation 13 is dealing with conditions *inside* the Tribulation. If the Rapture occurs prior to the beginning of it, then Christians are not going to experience these things. However, as stated, we have no real idea of how bad things will become *before* the Tribulation even starts, or just prior to the PreTrib Rapture if it is to occur.

We will present one final point about the mark of the beast. *"The three sixes **may elude to the satanic trinity**—Satan or the dragon, seeking to replace the Father, the beast seeking to replace the Lord Je-*

sus Christ, and the false prophet, seeking to replace the Holy Spirit. But they all fall infinitely short of the triune Godhead. No matter how far we carry the number 666 mathematically as 666666666 it never becomes seven. It always falls short. The point is that this man and his system can never do that which God has promised. Man promises peace but brings war; life, but brings death; liberty, but brings slavery; happiness, but brings misery; significance, but brings the loss of true meaning and purpose in life.

As the ancient church father Irenaeus proposed, the number may indicate that the beast is the sum of all apostate power, a concentrate of 6,000 years of unrighteousness, wickedness, deception, and false prophecy. The three sixes look at this wickedness in the past, the present and the future culminated in this end time system of the beast.

The general character of the Tribulation is clearly portrayed in this chapter. It is a time of slavery, blasphemy, apostasy, and gross satanic activity. Let us thank God that we have the blessed hope of the rapture (Titus 2:13). But let us not, as we contemplate on all this, forget our responsibility to be involved in the propagation of the gospel of Christ, the only hope for the world."[45] (emphasis added)

---

[45] J. Hampton Keathley III *Studies in Revelation* (Biblical Studies Press, 1997), 181-82

◆————————— 14 —————————◆

REVELATION 14

Revelation 14:1

"And I looked, and, lo, a Lamb stood on the mount Sion, and with him an hundred forty and four thousand, having his Father's name written in their foreheads."

The 144,000 are seen again here. This group first comes to our attention in Revelation 7, and is sealed for the work of evangelism. Here in Revelation 14, this same group is seen with the Lamb on Mount Zion. This is Christ's entry point, where He will "touch down" so to speak upon His return at the Second Coming. *"Prophetically in Scripture, Zion came to symbolize the place where Messiah would come as the deliv-*

erer of Israel and where He would gather together His people (Psalm 48:1f; Isa. 24:23; Joel 2:32; Zeph. 14:10; Rom. 11:26)."[46]

It seems clear enough that the picture John sees is of Christ on the physical Mount Zion *on earth*, with the 144,000 who will go into His Millennial Kingdom with Him. These 144,000 will have been protected from death and will actually go into the Millennium *alive*, never having experienced death or heaven.

The 144,000 make up part of the Last Days Remnant. As God has *always* kept for Himself a Remnant; this last group is that for the last generation. They will receive the same salvation that all believers receive, yet they will go into the Millennium alive, as human beings with human bodies. There, they will rule over nations with Christ and carry out His mission for the 1,000 years He will physically reign *on the earth*.

This group of 144,000 was sealed in Revelation 7, and again John points out that they were sealed with the Name of the Father. This sealing is the protection they enjoyed while living through the Tribulation.

Revelation 14:2-5
"And I heard a voice from heaven, as the voice of many waters, and as the voice of a great thunder: and I heard the voice of harpers harping with their harps:

"And they sung as it were a new song before the throne, and before the four beasts, and the elders: and no man could learn that song but the hundred and forty and four thousand, which were redeemed from the earth.

"These are they which were not defiled with women; for they are virgins. These are they which follow the Lamb whithersoever he

[46] J. Hampton Keathley III *Studies in Revelation* (Biblical Studies Press, 1997), 183

goeth. These were redeemed from among men, being the firstfruits unto God and to the Lamb.

"And in their mouth was found no guile: for they are without fault before the throne of God.

Immediately after John sees the Lord with His 144,000, we hear a voice from heaven. The voice is described as a *"voice of many waters...(and) great thunder."* This is none other than the pure and awesome voice of God. Picture the sound of Niagara Falls and then multiply it 100 or 1,000 fold. God's voice is overwhelming, terrifying to those who have rejected Him, and sweet to those who have received His salvation.

As God speaks (and we are not told what He says), He is joined by creatures playing their harps. The harp is what David, the Psalmist, played, and it is a beautiful sounding instrument. This is a *new song* to be sung at this point in the future, and it obviously has everything to do with the triumph of the Lamb and the vindication of His Creation.

We are told that the only individuals who were allowed to learn this song were those of the company of 144,000. They were specifically redeemed from the earth for a number of unique purposes, and this is one of them.

We are told that these men – they must all be men if they were not "defiled" by women – are virgins, having dedicated themselves to God. They view themselves as God's only. They are so dedicated to God that they follow God the Lamb wherever He goes. Whether or not these 144,000 are all men or John is referencing physical virginity is difficult to tell. Keathley states, *"One might assume these are all men because 'they were not defiled with women.' On the other hand, one might assume they are all women because they are literally called 'virgins,' the Greek parthenoi. Neither assumption, however, is necessarily correct. John is probably using these terms in a spiritual sense to declare their spiritual chastity and devotion to Christ. So the word 'virgin' in Scripture does not always have to refer to a woman. Further, the word 'defiled' is used by John in the Book of Revelation of moral or spiritual defilement or spiritual or cultic prostitution (cf. 3:4 where John also used 'defiled' or the Greek word moluno, with 2:14, 20, 22 for a setting of spiritual prostitution).*

"During the Tribulation there will exist a great apostate church, or religious Babylon, the mother of all harlotries and the great harlot of the Tribulation. This will be followed by the apostate and idolatrous worship of the beast (cf. Rev. 17 18:24; 13:1ff). But these 144,000 escape all spiritual defilement with these religious systems of the Tribulation. They remain pure, i.e., spiritual virgins. One might compare also a similar use of virgins in the parable of the ten virgins in Matthew 25:1-13. In both passages we have references to men and women. The emphasis is not on sex but on spiritual purity. It is for this reason the NASV translates the word parthenos as 'chaste.'

"This view fits with the following words, 'these are those who follow the Lamb wherever He goes.' The whole group has remained devoted and faithful to the Lord Jesus Christ; they follow and serve Him as obedient servants in contrast to a world that as a whole goes whoring after the beast."[47]

The idea that these 144,000 are stated to be *first fruits* who were redeemed unto God is another reason why the PreTrib Rapture may have occurred. If not, and the Church remains during the Tribulation, it is difficult to understand how these 144,000 could be considered first fruits, unless *all* who are ever saved from the time of Christ to His Second Coming are considered first fruits. Conversely, if the Church is gone, having been evacuated from earth in the Rapture, then the 144,000 who are saved and sealed in the Tribulation *are* the first fruits of that period. These in turn will go and witness to others who

---

[47] J. Hampton Keathley III *Studies in Revelation* (Biblical Studies Press, 1997), 185

will also become saved. Notice, though, that it is only the 144,000 who are referred to as first fruits and not the people who become Christians because of the ministry of the 144,000.

In any case, these 144,000 are completely devoted to the Lamb, following Him wherever He goes, and pure in thought and word. They are not sinless because as human beings, they still have the sin nature. However, God considers them to be pure without guile because of the level of dedication to Him and their willingness to do anything He asks of them. In other words, they are not alive for themselves, but for God, to be used of Him as He sees fit. This is really the perfect understanding of what it means to be an authentic Christian, and it is the very thing that all Christians should strive to become for Him.

Revelation 14:6-7

"And I saw another angel fly in the midst of heaven, having the everlasting gospel to preach unto them that dwell on the earth, and to every nation, and kindred, and tongue, and people,

"Saying with a loud voice, Fear God, and give glory to him; for the hour of his judgment is come: and worship him that made heaven, and earth, and the sea, and the fountains of waters."

Here an angel is given the privilege of announcing to all on earth that the Gospel of Jesus Christ is *the* truth! This angel is able to speak so that all nations and people of all languages hear his message. He states unequivocally that only God should be feared and given glory. It is God who made heaven, the earth, and everything that is contained within His Creation.

In other words, the rightful Owner and Creator is Almighty God, not the first beast, not the second beast, and certainly not the Dragon. God alone deserves all the credit, all the glory, and all the honor. None of it should be shared with another. The angel insists that all people must turn to Him.

This angel will go back and forth across the skies proclaiming his message. Picture a biplane with a trailing announcement tied to its tail. It flies back and forth so that all can read the message. The sense here is that this angel will do the same thing until all have heard his message of hope and warning.

Revelation 14:8
"And there followed another angel, saying, Babylon is fallen, is fallen, that great city, because she made all nations drink of the wine of the wrath of her fornication."

Immediately on the heels of the first angel, who preaches a Gospel message to all inhabitants of the earth, another angel comes along to announce that Babylon is fallen. That system is no longer. The angel's message is prophetic regarding what *will* in actuality happen to Babylon and its godless system.

Babylon is a city, having come into existence in Genesis 11. Here, under Nimrod's lead, the people became as if they were one in thought, deed, and word. Nimrod encouraged the people to build a tower to the heavens. As previously indicated, this tower may have only intended to be built to a point where a dimensional portal existed. From that point, it would be an easy "walk" right into heaven.

Though Satan and his angels had been tossed out of heaven, but allowed to go before God's throne to give reports and receive commands, the Nephilim (possibly like Nimrod) would have only had an imprint of heaven. Since Nimrod may have been the offspring of a fallen angel and human woman union, the concepts stored within the DNA of the angel would have passed down to Nimrod. It may have been for this reason that the idea to build a tower to "heaven," or the opening of heaven, was something that Nimrod opted to do. It also may have simply stemmed from Nimrod's desire to be *like* God and to have a place that ascended to the heavens.

In either case, Babylon had its start there, when God decided enough was enough. Since the people were acting as though they had one mind, God decided to split then up, and He did so by breaking them up into groups in which their language and culture matched.

The people would then find others who spoke their language and go off with these people in search of a place to put down roots. From Babylon (Tower of Bab-el) an entire system grew, which included a way of thinking, politics, and religion. All of it wrapped together is what constitutes Babylon.

During the reign of Saddam Hussein, he began rebuilding the famed city of Babylon. He did not get far, but that was one of his dreams.

Revelation 14:9-11
"And the third angel followed them, saying with a loud voice, If any man worship the beast and his image, and receive his mark in his forehead, or in his hand,

"The same shall drink of the wine of the wrath of God, which is poured out without mixture into the cup of his indignation; and he shall be tormented with fire and brimstone in the presence of the holy angels, and in the presence of the Lamb:

"And the smoke of their torment ascendeth up for ever and ever: and they have no rest day nor night, who worship the beast and his image, and whosoever receiveth the mark of his name."

Here is the point of no return for earth dwellers. They cannot say they have not been warned. An angel follows the previous angel announcing that anyone who receives the mark of the beast and worships the beast and his image will be cast out forever.

The description is horrific. The person who worships the beast and his image and takes the mark will:

- Experience the fullness of God's wrath, which includes
    - *Being tormented with fire and brimstone before the angels and the Lamb*
    - *Being tormented with fire forever and the smoke will never cease to rise*
    - *Having not one second of rest forever*

Is the above description scary to you? It is to me. Consider the fact that these individuals will never receive a reprieve. There are some who have a distinct problem with this; as if God has no right to do whatever He chooses to do. They believe that God should annihilate people instead of sequestering them to a furnace that burns day and night without letup. God has His reasons for what He does, and I doubt very seriously that humanity can appreciate the full ramification of God's plans or why He does many things.

We learned a bit about the number or mark of the beast in Revelation 13. It is difficult to be certain as to its meaning. We may not actually know until the world gets there and sees it. Could it be a microchip?

It's possible. Could it be some type of tattoo? It's also possible. Given the fact that so many people are into tattoos covering their bodies these days, it would not surprise me if the mark was something of a tattoo. Tattoos have become so common that no one would bat an eye if they had to add one.

If you watch a professional basketball game, it is extremely rare to see a player without tattoos. Many of them are literally covered with tattoos on both arms, shoulders, neck, back, and elsewhere, so that they look like walking billboards.

Irrespective of what the mark is, we see that it is the dividing line between those who stand with God and those who stand against Him. Everyone alive at that point in the Tribulation will be given the opportunity to reject the mark. Rejecting the mark, refusal to worship the beast, can lead to salvation. Accepting the mark automatically destroys any further chances of receiving salvation.

Revelation 14:12
"Here is the patience of the saints: here are they that keep the commandments of God, and the faith of Jesus."

This sentence ties in with the last group, but I have purposefully left it separate. It makes a statement and it says that in spite of the waywardness of most of the people of earth who receive the mark and worship the beast, the saints will *not*. God is stating that one of the facts that will keep saints on the road of perseverance is the knowledge of what will happen to those individuals who *do* take the mark.

I recall a brief discussion with someone opposed to the PreTrib Rapture. He himself believed in the PostTrib Rapture. He further believes that the PreTrib Rapture is a doctrine born of deception, therefore from hell itself. He indicated that those who are alive when the Tribulation occurs would be most deeply affected by their belief in a

PreTrib Rapture. When asked to elaborate, he stated that the people alive at the time that the Tribulation begins would realize that the PreTrib Rapture did not occur. This will so damage their psyche that because of their belief in the deception of the PreTrib Rapture, they will wind up taking the mark of the beast during the Tribulation to save themselves and therefore wind up losing their salvation.

It's a bit of a laughable proposition. What he's saying is that I believe in the PreTrib Rapture because I am deceived (since he assures me that the Bible does not teach a PreTrib Rapture). Since I am deceived in the first place, then if I am alive when the Tribulation period begins, the bottom will drop out for me and I will be so discombobulated that I will have no sense at all. Because there is no sense left in my brain, I will believe the Antichrist to be Jesus Christ and follow him to the loss of my salvation. This is extreme and highly absurd. As do many who do not believe in eternal security of the Christian, there is no mention or sense of God's sovereignty here. What is God doing while this is supposedly happening? Apparently, nothing.

Look, it is very simple. I believe in the PreTrib Rapture as I have previously stated because it is taught in Scripture. I know that people have argued about that for some time now. I see a PreTrib Rapture happening, but let me again say assuredly that if it does not occur and I am wrong in my understanding of Scripture, then I will enter into the Tribulation like all the other Christians (if I am alive at the point).

Once inside the Tribulation, God still has my life under control. No matter how much I may believe something to be true – like the PreTrib Rapture – if I have misunderstood Scripture, then the PreTrib Rapture will not occur. If it does not occur, I have actually lost nothing because I do not base my entire life on the PreTrib Rapture. I actually base my entire life on the fact that at any moment, of any day, I could die and be taken to the Lord. If the PreTrib Rapture is to occur, I have no idea when it will take place. I do not know when my death will occur either, but there is probably a greater chance of my death happening than any view of the Rapture. I simply do not know, and I am okay with that. I am not deceived, and if the PreTrib Rapture does not occur as I believe it will, then "oh well." Life moves on and I will move on with it.

Though many will find temporary respite from the wrath of the Antichrist in *this* life by *taking* the mark, it will only be temporary. Once these individuals die, they are met full force with God's unceasing wrath.

Conversely, while Christians are persecuted to death, the level of persecution may be extreme, but it also is only temporary. Once they die, they enter into God's rest, which is eternal. It is God who keeps His children, lest pride takes up residence in our hearts.

Eternal security of the believer is an important doctrine, but that may not in fact be what this verse is teaching. *"Because of the clause, 'the perseverance of the saints,' some take this passage as teaching the doctrine of the perseverance of the saints. Some confuse the Reformed doctrine called the perseverance of the saints with the doc-trine of eternal security, but they are not exactly the same. Eternal security says that once a person is saved he cannot lose his salvation because he is kept by the power of God through the finished and sufficient work of the Savior. The Reformed doctrine of perseverance says much more than this. It says that all who are truly saved will persevere in a life of godliness and holiness; that there may be temporary times of sin and carnality, but no true believer will persist in such a state for very long and will eventually come back to the Lord."*[48]

Revelation 14:13
"And I heard a voice from heaven saying unto me, Write, Blessed are the dead which die in the Lord from henceforth: Yea, saith the

---

[48] J. Hampton Keathley III *Studies in Revelation* (Biblical Studies Press, 1997), 195

Spirit, that they may rest from their labours; and their works do follow them."

The blessedness of this passage cannot be understated. Those who die because of their faith in the Lord are rewarded with an eternal rest. What a blessing.

The voice here is likely God, whereas the voices prior were from angels, and were listed as angels. God is announcing that those who are faithful will rest from their labors. Again, people tend to read into passages such as this to imply that there are those saints who are *not* faithful (or who *might not* be faithful). This is really not what the text states at all. Those who are faithful are rewarded.

15

REVELATION 15

Revelation 15:1-4

"And I saw another sign in heaven, great and marvellous, seven angels having the seven last plagues; for in them is filled up the wrath of God. And I saw as it were a sea of glass mingled with fire: and them that had gotten the victory over the beast, and over his image, and over his mark, and over the number of his name, stand on the sea of glass, having the harps of God. And they sing the song of Moses the servant of God, and the song of the Lamb, saying, Great and marvellous are thy works, Lord God Almighty;

just and true are thy ways, thou King of saints. Who shall not fear thee, O Lord, and glorify thy name? for thou only art holy: for all nations shall come and worship before thee; for thy judgments are made manifest."

We arrive at chapter 15 with John seeing another sign in heaven. This one – great and marvelous – is seven angels who will pour out the last seven plagues onto the earth.

In each plague, God's wrath is evident. Again, there is no point in time when any of the plagues or judgments from God, either from the Seals, the Trumpets, or now from the Bowls, comes forth from any-one other than God, the Lamb. Satan and his minions along with An-tichrist do God's bidding. Their "freedom" to move is only within the confines of each judgment, not outside of it. God is in full control not only of each judgment or plague, but in the timing and duration of each as well. Those who erroneously believe that Satan has control of certain things apart from God's will, or that Satan's wrath is on display *above* or *to preclude* God's wrath, appear to be in error.

John says he sees (as it were) a sea of glass mingled with fire. Since John says "as it were," he could very well be referring to something that is *representative* of something else. He did not say that he saw a sea of glass mingled with fire. He said he saw something *like* a sea of glass mingled with fire.

It must be remembered that John is describing things as he sees them in the language he understands. For those things that he sees but can only describe figuratively, we must be careful to not assume our meaning into the passage.

This particular "sea" that is "mingled with fire" could very well be the shining brightness of the "floor" of heaven, as it is before God's throne.

If this heavenly floor is like nothing John has ever seen before, then it is natural to suppose that he would use descriptors of things he *has* seen that remind him of what he now sees. This floor is before the throne of God. It stands to reason that if this is what John is actually attempting to describe, then he would really have little to compare it to, but what he does compare it to is like the shiny sea mixed with the brightness of fire.

The text states that those who gained the victory over the beast stand on this "sea of glass." It appears to be a scene in which these martyrs, who in Christ's strength stand victoriously before Him, are receiving their reward. They recognize that Christ is the Lamb, and is the same One that Moses sang about.

These martyrs also recognize that all nations will come before Him, bowing to His Lordship. Notice the last statement of this section, which states, *"for thy judgments are made manifest."* What judgments are those? The judgments that have poured forth from the throne throughout the entirety of the Tribulation.

Revelation 15:5-8

"Then I looked and saw that the Temple in heaven, God's Tabernacle, was thrown wide open. The seven angels who were holding the seven plagues came out of the Temple. They were clothed in spotless white linen with gold sashes across their chests. Then one of the four living beings handed each of the seven angels a gold bowl filled with the wrath of God, who lives forever and ever. The Temple was filled with smoke from God's glory and power. No one could enter the Temple until the seven angels had completed pouring out the seven plagues."

Things have literally broken wide open by this point. Here we see the final plagues, carried by seven angels. These angels are each given a gold bowl by one of the four living beings. Each bowl is filled with God's wrath.

We also see in this scene that the Temple in heaven is filled with God's power and glory, which emanates as smoke. The Temple is completely off limits to everyone until the seven angels complete their assignment. The contents of all seven bowls must be poured onto the earth before the Temple can be approached again.

What should be understood is that God is angry. His anger is represented in each of the seven golden bowls. The angels stand in the Temple and until God's wrath is poured out of all the bowls, no one could approach.

This is very reminiscent of the manifestation of God's presence on the mount with Moses. The rumblings, the lightning, the dark clouds – all of it represented God's presence and it terrified the Israelites, so much so that they begged that God should only speak to and through Moses, but not directly to them.

In the heavenly Temple, God's wrath is at its full level, and with finality it will pour out of each bowl onto earth and its citizens. God, who has poured out judgment after judgment during this seven-year period, has also extended grace. With each new judgment there remained the possibility of people bowing the knee to Him willingly, gratefully acknowledging His power, His might, His love, His holiness, and His salvation.

Most on earth resolutely refuse repeatedly to acknowledge God, much less bow to Him. The length of the Tribulation with all of its accompanying judgments is in one sense a show of God's mercy.

Just as a loving parent chastises and disciplines his children, so also does God bring His discipline to bear on a wayward world. Though most will refuse His mercy, many will be embrace Him and His salvation, which is why there are so many martyrs during this period.

God here is at the height of His anger and His severe wrath is manifest toward those on earth who continue to refuse recognizing His

Lordship. His own Temple in His heavenly realm is filled with the smoke of His wrath.

This brief interlude sets the tone from the release of these seven last judgments. All things are ready. Those in heaven worship God as God and await His final display of severity to those who continue in rebellion.

16

REVELATION 16

Another "great voice" speaks in heaven, speaking to and providing direction for the seven angels. This great voice could very well be the mighty angel we have seen and heard from on numerous occasions.

Revelation 16:1
"And I heard a great voice out of the temple saying to the seven angels, Go your ways, and pour out the vials of the wrath of God upon the earth."

Each angel is commissioned to pour out the vials (or bowls) of God's wrath upon the earth. These coming judgments are not pleasant, and since the opening of the First Seal things have become progressively more complex and fierce. We arrive at this point with God having given the world a last chance to catch their breath before He pours out the final phase of His wrath.

While some may balk at this entire scenario (and many have done just that), the reality is that God has persevered in patience for thousands of years. He has given humanity in each generation every chance they need to repent and come to Him in humility, asking for forgiveness.

While many from each generation have done this, the majority have not, with the world becoming more evil as time goes by. Here in 2010, we see a world that is quite different from the world that God created.

People have become just what Paul prophesied they would become, as he told Timothy:

> *"This know also, that in the last days perilous times shall come.*
>
> *For men shall be lovers of their own selves, covetous, boasters, proud, blasphemers, disobedient to parents, unthankful, unholy,*
>
> *Without natural affection, trucebreakers, false accusers, incontinent, fierce, despisers of those that are good,*
>
> *Traitors, heady, highminded, lovers of pleasures more than lovers of God;*
>
> *Having a form of godliness, but denying the power thereof: from such turn away.*
>
> *For of this sort are they which creep into houses, and lead captive silly women laden with sins, led away with divers lusts,*

Ever learning, and never able to come to the knowledge of the truth.

Now as Jannes and Jambres withstood Moses, so do these also resist the truth: men of corrupt minds, reprobate concerning the faith.

But they shall proceed no further: for their folly shall be manifest unto all men, as theirs also was," (2 Timothy 3:1-9).

Pretty sad, isn't it? Men *have* become lovers of themselves in 2010. They are proud, boastful, blasphemers, disobedient not only to parents, but to most forms of authority. They are unthankful and unholy, completely irreverent.

People today can lie as if they are telling the truth with no compunction, they will break a promise as quickly as they can change directions, many always seem ready for a fight, and they hate people who prefer to do the good things that God requires of His children.

Many of these individuals have a form of godliness, meaning they attend church, they profess to know Christ, and they even look and/or sound like authentic Christians. However, the power they do not have is the power that comes only from God to change lives. This they do not possess.

These types of professing Christians know nothing of God, because they do not have the indwelling Holy Spirit to guide them. They have merely *put on* Christianity, like a jacket that they can remove at will.

In spite of what evolution teaches, people are *not* getting better. In fact, evolution cannot tell us where our sense of morality comes from, nor can it show that man – while allegedly evolving – has actually improved his character. Quite the opposite seems to be the case.

I recall when I took in Biology in college. The professor – a staunch evolutionist – rejected Creationism hands down, and he also had an interesting reason he put forth as to why people are the way they are now.

He stated that it is only since man became "civilized" that things started going wrong. When man entered the phase we call civilization, he learned how to control things like how many babies should be born, and how to react to certain things.

In other words, apparently, when man still lived under the rote method of living and acting by natural instinct, life was better in many ways. Then civilization came into the picture and man changed, but not necessarily for the better.

It would seem then that evolution also stopped there, because man can now decide his fate. Evolution, like the New Age movement, teaches that man can now determine the direction and outcome of his life. If so, one would think that humanity would become far better than our distant ancestors would. This is certainly not the case, as we can readily see.

Humankind has not only *not* become better, but is also becoming far worse. This is obvious, or should be to anyone who can look beyond their presuppositions.

This is what Paul said would happen, and it is clear that this is where we are now. These are terrible times in many ways. Look at people today and for the most part you will see people who act tough and who have exterior countenances to match the way they feel.

People believe they add to their toughness by tattooing themselves from their toes to their heads. People have become walking billboards. Does anyone really think the average person will have a problem taking the mark of the beast, whatever it happens to be? If it is something that is visibly placed on the skin, most people will simply see it as another tattoo, added to the many pieces of artwork that already adorn their bodies.

Everything humanity has done and become warrants God's judgment. That is *not* why He created the earth or the creatures on it. He created everything and He does everything to bring glory to Himself, and we have fallen far from that purpose.

God's judgments come not because He is somehow "mean-spirited" or "evil." His judgments are sent – via Seal, Trumpet, and Bowl – because He desires us to turn to Him. Those who refuse will have been given every chance to submit to Him. Their constant refusal results in their own eternal demise. However, they will never be able to say that they did not receive enough chances.

God's final seven judgments are being poured out, and the question is: what will the world do in response to those judgments?

Revelation 16:2 – First Bowl

"And the first went, and poured out his vial upon the earth; and there fell a noisome and grievous sore upon the men which had the mark of the beast, and upon them which worshipped his image."

This first bowl judgment, along with the other six, likely all came from the seventh trumpet judgment since there is no specific judgment associated with the seventh trumpet.

Here we see the first angel pouring out the contents of his bowl onto the earth, and the result is seen in terrible sores that cover the skin. These sores are noted as "noisome and grievous." They are noisome because of the bother they create, along with the constant groaning in agony.

Imagine the worst cold sore or boil you have ever had. Now multiply that by 1,000. Now imagine boils like that covering you from head to toe! It does not take long to realize that with that many sores and as painful as they are, just moving would be extremely difficult. Your body would go into spasms due to the pain. This is not a pretty sight at all.

Also note that there seems to be no relief at all. Once the angel pours out the contents of the bowl, people suffer and there is no let up. No one – including the beast or Antichrist – can do anything to alleviate the pain. God is in charge.

Revelation 16:3 – Second Bowl

"And the second angel poured out his vial upon the sea; and it became as the blood of a dead man: and every living soul died in the sea."

The contents of this second bowl are poured out onto the sea. The reaction is instantaneous, as it becomes as the blood of a dead man. Note that the text is not saying that it symbolically becomes like blood. It is saying that it becomes blood, like that of a dead person.

What happens when any living mammal dies? It begins the process of decay. Since the blood is no longer circulating with fresh supplies of oxygen throughout the body, all organs, skins, bones – everything – begins to decay.

Anyone who has had the unlucky proposition of having to take a dead animal (like a rat) out of the attic knows all too well how badly a carcass can stink. Since the sea has turned to stagnant blood, everything that lives in the sea dies.

All creatures need oxygen, including those in the sea. We know that fish, for example, extract oxygen out of the water through their gills. The oxygen keeps them alive. We know that whales need air, though they can stay under the water for long periods of time. They have to come up for air, while other fish and creatures can remain under the water, absorbing oxygen from the water itself.

Since the sea has become blood, there is no longer any useable oxygen in it. No oxygen means death to everything. Beyond the fact that there is no longer fresh oxygen in the sea, blood acts differently than seawater (or even fresh) does with respect to how creatures and fish can swim. Blood is far thicker than water, making it difficult to move. in little time, creatures that need to move constantly in order to say alive (like sharks) will be unable to do so, bringing about their deaths.

Imagine the stench! Every creature in the sea dies. The blood sea already stinks because it is stagnant blood. Add to that every creature within the sea and the stench will likely become unbearable throughout the world!

This second bowl, like the ones coming afterwards, does not create a picture of beauty. It is judgment, directly from God, based on His wrath – His severe anger. This judgment is designed to show people how wrong they have been about Him and those who serve Him.

Revelation 16:3-7 – Third Bowl

"And the third angel poured out his vial upon the rivers and fountains of waters; and they became blood.

"And I heard the angel of the waters say, Thou art righteous, O Lord, which art, and wast, and shalt be, because thou hast judged thus.

"For they have shed the blood of saints and prophets, and thou hast given them blood to drink; for they are worthy.

"And I heard another out of the altar say, Even so, Lord God Almighty, true and righteous are thy judgments."

As the second bowl sullied and polluted the sea, this third bowl does the same to the fresh water sources. What is interesting here is what the angel says as he pours out the contents of his bowl. He says that just as those in opposition to God have shed the blood of saints, they deserve (are worthy) to drink blood as a result. *"These apostate and rebellious people have slain and shed the blood of believers, thus, just as the saints receive rest and reward for their faith, so these will receive punishment fitting the nature of their crimes. They have only blood to drink. They have been blood thirsty—now they get their fill. This gives us another indication that during the Tribulation the shedding of the blood of believers will be without parallel in history."*[49]

The seven-year Tribulation period will be the bloodiest period known to man. The blood of the martyrs will flow like rivers, and so God repays the people of the earth in kind. The fountains of waters here may refer to the source of the rivers, where the river originates. Once the source is polluted and turns to blood, the entire river will become blood as well.

It seems that the picture here is that not just parts of these freshwater rivers become blood, but the entirety of the rivers becomes blood. While in the second bowl only the seas were affected, here the fresh water, or potable water, is affected, leaving very little water to drink. Again, with the fresh waters becoming blood, nothing will survive, and the stench will also be unbearable.

Notice in the last verse of this section, the angel agrees with God that His judgments are righteous and true. We often tend to forget that. We think we know better than God. We think that it is unloving for God to actually put people in a place where they will be eternally tormented. That's not fair, we say. It is unconscionable, others would say. It is fully unloving, some think.

The trouble is that human beings are the ones who allowed God's Creation to become the mess it has become. If Adam and Eve had not sinned, no problem would now exist! Often people ask why God al-

---

[49] J. Hampton Keathley III *Studies in Revelation* (Biblical Studies Press, 1997), 208

lows suffering. Suffering is the natural consequence of the fall of man. Suffering is part of the package to which Adam and Eve gave themselves over. How is it possible to be a fallen human being (which also affected the Creation; the animals, the earth, etc.) and not experience suffering? It is impossible. Why is God to blame for that? Simply put, He is NOT.

Whatever God does is righteous and just. There is no question. Those who deign to question Him do so because of their ego and pride. They kick against the goads because they have no real understanding of God and His ways.

Kicking against the goads is a term used by farmers. When animals were guided through a gateway, they might become stubborn and refuse to go. As they kicked against the sides of the railings, they would often hurt themselves because the farmers had placed "goads" or spiked sticks along the fence to keep the animals from going backwards from where they came.

Human beings know little at best. The sooner we realize that, the sooner we can come to depend upon God, trusting Him for everything He accomplishes in this world as being the best option. God will only do what is in keeping with His character.

People like to say, "God is love." Yes, He is absolutely love. He is also just, holy, perfect, sinless and much more. He is not just love, as if we can think that God is some old man in a rocking chair doting on His grandchildren. Love often makes difficult decisions. Love can appear to be very tough at times. Love can make people cry. Love does what is best for a person, not what they want done.

Revelation 16:8-9 – Fourth Bowl
"And the fourth angel poured out his vial upon the sun; and power was given unto him to scorch men with fire.

"And men were scorched with great heat, and blasphemed the name of God, which hath power over these plagues: and they repented not to give him glory."

This is another tragic event. It is another aspect of God's wrath, as were the previous seals, trumpets, and bowls. This one is designed to scorch people on the earth. They will experience the worst sunburn they've ever experienced, and unfortunately, it will be but a taste of what is in store for them after their life on earth ends.

Notice the reaction of the people on the earth. They not only "repented not" because of their own sin, but they "blasphemed" God. The searing heat caused them to continue to reject God, in anger and with epithets.

It is likely that the people who are affected by this scorching heat are the ones who have worshiped and have taken the mark of the beast. It seems reasonable to state that those who are *believers* will be kept from this, just as God protected the Israelites supernaturally from being affected by the plagues He sent during the plagues of Egypt. Literally, the Greek has "to scorch the men with fire." *"The use of the article specifies a particular group of people, those mentioned in connection with the first bowl, unbelievers, worshipers of the beast. Evidently, believers will somehow be protected from this."*[50]

I have often heard people argue that the Lake of Fire cannot be a real place, and even if it is, how could God cause people to be there forever, for all eternity? Here is a mini-picture of what that Lake of Fire will be like. There, human beings (along with the devil and his angels) will burn forever. Please notice that based on this passage alone, it is very likely that just because people have died and their constant rejection of God caused them to go the place He originally

---

[50] J. Hampton Keathley III *Studies in Revelation* (Biblical Studies Press, 1997), 209

created only for the devil and his angels, they *continue* to rebel, blaspheme and *sin*.

Just because people are in the Lake of Fire, it does not mean that they *stop sinning*. That is not the case, as this text shows. They hate God, they continue to call Him names, they continue to reject Him, and they continue to sin. The sin of those who end up in the Lake of Fire (through their continued rejection of God and His salvation) will continue on throughout eternity. Their sinning does not cease simply because they are dead. If anything, it will *increase* as they experience God's wrath without letup. It is the choice they made in *this life* through their constant desire to push God away from them.

Authentic Christians (the ones who have actually been born again, or born from above; cf. John 3) are given new natures in this life at the moment of salvation. This occurs when the Holy Spirit takes up residence within the person. Though the sin nature is still present, the devil's claim on us through the sin nature is broken.

After the death of authentic Christians, the sin nature is completely removed and we become just like Jesus in character. His perfection, His lack of sin, His perfect submission to the Father is mirrored within each authentic Christian. Never again does the Christian have to deal with temptation or sin of any kind.

Those who do not receive Christ in this life go into the next life with their sin nature intact. It is not removed, nor do those people have a new nature. They die in their sins and they exist throughout all eternity as objects of God's wrath.

It needs to be clearly understood that sin is the sole object of God's wrath. All sin and any sin is hated by God. The only place to put that sin is in a place where it will, for all eternity, be burned for purification. Of course, the problem is that because sin continues, it will *never* be finally purified; never. It will remain for all eternity as sin.

This is a troublesome doctrine to many, but that is because they are fully unable to see this situation from God's perspective. They see it only from their perspective, and it is tainted at best. People are not perfect – even Christians – in this life. Fallen individuals who never receive God's salvation and never learn to see things from God's perspective. Because of that, it is not unusual that people arrive at conclusions that they believe means they are wise; however, God says they are fools (cf. Romans 1:22).

Unsaved people never want to give the glory to God. They want to give it to other human beings or themselves, but never to God, who is the only One who should have any and all glory. Unsaved people are unable to see their own inherent evil, nor are they able to understand most spiritual doctrines, because these are from God, not their own natural, darkened thinking.

Revelation 16:10-11 – Fifth Bowl

"And the fifth angel poured out his vial upon the seat of the beast; and his kingdom was full of darkness; and they gnawed their tongues for pain,

"And blasphemed the God of heaven because of their pains and their sores, and repented not of their deeds."

Here we see the reaction from the contents of the fifth bowl. This angel pours the contents of his bowl onto the seat of the beast. This has a direct connection to the beast's kingdom. The fifth bowl ushers in darkness and it begins with the throne of the beast, continuing throughout his kingdom. Keathley states, "*the beast refers to a person as well as to a political system, therefore, his throne is a definite place. I be-lieve it will be rebuilt Babylon on the Euphrates River, the ancient capitol of Satan's wickedness in the land of Shi-nar (Zech. 5:5 10). This is the land beast of Revelation 13 who will receive his power from Sa-tan and who will become the object of man's worship. Men will marvel at the beast and proclaim "who is like the beast, and who is able to make war with him" (Rev. 13:4). Remember, he will be seen as the solution to the world, the answer to man-kind, the hope of the world."*[51]

There is a good deal of imagery here for us to consider. This darkness appears to be so thick that you could cut it with a knife. Notice how the people react to it. They "gnawed their tongues for pain." Looking at Jesus' words in the gospels, He stated that those who reject Him will be cast into outer darkness where they will gnash their teeth (cf. Matthew 22:13). Why would outer darkness cause people to gnash their tongue or teeth? Simply put, it is because of the tremendous fear that people will feel due to this darkness.

People will see nothing...absolutely nothing. They will hear things, but they will see nothing. They may bump into things – other people, demons, the devil himself – in this outer darkness of eternity, and it will cause an even greater fear within them.

Imagine being in the darkest place you can think of and how that would feel. Years ago, one of my favorite books was "Tom Sawyer" by Mark Twain. In that book, Injun Joe gets stuck in the cave toward the end of the story. It's a pitiful sight. As the rescuers open the blocked cave entrance, they see Joe, dead. Near him are pieces of candles, some used for light, and others he ate because of his hunger. There were great scratch marks on the heavy door that had sealed the cave as he attempted to claw his way out.

I have thought of what it must have been like when the last candle went out and there was nothing but darkness...and complete quiet. How unnerving that would be. This is what the earth will be like when God literally turns out the lights.

It almost implies that all electricity at this point is not working. What is the big deal, we might think, to have no moon or stars if we still have lights in our home? Consider what the world would be like if a

---

[51] J. Hampton Keathley III *Studies in Revelation* (Biblical Studies Press, 1997), 210

solar flare caused a large electromagnetic pulse (EMP) throughout the globe. Anything that relied on electricity would be affected, depending on how large the EMP was when it hit the earth.

It is also likely that at least some of the previous judgments will continue, as there is no real indication that the sores, for instance, last only until the next judgment is poured out. People are probably still suffering from the sores, lack of fresh water, stench from the seas and rivers, and now this complete darkness that seems to envelope them. Would this not be enough to cause anger on top of their existing pain? Instead of repenting, they continue in their stubborn rebellion. *"There will, at this time, be no more atheists or agnostics. All men will know, like the demons, that God exists, but they remain stubborn in their rebellion."*[52]

Revelation 16:12-16 – Sixth Bowl

"And the sixth angel poured out his vial upon the great river Euphrates; and the water thereof was dried up, that the way of the kings of the east might be prepared.

"And I saw three unclean spirits like frogs come out of the mouth of the dragon, and out of the mouth of the beast, and out of the mouth of the false prophet.

"For they are the spirits of devils, working miracles, which go forth unto the kings of the earth and of the whole world, to gather them to the battle of that great day of God Almighty.

"Behold, I come as a thief. Blessed is he that watcheth, and keepeth his garments, lest he walk naked, and they see his shame.

"And he gathered them together into a place called in the Hebrew tongue Armageddon."

---

[52] J. Hampton Keathley III *Studies in Revelation* (Biblical Studies Press, 1997), 210

This particular judgment is extremely interesting in many ways. First, there are a number of things that occur after the bowl's contents are poured out. Second, there is one main reason why this judgment occurs.

First, the Euphrates River dries up. This is no small river! If you know anything about this particular river, you know that this river is roughly 1,800 miles in length and forms natural boundaries between countries. It has played a large role in biblical history. It ranges in width from 450 feet across to 750 feet across. The river has been a major source of water for irrigation for crops and animals, allowing areas to flourish.

All of a sudden, the Euphrates River is no more. It has completely dried up. That becomes a HUGE problem! However, the point here is that God's purpose in drying up the river is to bring something *about*. That something is to allow the troops to move into the Valley of Megiddo for the last battle upon the earth, the Battle of Armageddon, which is essentially Satan's last stand against God Himself.

Notice the text, "and he gathered them together," in the last part of the verses. The "he" in this verse refers to God. God is gathering all these troops and armies as they make their last stand against the God of the universe. Does this make you think of Psalm 2?

> *"Why do the heathen rage, and the people imagine a vain thing?*
>
> *"The kings of the earth set themselves, and the rulers take counsel together, against the LORD, and against his anointed, saying,*
>
> *"Let us break their bands asunder, and cast away their cords from us.*

> *"He that sitteth in the heavens shall laugh: the LORD shall*
> *have them in derision"* (Psalm 2:1-4)

Led by Antichrist, the rulers and kings, along with their armies, will come together in preparation for Jesus Christ's physical return to the earth. This is not a welcoming committee! They intend to stop Jesus from returning! Satan's goal as incarnate Antichrist is to direct all of his supernatural power against the God of the universe! Do you think Satan actually believes he has a chance of destroying God? I do, and I believe it because it seems clear that Satan himself has fallen prey to his own lying. He has come to believe that he actually has a chance to bring an end to God. It is absurd for him to think this, because he is a *created* being. Because he is created, he is nowhere near infinite. God is infinite, uncreated. He has always been and always will be.

The text also indicates that *three spirits* that looked something like frogs come out of the mouths the dragon (Satan), the beast (Antichrist), and the false prophet. These frogs are the devils that empower the visible dragon, beast, and false prophet. The frogs are they which hold the strings to these beings.

Beyond that, these frogs are being *breathed* onto the kings and rulers of the earth. Notice the next verse states, "***For they are the spirits of devils, working miracles, which go forth unto the kings of the earth and of the whole world, to gather them to the battle of that great day of God Almighty.***"

Occultists tell us that when they breathe on someone, it can actually transfer the demon or familiar spirit attached to them onto someone else as well. Often, demons can be transferred through touch, as well as through spells.

Take a look at John 20. Here, Jesus has risen from the grave. He has a glorified body and He will remain with them over the period of 40 days before He ascends into heaven. In John 20:22, we read the words, "*And when he had said this, he breathed on them, and saith unto them, Receive ye the Holy Ghost.*" Here, Jesus breathes on the people gathered there for the purpose of receiving the Holy Spirit.

Satan does the same thing. Breathing on someone like this means to pass or transfer something from one person to the other. God did it in Genesis 2 where He breathed into Adam so that Adam became a living soul. He had not done this to the angels, or to any of the animals. He did this to Adam.

In John 20, to pass the Holy Spirit onto the disciples, Jesus breathed on them. This transference sets in motion an act whereby the individual being breathed on receives what the person doing the breathing intends for them to have.

With Satan there is no originality. He only knows how to *copy*. He has learned by watching God work and by trial and error. He knows what works and what does not work.

In order for people to have demons or familiar spirits attached to them, they must want it by opening a door. They may not realize that they are opening the door at all, but by doing certain things – drugs, meditation, or even playing with an Ouija board "for fun" – they are opening the door to Satan's kingdom. Satan will take that open door as an invitation, and he or one of his minions (or many) will walk through it.

Here in Revelation 16, we see that Antichrist, the Dragon, and the False Prophet all breathe onto the world at large, specifically the leaders, rulers, and kings. They want the power that is within them to become part of those kings and rulers.

The more the evil power and influence comes over to this realm from the spiritual realm of Satan's kingdom, the more power that Satan has *in this realm*. As Antichrist, he will physically dwell within this realm. He will also continue to be fully connected to his dark, spiritual realm. His need is to make this realm as powerfully evil as the spiritual realm that he fully controls. He can only do this by opening more and more doors. He can only do that by causing people to want to open those doors. Once they open the door, evil comes in.

It is no different than when God saves someone. They must open the door. Once they open the door, God will enter in the form of the Holy Spirit, bringing eternal life.

Notice at this point in the Tribulation, just prior to Christ's physical return, these frogs come out and work directly to gather the kings and their troops throughout all the world. They are able to gather them or win them over through the many false miracles and signs they are able to perform. They literally "work miracles" to impress these rulers, convincing them that they (Dragon, Antichrist, and False Prophet) are the real deal and they should not hesitate to join them.

Once these spirits deceive these kings and rulers through grandiose miraculous signs, they are then able to gather them to fight against God. It is clear that Satan is aware of much that will occur in the future. He obviously knows that Jesus is going to return physically, though he has worked to ensure that many people take this literal event as *figurative*. Some believe Jesus returned *spiritually* in A.D. 70 when the Romans destroyed Jerusalem and the Temple. This is in spite of the fact that two angels in the first chapter of Acts state unequivocally that Jesus will return the same way He left – physically – and every eye will see Him.

So which is it? Is God the one who gathers the kings and their troops against Him, or is it Satan? The answer is both. God is ultimately in control and allows Satan to bring his puny plans to fruition. God knows what is in Satan's heart (to come against God). He is not surprised by it, nor does He at this point stop it from occurring. This shows that God is sovereign in all things, and that man (or in this case, Satan) is fully culpable for all that he does.

Whether the kings of the earth and their armies realize that they are ultimately going to fight God is not fully clear from this passage, but if the Bible here is to be considered against other portions of the Bible, the sense we get is that they are willing participants, knowing that Jesus is getting ready to return. Because they are sold out to Antichrist, they want to keep Jesus from returning as well.

People have forever been standing up to God in rebellion of some kind. Here, though, it goes way beyond that. Now, the Antichrist, empowered by Satan, leads the charge to overthrow God and destroy God. How asinine. However, it will be no contest. Christ is already victorious!

Anyone who believes things in this life are happenstance is unaware of the fact of God's *sovereignty*. He controls (by permitting or causing them directly) all events for His good pleasure. Too many human beings are unwilling to admit or give credence to that truth.

Notice that toward the end of this section of Scripture, an aside is issued to believers. Believers are told to be awake, be aware, because He will come like a thief. God is saying that believers should be prepared for His return because it will come quickly. Believers should be living lives that glorify God. If they are, they will be looking up. This will be very difficult to do at this point in the Tribulation.

This is the interesting truth about prophecy and Eschatology (the study of Last Days). This section of the text is reminiscent of 2 Peter 3 where he speaks of the fact that the coming of the Lord is like a thief and that people should live rightly so that they will not be ashamed at His return. John states those who look forward to His return purify themselves (cf. 1 John 3:3).

Revelation 16:17-21 – Seventh Bowl
"And the seventh angel poured out his vial into the air; and there

came a great voice out of the temple of heaven, from the throne, saying, It is done.

"And there were voices, and thunders, and lightnings; and there was a great earthquake, such as was not since men were upon the earth, so mighty an earthquake, and so great.

"And the great city was divided into three parts, and the cities of the nations fell: and great Babylon came in remembrance before God, to give unto her the cup of the wine of the fierceness of his wrath.

"And every island fled away, and the mountains were not found.

"And there fell upon men a great hail out of heaven, every stone about the weight of a talent: and men blasphemed God because of the plague of the hail; for the plague thereof was exceeding great."

This seventh bowl is emptied into the *air.* Immediately a *great voice* that can only be understood as God's voice announces, *"it is done."* The natural question is, *what is done?*

Immediately after the pronouncement that it is done, there were voices, thunders, and lightning, coupled with a tremendous earthquake on the earth. The quake is so great that there has never been anything like it in all of earth's history.

The results of this earthquake on the earth are catastrophic, with absolute chaos. This is connected with the *"wine of the fierceness of his wrath."* Once again, these events are the direct result of God's severe anger, and He causes them. Cities like Babylon topple. They become rubble. One can only wonder what is left of the earth to destroy.

The earthquake causes all islands to move out of place. The mountains become flat lands. Moreover, due to the thunder, lightning, and atmospheric problems, large hailstones fall from the sky. These hailstones are not small or light. Weighing roughly 90 pounds or so each, they would easily kill any person or animal they hit even if they did not fall from a great height. Since they are falling from the sky, with that much weight, they will strike the earth with devastating force.

You have probably watched some of those documentaries about people who chase storms. They want to find out more about tornados and how a tornado develops, so they go into areas that are known for tornadic activity and get as close as possible to them.

It is not uncommon for large hailstones to develop and literally be thrown to the ground during the final stages just prior to the full development of a tornado. In many cases, these hailstones have smashed windshields, caused deep dents in vehicles and done tremendous damage to other things as well. To be hit with one of those hailstones could cause a concussion or even death, and they weigh nowhere near 90 pounds! Now, imagine a 90-pound hailstone falling on you. Lights out.

The reaction of the people is, once again, to curse God. It is interesting that they know who is behind these judgments. They at least give credit where credit is due, though their heart remains hardened to Him. It is too late for anyone who has taken the mark of the beast anyway. They have already – with finality – sold their soul to the devil, from which there is no return.

The reaction of these fallen people is in keeping with their fallen nature. They blame God instead of blaming themselves for their own failures to receive the salvation that He has consistently offered them. This is the tragedy of man's constant rejection of God due to man's rebellious nature. No one – unless God opens their eyes and He draws them to Him – will ever seek God. If left to themselves, all people would follow their ego, their pride, and their stupidity that says they need nothing and they certainly do not need God.

During this time, the New Age movement's tenets, which teach that each person holds the key to their own divinity, will be rampant. The beliefs will go from one end of the planet to the other. All people except authentic believers will follow their pride in rejecting God because they believe that they themselves are, in some form, god. Because they are god, why would they possibly need any other God? The futility of their thinking is ultimately shown for what it is through the series of judgments that occur throughout the book of Revelation. God takes His time to ensure that the people of the world understand that He alone is God.

They think they are god? Then why can't they extricate themselves from the very judgments God hurls their way? They worship an Antichrist whom they believe to be god? Then why is he unable to help them when they need his help the most? It is because there is One who is greater – infinitely greater – than all other pretenders and wannabes. God alone is sovereign. God alone is just, holy, loving, righteous and true. God is alone is all knowing, everywhere at once, and fully able to see into the hearts of every man. Nothing hides from Him. Only God is God and no other.

◆——— 17 ———◆

REVELATION 17

The first judgment poured out from the first of seven bowls is a big one. It takes on one of the biggest thorns in God's side since nearly the beginning of time. In fact, it started in Genesis 11 and continued on from there in one form or another.

Revelation 17:1-2

"And there came one of the seven angels which had the seven vials, and talked with me, saying unto me, Come hither; I will shew unto thee the judgment of the great whore that sitteth upon many

waters: With whom the kings of the earth have committed forni-
cation, and the inhabitants of the earth have been made drunk
with the wine of her fornication."

The first angel with the first bowl (which the King James renders *vi-al*) calls John's attention to what the judgment will be poured out on-to. It turns out to be the "great whore" that sits on many waters.

Now, if we were to be literal*istic*, we would say that this is a huge woman that is so huge she can straddle across many waters. What is actually going on here, though, is that the angel is using a figure of speech, or figurative language. We know that every figure of speech has a specific meaning.

In this case, the angel is saying that this whore – whatever it is – has mingled with many nations. The leaders of these nations have com-mitted fornication with her. Essentially, what the angel is saying is that the whore has caused the leaders of the world's nations to forni-cate with her, because they treated her *as though she were God.* In other words, their *worship* of her is called fornication by the God of the Bible.

The kings and leaders are guilty of committing fornication with (worshiping) someone other than the true, living God. This whore is worshipped as though God, and the true God is ignored.

What does this have to do with Genesis 11? Let's take a look and see:

> *"And the whole earth was of one language, and of one speech.*
> *And it came to pass, as they journeyed from the east, that they*
> *found a plain in the land of Shinar; and they dwelt there. And*
> *they said one to another, Go to, let us make brick, and burn them*
> *thoroughly. And they had brick for stone, and slime had they for*
> *morter. And they said, Go to, let us build us a city and a tower,*
> *whose top may reach unto heaven; and let us make us a name,*
> *lest we be scattered abroad upon the face of the whole earth.*

"And the LORD came down to see the city and the tower, which the children of men builded. And the LORD said, Behold, the people is one, and they have all one language; and this they begin to do: and now nothing will be restrained from them, which they have imagined to do. Go to, let us go down, and there confound their language, that they may not understand one another's speech.

"So the LORD scattered them abroad from thence upon the face of all the earth: and they left off to build the city. Therefore is the name of it called Babel; because the LORD did there confound the language of all the earth: and from thence did the LORD scatter them abroad upon the face of all the earth" (Genesis 11:1-9).

We are all familiar with the debacle of the Tower of Babel. As we see from the text, the people (led by Nimrod; cf. Genesis 10:9) decided to build a tower that extended to the heavens.

Tom Horn has an interesting take on this from his book *Apollyon Rising 2012*. Paraphrasing his theory, he believes that Nimrod may have been one of the Nephilim that came about from the union of fallen angels with human women. How that was done we do not know, but Horn believes it may not have been actual physical union so much as the fallen angels simply manipulated the human DNA and mixed it with their own, creating a hybrid race called Nephilim.

If this is so, then the angels that had fallen from heaven would certainly have remembered what heaven looked like and even *where* the entrances to heaven were from earth. In Horn's mind, the possibility exists that these Nephilim, having come from fallen angels, might also have had the heavenly imprint within them, and decided to gain access to heaven once again. This they might have done by building a huge tower that would have given them access through a porthole or wormhole from earth to heaven.

In this author's mind, it is a reasonable and very possible scenario. Of course, it hangs on the fallen angels, the Nephilim (if they actually existed), and so on. However, if these things did occur, with the result being a hybrid race of human-angel, then it is conceivable that portholes or wormholes do exist, as in the case of Jacob's Ladder, recorded for us in Genesis 29:11-19.

Can we prove these things with finality? No, we cannot, but neither can we disprove them. With that in mind, it is sometimes best to keep an open mind.

Nonetheless, what began at Babel continued in some form or another since then until we arrive at the present. In today's world, we have another movement that is pushing humanity to the same oneness that existed during the attempted building of the Tower of Babel.

Today, English is becoming the global language. This alone is making it far easier for nations to communicate with other nations. If we couple this with the tremendously fast ways of communication at our disposal today, the possibilities are, in reality, limitless.

This problem faced those building the Tower of Babel. They were quickly becoming *one*. In fact, God proclaimed that the people had indeed become *one*; one in language, and one in purpose. His response to this was that as such, they would be able to accomplish anything they set their minds to doing. He also knew the problems that would result from this. To stem the tide, God divided the people according to languages and cultures. He introduced to them a variety of languages and people then formed groups according to languages, which makes sense. It would be normal to hang around with people that could be understood and who could understand you.

It has taken thousands of years, but the world is once again fast becoming one. Not only is the global language becoming English, but more and more leaders of countries (and citizens within those countries) are calling for the elimination of borders in order to become a true global people. This will mean that eventually, there will be of necessity one leader to govern *all* people. In other words, there will come a time when there is a final global empire headed up by one individual, and that person will be the Antichrist.

This already exists in much of Europe where the European Union exists. While countries continue to exist, the European Union flag is flown *above* the individual country flag, which places the individual country in a less important role.

The New Age movement is fast becoming the one-world religion. The reason is simple. The New Age movement offends no one, except authentic Christians. Who cares about whether Christians are offended or not? Very few. The mentality and attitude that existed during the days of the leader Nimrod has come back to roost.

We now have a political push to become one world, and the religion of choice is the New Age movement that is understood in a variety of modes. Ultimately, the main tenet of New Age is that each person is god. His or her inherent deity resides within and all that is needed is for each person to realize it through self-actualization. Once this is achieved, that person encounters his or her own godhood. They then realize that they can and should create their own reality. Heretofore they have done this, albeit unconsciously, without knowing it. What is needed is for each person to come upon his or her own deity so that each reality can be created *consciously*.

This is the religion of Babel. It is in pursuit of the inner deity. It is what both Eve and Adam chased while still in their yet untainted creation, as God had made them. Like Lucifer before them, they both succumbed to the lie that they could become like God. Lucifer, now Satan, plied his web of lies and our first parents took the bait.

This is what people have been trying to do for thousands of years, and it is a good bet that those who were building the Tower of Babel were doing so to invade God's very presence. That possibility exists. They were foiled then and God will foil the world once more.

The angel speaks to John of this whore, inviting him to witness the judgment that will come upon her.

Revelation 17:3-7

"So he carried me away in the spirit into the wilderness: and I saw a woman sit upon a scarlet coloured beast, full of names of blasphemy, having seven heads and ten horns.

"And the woman was arrayed in purple and scarlet colour, and decked with gold and precious stones and pearls, having a golden cup in her hand full of abominations and filthiness of her fornication:

"And upon her forehead was a name written, MYSTERY, BABYLON THE GREAT, THE MOTHER OF HARLOTS AND ABOMINATIONS OF THE EARTH.

And I saw the woman drunken with the blood of the saints, and with the blood of the martyrs of Jesus: and when I saw her, I wondered with great admiration.

"And the angel said unto me, Wherefore didst thou marvel? I will tell thee the mystery of the woman, and of the beast that carrieth her, which hath the seven heads and ten horns."

So the angel takes John away in spirit (probably through a vision) into the wilderness. There he sees a woman and the woman is astride a scarlet-colored beast. The beast was also filled with blasphemous names, and had seven heads and ten horns.

Full of Names of Blasphemy:

1. *Denies the absolute authority of Holy Scripture.*
2. *Blasphemes the single source for the cleansing of human sins.*
3. *Rejects the fear of God, which is God's lasting means of wisdom.*
4. *Denies the absolute demand of holiness in the human temple (our body).*
5. *Blasphemes the created sacredness of male and female.*
6. *Forsakes the great depth and beauty of the human spirit.*
7. *Transfers the center of human life from the spirit to the soul or the fallen nature.*

By now, we should be seeing some things that cause us to think back to Daniel. The woman has seven heads and out of the heads come ten horns. We also know that out of these ten horns will come an eleventh horn, who will be the Antichrist.

The woman herself was clothed in purple as well as the same scarlet color. She was all decked out in gold and jewelry. The gold cup she carried was filled with the full measure of her wickedness from her many fornications.

This is the Mystery Religion of Babylon, the very one started by Nimrod. Though it has taken centuries to get to this point, it *does* come back once again to this point. This mystery religion is the mother of all harlots. This religion claims the lives of many, both within and without the invisible Church.

John is stupefied with wonder at this sight, and even though he sees that she is drunk from the blood of the martyrs, he cannot help but exhibit admiration for her. She must have been one truly bedeviling sight for John. The angel immediately snapped John out of it by asking him why he admired her. He then went on to explain the meaning of the beast and the woman.

Revelation 17:8-14
"The beast that thou sawest was, and is not; and shall ascend out

of the bottomless pit, and go into perdition: and they that dwell on the earth shall wonder, whose names were not written in the book of life from the foundation of the world, when they behold the beast that was, and is not, and yet is.

"And here is the mind which hath wisdom. The seven heads are seven mountains, on which the woman sitteth.

"And there are seven kings: five are fallen, and one is, and the other is not yet come; and when he cometh, he must continue a short space.

"And the beast that was, and is not, even he is the eighth, and is of the seven, and goeth into perdition.

"And the ten horns which thou sawest are ten kings, which have received no kingdom as yet; but receive power as kings one hour with the beast.

"These have one mind, and shall give their power and strength unto the beast.

"These shall make war with the Lamb, and the Lamb shall overcome them: for he is Lord of lords, and King of kings: and they that are with him are called, and chosen, and faithful."

Let's line up the facts, based on what the angel tells John:

- *The beast was and is not*
- *The beast will ascend out of the bottomless pit*
- *He will then go into perdition (the Lake of Fire)*
- *The people of the earth will marvel because of the beast who was and is not*
- *These people do not have their names written in the book of life from the creation of the world*

Those are the main facts concerning the beast. Commentators and biblical scholars have long debated about the identity of this beast. What is he? Who he is? These are reasonable questions. Can we arrive at *the* answers with 100% accuracy? Probably not. The most we can do is come away with our best educated guess, not based on how we feel about something, but based on the facts of history and the biblical text.

The angel also reveals that the beast will rise out of the bottomless pit. We have already seen that Apollyon comes from the bottomless pit and is destined to return there for all eternity.

During the time he is on the earth, people will "wonder." In other words, these people will be absolutely amazed with the beast, his power, his charisma, his intelligence, and his ability to perform miracles. These are the people whose names are not written in the book of life. Notice the text tells us that from the time that God laid the foundations of the earth (and implicitly before that) these individuals did not have their names in the book of life. They did not have their names written in the book of life because of their continued rejection of God.

This is a testament to election, which is something that is very difficult for the human mind to comprehend. How can God choose people who will receive Him, while others are not chosen? Obviously, in our fallen state it is impossible to fully come to grips with this all-important doctrine. It is best left up to God, and in the meantime authentic Christians are commanded to fulfill the Great Commission by evangelizing the lost. No human being can save another human being. No human being can even cause another human being to understand his or her need for salvation. All we can do is explain salvation the best way we know how. God does everything else.

In fact, who can fully understand the process of salvation at all? Who can comprehend the full portent and meaning of salvation and all the intricacies of how it works itself out in and through the individual? These things are best left to God. It is good enough for us to know that some will be saved, and it is God who does the saving. Our job is to tell and let God take care of the rest.

The seven mountains is understood by different people to mean different things. In this author's opinion, it seems best to recognize these mountains as the seven previous kingdoms that lead into the final one-world rule. In each case, the previous kingdoms all bowed down to the spirit of Babylon found within each one. The Antichrist and his one-world government will be the final and most vehemently opposed to God and God's rule over the entire world.

It is easy to appreciate the simplicity of Keathley's understanding of these *mountains*. *"Verse 10 tells us that 'five are fallen.' As mentioned previously, this refers to the past history of Egypt, Assyria, Babylon, Medo-Persia and Greece. 'One is' refers to Rome of John's day, the sixth. 'The other is not yet come' refers to the revived Roman empire, or the Ten Nation Confederation of the first half of the Tribulation and will truly be a work of the Devil. This seventh kingdom will continue only for a little while, specifically, 3 1/2 years (the first half of the Tribulation)."*[53]

Many forget that John is hearing things spoken *to* him that reference the time in which he lived. So when the text states, "one is," it makes sense that this would be referring to the Roman Empire that existed during John's day. The empire that is yet to come was obviously referencing a point in the future from John's perspective. It remains that this is yet future from our perspective as well.

Since the fall of the Roman Empire there has been no "world ruler," and even though Roman rulers did not technically rule the entire world, they ruled what was then understood to be the *known* world.

---

[53] J. Hampton Keathley III *Studies in Revelation* (Biblical Studies Press, 1997), 231

The description in verse eleven is interesting as well. *"Verse 11 then informs us this beast which was, is not, and would come again actually becomes an eighth kingdom; he is one of the seven and will go into destruction. The revived Roman empire will take on the form of an imperial dictatorship and by this change actually become an eighth kingdom, a whole new and vicious form of government, the blasphemous form seen in Revelation 13. This occurs in the last half of the Tribulation and lasts for 3 1/2 years, but then is destroyed by the return of Christ (Rev. 19)."*[54]

It appears that the beast that *was* and *is not* represents a *system*. Some believe that it speaks of a person who died and will be resur-

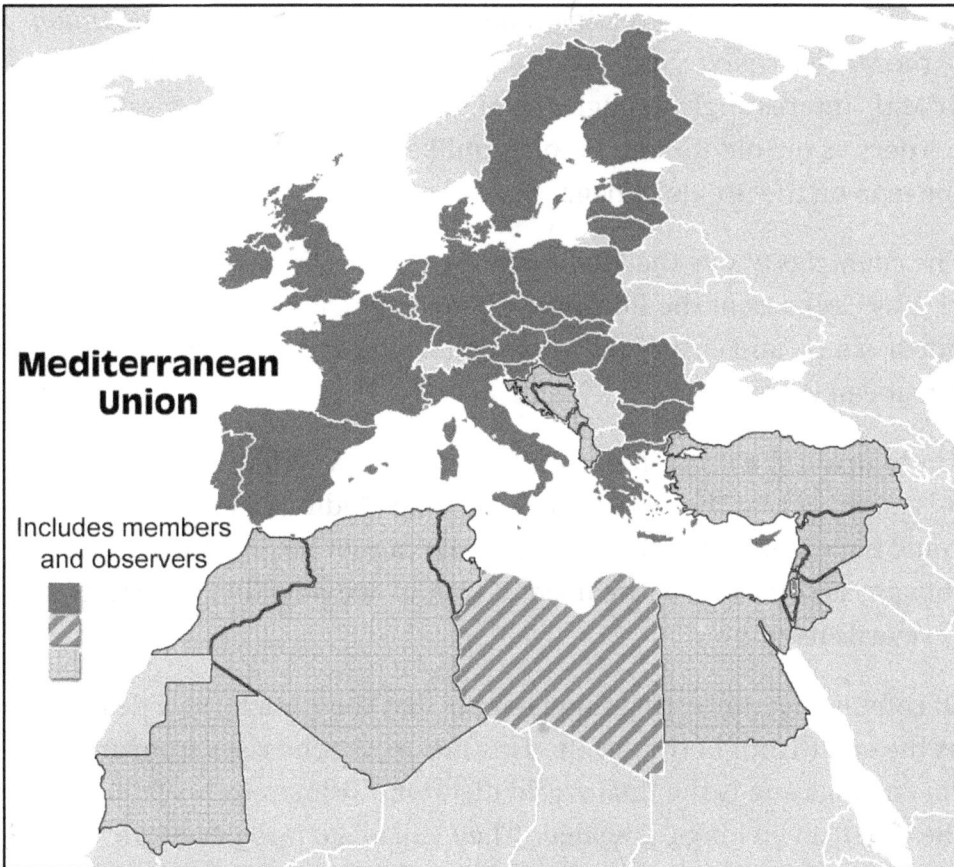

Mediterranean Union

Includes members and observers

[54] J. Hampton Keathley III *Studies in Revelation* (Biblical Studies Press, 1997), 231

rected. This is also possible *if* we are talking about an incarnation.

There are some who believe this person to be Nero; however, they might be disappointed to learn that Nero himself is not resurrected – but quite possibly the demon(s) that animated Nero is used once again in this last world emperor, the Antichrist.

If it represents a system, then we will have a *resurrection* of a system of government that came before today, one that we will see in the future. Some believe this to be the resurrected Roman Empire. This is also possible, as they see the current European Union as the resurrected Roman Empire.

What is even more interesting than the European Union is the *Union of the Mediterranean*, otherwise known as the *Mediterranean Union*, or M.U. Interestingly enough, the M.U. has nearly the exact same borders as the old Roman Empire, unlike the E.U., as can be seen on the map on the previous page.

The countries above the Mediterranean Sea on the map (in the darker gray), represent the European Union countries, while all countries north, south, and east of the Mediterranean Sea represent the Mediterranean Union.

Therefore, if the *beast* in this case represents a *system* or *empire*, then it is possible that the current and growing Mediterranean Union could have something to do with it. We cannot be dogmatic about it though, as some are, as we need to wait to see how God's Word plainly reveals itself.

Of course, the interesting thing here is that the Antichrist is described as the eighth, but of the seven. This means that he rises from amidst seven kings and is the final world dictator. Ultimately, his fate, like the other seven kings, is sealed. They will all go into perdition.

Depending upon how the text is understood it would be reasonable to assert that the ten horns (v. 12) is referencing the ten kingdoms that the world is divided up into before the Antichrist gains control of the world, creating a one-world government. This rule of his will essentially be a rule of Imperialism. Antichrist will be the imperial ruler over the earth. The ten kings will give total allegiance to the Antichrist. In other sections of Scripture (Daniel), Antichrist is referred to as coming from the ten, and is the eleventh (cf. Daniel 7:7-8). On one hand, Antichrist it the eighth, rising from seven (cf. Revelation 17), as well as the eleventh, rising from ten.

In Daniel 7, the Antichrist is referred to as the little horn, which has eyes of a man and a mouth speaking great blasphemies. This horn represents a system as well as an individual. This horn – Antichrist – will make war with the Lamb. He will do so as Jesus returns to earth physically. This will be Satan's final stand against Jesus Christ. The attempt of Satan to mount an insurrection against Jesus and His saints after Satan is released from the bottomless pit following the Millennial reign of Christ amounts to nothing, in spite of the fact that he is able to persuade many human beings to turn away from Jesus.

The Battle of Armageddon will be Satan's real last attempt to thwart God's purposes as rightful Ruler of all. Please notice the text of verse 14 in Revelation 17. The reason that Jesus overcomes the Antichrist and his followers is because Jesus is *"Lord of lords, and King of kings: and they that are with him are called, and chosen, and faithful."*

Jesus overcomes because of *who* He is as God. Nothing can withstand Him or thwart His purposes. Nothing. God allows Satan's attempts to do so in order to *prove* beyond doubt that this is the case.

Revelation 17:15-18
"And he saith unto me, The waters which thou sawest, where the whore sitteth, are peoples, and multitudes, and nations, and tongues.

"And the ten horns which thou sawest upon the beast, these shall hate the whore, and shall make her desolate and naked, and shall eat her flesh, and burn her with fire.

"For God hath put in their hearts to fulfil his will, and to agree, and give their kingdom unto the beast, until the words of God shall be fulfilled.

"And the woman which thou sawest is that great city, which reigneth over the kings of the earth."

Here is an example of Scripture interpreting itself. It is plain (because it is stated) that the waters represent the *people, multitudes, nations,* and *tongues.* There should be no reason to miss this or to assume that the waters mean something else. The waters represent all the people throughout the world that the whore has infected and affected with her blasphemy.

What is interesting here is that we are told that the ten kings shall rise up against the whore, or the religious system. Having no more use for her, they get rid of her. In other words, the system of Babylon, which is religious harlotry and idolatry, will have outlived her usefulness. Through it, the kings were able to capture the hearts of the people all over the world. Now that they have done so, what more reason do they need her around? Since these kings decide that they themselves will give their allegiance to the beast, then all the world should do the same.

In essence, the system of Babylon has merely been a decoy or cover, used to ensnare people so that they come to worship something other than God. Once the world has been completely captivated through the system of the whore, by removing her the kings can simply shift the gaze of the people from the whore to the beast. The people will then wind up worshiping the beast.

Verse 17 states, *"For God hath put in their hearts to fulfill his will, and to agree, and give their kingdom unto the beast, until the words of God shall be fulfilled."* Is there any doubt that God is fully sovereign? It is God who turns the hearts of the kings to fulfill His will. This they do by giving their individual parts (their 1/10ᵗʰ of the world) to the Antichrist. This is done so that God's Words will be fulfilled.

It seems that the final verse of chapter 17 is referring to not a specific city, but to an attitude, demeanor, or stance against God. Ever since Nimrod attempted to unify the world's people under him in order to build a tower to the heavens, the world has had its share of leaders who have attempted to do the same in one way or another. In this final stage, the Antichrist attempts to unite all people under heaven in order to overthrow God's rule in Jesus Christ. It is, as Keathley states, *"the final form of Babylonianism."*[55]

---

[55] J. Hampton Keathley III *Studies in Revelation* (Biblical Studies Press, 1997), 233

18

REVELATION 18

C hapter 18 begins with the sight of another angel coming down from heaven. He comes down to announce what the earth has been waiting to hear ever since Nimrod.

Revelation 18:1-3

"And after these things I saw another angel come down from heaven, having great power; and the earth was lightened with his glory.

"And he cried mightily with a strong voice, saying, Babylon the great is fallen, is fallen, and is become the habitation of devils,

and the hold of every foul spirit, and a cage of every unclean and hateful bird.

"For all nations have drunk of the wine of the wrath of her fornication, and the kings of the earth have committed fornication with her, and the merchants of the earth are waxed rich through the abundance of her delicacies."

This powerful angel comes down toward the earth. The glory that he has, due to his position, power, and might, is reflected over the earth and comes from the fact that God is who He is, and the glory that the angel possesses comes from God alone. It is not the angel's glory by himself. It is from God. It is doubtful that this is Jesus, simply because the text tells us that it is *another angel*. The use of the word *another* signifies that this being is of like kind to the previous angel, yet more powerful.

Keathley states, "*First, he is 'another' angel. 'Another' is allos meaning another of the same kind as those angels that preceded him. This is not the Lord nor is there any reason to see this as the Lord since angels do have great power and often display great glory. Second, that 'he comes down from heaven' points to the fact this judgment comes from God. Third, he has 'great authority.' 'Authority' is exousia which means 'liberty, or authority' and then 'power to act.' As an angel and messenger of God, he comes possessing supernatural authority and power to execute judgment on behalf of God. Fourth, 'the earth was illumined with his glory.' Literally the Greek says 'and the earth was made bright from or out of the source of his glory.' Grammatically it may also mean 'by his glory.' The word 'illumined' is the Greek pho, tizo, a causative verb meaning to 'illuminate or make bright'.*"[56]

The angel comes down to announce the fall of Babylon. Here he is obviously referring to the *system* that literally began in Babylon and

---

[56] J. Hampton Keathley III *Studies in Revelation* (Biblical Studies Press, 1997), 235

has been carried through from Nimrod to the present day and into the Tribulation. It also seems clear though that a new Babylon will exist at least during the Tribulation. As stated, Saddam Hussein attempted to rebuild the actual city of Babylon during his dictatorship. While he managed to uncover the ruins of some of it, he was unsuccessful in completely rebuilding it.

It is also possible that the Antichrist will be able to rebuild Babylon, or set up another area he dedicates to the system of Babylon. In either case, when this Babylon is felled by God, it is left only to become a prison for *"the habitation of devils, and the hold of every foul spirit, and a cage of every unclean and hateful bird"* (v. 2b).

Babylon is a system *and* city that has always been the home of demonic activity. At one point, Babylon was part of the Persian Empire. Prior to this, Babylon was the capitol of Nebuchadnezzar's kingdom, and it was to this kingdom that Daniel and many other Jews were deported.

Over time, this kingdom changed hands from Nebuchadnezzar to the Medes and the Persians. Interestingly enough, a powerful demon named the prince of Persia kept Gabriel from arriving to Daniel with an answer to prayer for twenty-one days (cf. Daniel 10). Tremendous satanic activity has always been associated with Babylon and as the Tribulation winds down, the world will once again focus on this area.

The world will see it fall, yet in a very real sense, prior to its ultimate fall it will become Satan's last hurrah, as he attempts to convince the world to follow him through the variety of lies and deceptions that emanate from the system of Babylon. The city of Babylon is merely a physical representation of the system that moves it.

There are really two aspects of philosophies built into this Babylon system. They are 1) New Age mysticism, and 2) chasing after riches.

That the New Age inhabits this system is becoming more obvious as time goes on. Mysticism, the idea that we are gods and all that remains is to unleash or unlock our inner godliness, is what lies at the heart of Babylon. It is man's attempt to elevate himself up to God's position, which is simply a mirroring of the same sin that overcame and ultimately cast down Lucifer, who became Satan.

People from all walks of life use many of the mystical tenets within the New Age to change their lives for the better. It is a way they believe they can focus their own energies to create their own reality. We have seen and heard this mantra from everywhere, and it has made tremendous gains in popularity from books, movies, talk shows, and more. People from all avenues are being told that they are their own gods. They control their lives, if they are but willing to look deep inside to unlock the deity that resides within each person.

This type of thinking promulgates the view that says, "*I can do anything and I can create my own reality!*" Normally, once a person begins to believe this, it is interesting to see that they often direct their energies toward making their lives more *comfortable*. They do so by seeing themselves as already financially wealthy. They believe that as they see themselves, so will they become.

One particular famous celebrity used this technique long before he became famous. He wrote himself a check for $20,000,000 and would sit overlooking Hollywood. He meditated and contemplated his life as a multi-millionaire. His desires drew that wealth to him. Eventually, he was paid $20,000,000 for one particular movie he did and his wish became reality. Did it really work? Does mysticism honestly bring about what we desire because we are our own gods?

There are many ultra-rich people in this world today. They have more money than they could possibly spend if they had ten or twelve lifetimes in which to spend it. In some ways, it is truly sinful that some people have so much money, and too many others have little to nothing. This is *not* God's method or system. While the world has tried Socialism and even Communism, it has been proved repeatedly that Socialism as a system that governs a nation does not work. It has too many failures, and it fails because there are always people who want more than they have now.

It is the same with gun regulation. As long as guns exist, criminals will get them. Outlawing guns only truly applies to the law-abiding citizens of the world, those who obey the laws. The criminals, on the other hand, pay no attention to laws or gun regulations. They are not affected by them. Guns have been invented. There is no going back to the time before guns existed. As long as people exist who want to harm others it is ridiculous to try to outlaw guns, as it will never have any effect on the criminal element.

Socialism will only be perfected during the reign of Jesus Christ, the Millennial Kingdom. He will rule with a rod of iron, which simply proves that problems will still come to the fore during his rule, though He will deal with them instantly.

As long as people are imperfect and guided by the sin nature, ideals such as "all we need is love" and "end wars" will only be wishful thinking. There will always be some maniacal dictator somewhere who believes he can overrun the country next to his, thereby adding that land to his.

During the Tribulation, it appears that Antichrist will bring to those who follow him great wealth and anything they want as long as they *serve* him. This they will do so gladly because of the return on their investment of serving Antichrist.

People who simply amass wealth, gathering as much as they can, do so for their own power, yet it is also to their own spiritual detriment and the physical detriment of the poor who struggle to survive. The rich are often treated as if they are royalty, or even gods. They are

given special privileges – free this, free that – all because those be-
stowing these gifts believe that it will cause those same rich people
to invest in their product or business.

Consider the fact that on most airplanes, there are very few seats that
are designated First Class compared to the amount of Coach seating.
Even if it costs something like $2,500 for one of those seats in First
Class, compare that to the eighty, one hundred, or more (depending
upon the size of the plane) that fly coach. Together the cost of all
their seats combined far outweighs the cost of all the First Class
seats, yet who are the ones who are treated as if they own the plane?

Keathley (as well as numerous other commentators) points out that
God had strict rules for Israelite kings, as we can see from the Old
Testament. They were not supposed to simply gather horses, gold, or
material possessions (cf. Deuteronomy 17) for the sake of gathering
them, or because they wanted more and more. Many did, though, including Solomon. This causes us to become reliant on ourselves rather than the Lord. God wants us to be reliant on Him, but by accu-
mulating large amounts of wealth we come to believe that we are dependent upon no one, not realizing that God could take away our
wealth in a heartbeat.

Those who chase after wealth are never done chasing after it. They
usually want more than they have in spite of the fact that they would
never be able to spend what they have in their lifetime, especially
considering the fact that they have no idea how much longer they
will live before their soul is required of them.

Revelation 18:4-8
*"And I heard another voice from heaven, saying, Come out of her,
my people, that ye be not partakers of her sins, and that ye receive
not of her plagues.*

"For her sins have reached unto heaven, and God hath remembered her iniquities.

"Reward her even as she rewarded you, and double unto her double according to her works: in the cup which she hath filled fill to her double.

"How much she hath glorified herself, and lived deliciously, so much torment and sorrow give her: for she saith in her heart, I sit a queen, and am no widow, and shall see no sorrow.

"Therefore shall her plagues come in one day, death, and mourning, and famine; and she shall be utterly burned with fire: for strong is the Lord God who judgeth her."

In the above verses, we read of the depth of sin to which the system of Babylon will cause men to stoop. A voice from heaven (speaking for God) calls to God's people to come out of her, to not partake of her sin. The angel is obviously speaking to those believers during the Tribulation period. What is Babylon's sin?

In essence, he is warning God's people to not succumb to the temptations found within the system of Babylon. Believers should avoid partaking of the cheap and temporary thrills of Satan's kingdom. This is likely the biggest problem that Christians of every age have to contend with, the enticements of the enemy.

As we grow in maturity in Christ, the idea of thrill seeking with the things of this world should become less of a pull within us. As we draw closer to God, over time He changes our desires so that we find no interest in the things of this world.

There are so many things that the average individual seems to get into these days. They go for the thrills the world offers, yet they have no lasting value. They wind up offering temporary happiness, and long-term emptiness.

If you spend any time flipping channels on the TV, you will run across numerous reality shows that defy explanation. If not reality shows, there are numerous "Spring Break" specials from various locations throughout the world. Glimpsing these shows highlights scantily-clad women and men, and all of them drinking until they get drunk. They spend hours on the beach during the day, and in the nightclubs at night, all the while being wild and imbibing drugs and alcohol until they are senseless. Then the stupidity *really* comes to the fore!

That this is what people do for *fun* is strange. I recall that when I was younger and living on the east coast, my friends and I would some-times go to a lounge or club to hear a local band play. We might have a few drinks, but none of us drank to get drunk. There were plenty of people around us, though, who *did* drink to get drunk. It was not long before I realized that there was little fun being in a bar where other patrons came to drink and get rowdy.

God has always been *more* gracious to me than I have deserved. Soon after this, I decided bars were not for me. In fact, I soon learned that I had no interest in drinking at all. My biggest fear was that I would get drunk, drive home and accidentally kill someone as I drove, which would then put me in jail for some time. The idea of killing someone in a drunken stupor did not set well with me at all, and I am thankful that God chose to use that picture to keep me from doing that. Having that on your conscience is something I cannot im-agine.

But the band plays on with the Babylon system. People drink daily, they carouse, they smoke, do drugs, buy expensive cars, live the high life, hop from one bed to another, going through many partners every year, and in general, they live only to please themselves. They live to get what they can out of life, ignoring the most important aspect of life: *the question of salvation.*

God is warning His people that they must not give into the temptation to join the world. He says to come out of Babylon so that they will actually leave the temptation behind. If you remove yourself physically from the temptation, it cannot touch you. Christians also need to remove themselves *mentally* from temptation when they are unable to remove themselves physically. Doing so is the best way to avoid temptation. If the things of Babylon never capture your mind, you will not sin.

We should not be involved in things that will cause our minds to wander from God. In fact, there may be situations where we cannot remove ourselves physically from a situation, and in that case, we must remove ourselves mentally.

Believers during the Tribulation will have difficult choices to make because temptation will be so great. They need to hold on tightly to God, depending upon Him for strength to avoid succumbing.

Like Lot, the angels came to remove him and his family from the situation so that God could destroy Sodom and Gomorrah. Had Lot not gotten out, he would have been destroyed as well, though in his case the city was not to be destroyed until Lot and his family was safely removed. Even though Lot's wife was physically being removed from the city that was to be destroyed, she had not removed herself mentally. As they fled, she could not help but to turn and look back, and the result was that she turned into a pillar of salt (cf. Genesis 19).

In this section of Revelation, God is calling His people to come out from among the "Babylonians" because of the wrath of God that is coming upon those who are part of that system. The best way to become impervious to temptation is to not allow it to get hold of your mind at all. Once it gets hold of your mind, it is extremely difficult to avoid giving into its temptation. As we have seen with Lot's wife, being *physically* removed from a situation is no guarantee, because the person may still be connected *mentally*.

The last verse in this section speaks of the horrors of God's judgment that will come upon the system and people of Babylon in a single day. The complete bottom will fall out of Babylon – *death, mourning, famine, fire*. Babylon will be *consumed*. Babylon will become a graveyard, fit only for *demons*.

Revelation 18:9-10

"And the kings of the earth, who have committed fornication and lived deliciously with her, shall bewail her, and lament for her, when they shall see the smoke of her burning,

"Standing afar off for the fear of her torment, saying, Alas, alas that great city Babylon, that mighty city! For in one hour is thy judgment come."

Look at their reaction to God's wrath. When Babylon collapses, people *mourn*. Here we see the kings of the earth – the leaders of nations, or the ten kings of the ten kingdoms that eventually become a one-world government. These people act like their life is over because Babylon is gone. The system, which propped them up in luxury and wanton waste, is now kaput. They cry. They actually shed tears!

Notice also that they stand afar off for fear of her torment. In other words, it will be such a sight that it will create deep fear within them. Yet this fear does not deter them from mourning the loss of the city and system that has continually fed their desires! From a human standpoint it makes sense, doesn't it? Those who control commerce control *people*. Because commerce has literally crashed and burned, with it goes the ability to control people and direct their lives, proving that these leaders only care for themselves and nothing more.

Look at what they say when they realize what has happened. *"Alas, alas that great city Babylon, that mighty city! For in one hour is thy judgment come."* Their concern is for the system that made *them* rich. They are still not concerned for their own eternal soul or anyone else for that matter, though it is too late by this point anyway because they have already taken the mark. Still, they do not realize the abject horror they face. They are still linked to the destroyed system of Babylon, the Beast. Their concern is for their own welfare, and from that standpoint, it is gone. What will they do now?

Revelation 18:11-16
"And the merchants of the earth shall weep and mourn over her; for no man buyeth their merchandise any more:

"The merchandise of gold, and silver, and precious stones, and of pearls, and fine linen, and purple, and silk, and scarlet, and all thyine wood, and all manner vessels of ivory, and all manner vessels of most precious wood, and of brass, and iron, and marble,

"And cinnamon, and odours, and ointments, and frankincense, and wine, and oil, and fine flour, and wheat, and beasts, and sheep, and horses, and chariots, and slaves, and souls of men.

"And the fruits that thy soul lusted after are departed from thee, and all things which were dainty and goodly are departed from thee, and thou shalt find them no more at all.

"The merchants of these things, which were made rich by her, shall stand afar off for the fear of her torment, weeping and wailing,

"And saying, Alas, alas that great city, that was clothed in fine linen, and purple, and scarlet, and decked with gold, and precious stones, and pearls!"

What can be said? Here is probably one of the biggest pity parties in the Bible. Merchants that were made rich by the commerce are crying for themselves because no one is able to buy their merchandise anymore due to Babylon's destruction and the system with it.

In these verses we read one long list of all the things that these merchants anguish over. It's a tragedy as far as they are concerned. Their reaction, like that of the kings and leaders, if one of self-pity and sorrow for what they had, and what they have now. This is not a pretty picture, is it? So many people have lived their lives through the system that has guided this world that the realization of no longer having that life is disheartening.

I recently watched a documentary on TV about mega-disasters. In one scenario, the experts ran through what might happen if a major earthquake occurred in or near New York City. It would devastate, causing 100-foot tsunamis which would not only flood but also destroy much of Manhattan and other suburbs of NYC. The devastation would last for years before it could be successfully and finally cleaned up. Rebuilding New York City would take just as long.

The reality is that if something of this magnitude occurred in or near one of the major business or commercial hubs of the world, consider it gone forever. It would probably be pointless to try to rebuild it. If only one major commercial city collapsed like that, it would affect all other commercial hubs and areas.

If you consider this world and its system of commerce, in one sense, it is merely moving money from one hand to another. The game for most, though, is to try and keep as much of it as possible. This has led to all sorts of shortcuts, bad, illegal, and even dangerous decisions to the public all because people want riches more than anything. Money is their god, and they will do whatever they need to do to get it and keep it.

I'm sure you can think of situations in which you became aware of some product that needed to be recalled because it was faulty. One wonders why that same product was not thoroughly tested prior to being sold. There is only one reason: *money born of greed.*

Recently, a well-known auto maker was forced to recall thousands upon thousands of their vehicles because the gas pedal seemed to stick, causing crashes and injuries. After the recall, this same company began producing commercials in which they attempted to show how much they care for Joe Public. They spoke of how much testing they now did, and the spokesman was Joe Average who stated that he wanted to know his family was safe too. The question is why this auto manufacturer not take the time to really test the car thoroughly prior to selling them? The answer is *money*. If people have it, they do not like giving it away.

Go to one of the big discount stores some time. You might see a parking lot filled with Mercedes, BMWs, and many other high-end and expensive cars. Why? It is because people who have money like bargains as well as the next person.

Not long ago as this is being written, there was a major oil leak in the Gulf Coast because of a deep oil well. Somehow the well head broke off or began leaking. The oil company tried this, they tried that, and little worked. Eventually, after a few million (or was it billion) barrels of oil leaked into the Gulf of Mexico, they were able to cap the well. Cleanup began in earnest, and during the process information came to light that this oil company had ignored warning signals before the oil well failed. Why did they ignore the signals? *Money*.

Years ago, another auto manufacturer produced a small car that often exploded into flames during a rear-end collision. A number of the victims had to take the auto company to court before the auto company would do anything at all. Money was the root of the problem. The auto maker did not want to part with any of it, so they fought by digging in their heels until they were forced by the courts to do something. Eventually, they opted to settle rather than drag on a protracted appeals process that would have cost a good deal of money anyway. One way or another, they wanted to give away as little money as possible, so they chose the best route for them.

This mentality is tragic. It should not exist, yet it does, and will continue to exist until Jesus Christ returns to establish His physical rule over this earth.

Greed is at the heart of the Babylon system. It is greed for money, and *more* money. Most people believe that money is the root of all evil. It is not. Paul tells us, "*For the **love** of money is the root of all evil*" (1 Timothy 6:10; emphasis added).

People who love money chase it continually. They can never get enough of it, and they become willing to cut corners to get more of it to satisfy the drive in them that will not be satisfied. Some are even willing to do things that are illegal to attract more of it.

I was speaking with an attorney not long ago who was previously a State Police Officer. His job as a police officer was to investigate false insurance claims, mainly through doctor's offices.

He told me of one case in which a doctor was caught trying to submit fake medical documents to the insurance so the insurance would pay the bill. He was in collusion with someone else. He was caught, lost his medical license and went to jail. How much did he get paid to attempt to pass the fake medical documents through the insurance company? The individual who approached him paid him $700. Yes, seven *hundred* dollars. That's all. It is such a paltry sum compared to his yearly earnings, yet he was willing to risk it, and lost his medical practice and his freedom.

This is what loving money will do for you. It is what undergirds the Babylon system, because it starts and ends with self. Love of money, love of self, a desire to create your own reality; all these things are part and parcel of the system that Satan created thousands of years ago at the Tower of Babel, and still exists today.

I was thinking of one of the richest men in the Arabian world and found Al-Waleed bin Talal, who by most accounts is the Arabian

Warren Buffet. He has amassed a fortune, millions upon millions of dollars, mainly through real estate ventures. He is part owner of News Corp., which owns Fox News among others.

Because he has so much money, he can and does buy anything he wants to have, whether it is another castle/mansion or the world's biggest yacht. He is using all of his money for *himself*. While he gives some of his money to charities, or non-profits, a number of those non-profits are directly or indirectly connected to the Muslim world of Islam. So even there, he is benefitting himself.

Talal loves money, and he is rich enough to give a few million here and a few million there without even noticing that it is gone, compared to his entire fortune. This is simply giving out of his excess and it causes no pain to do it.

This is the Babylon system. It is carried along by greed for money, greed for self-pleasure, and greed for self-fulfillment, and greed causes people to do what are wrong and even illegal things to continue to *have* money. The more money a person has the more power he wields.

Babylon will come crashing down in a burning heap one day and God will cause it to happen. As Christians, we are not to be caught up in the world's system of getting as much as we can any way we can get it, especially if it is illegal. That is the world's system, but it is not God's. God will destroy that system and all who continue their association with it will suffer loss when it is destroyed.

The Millennial Kingdom, which we will get into shortly, will not be run by *greed*, or *money*, or *power*. It will be ruled *justly* by Jesus Christ, who will rule with a rod of iron.

Revelation 18:17-19
"For in one hour so great riches is come to nought. And every

shipmaster, and all the company in ships, and sailors, and as many as trade by sea, stood afar off,

"And cried when they saw the smoke of her burning, saying, What city is like unto this great city!

"And they cast dust on their heads, and cried, weeping and wailing, saying, Alas, alas that great city, wherein were made rich all that had ships in the sea by reason of her costliness! For in one hour is she made desolate."

Here we see more of the same, except this is from the captains of ships and those who work on them, carting commodities from one part of the earth to the other.

The reality here is that God is telling us that this is a worldwide failure. The entire system of commerce, buying and selling, collapses. If we consider that the debt just in the United States as of this writing is $13,376,631,687,586.03[57] and it grows by just over 4 billion dollars per DAY, it is astounding! Who can visualize that amount of money – and that is only for America. Other countries are much worse off. Eventually, something has to give, and it does. At just the right time that God foreordained, the system crashes and burns, never to rise again. That is scary, isn't it? Those who put their faith in that system are destined to crash and burn with it.

The text here continues to refer to a "great city" called Babylon. It may well be that the Bible is referring to one major hub at some point in the future through which all financial transactions travel. In effect then, when that city or hub collapses under its own weight of debt, everything connected to it collapses as well. Considering the fact that the world is becoming smaller and smaller due to technology, this is not at all hard to imagine.

---

[57] http://www.brillig.com/debt_clock/

Revelation 18:20-24

"Rejoice over her, thou heaven, and ye holy apostles and prophets; for God hath avenged you on her.

"And a mighty angel took up a stone like a great millstone, and cast it into the sea, saying, Thus with violence shall that great city Babylon be thrown down, and shall be found no more at all.

"And the voice of harpers, and musicians, and of pipers, and trumpeters, shall be heard no more at all in thee; and no crafts-man, of whatsoever craft he be, shall be found any more in thee; and the sound of a millstone shall be heard no more at all in thee;

"And the light of a candle shall shine no more at all in thee; and the voice of the bridegroom and of the bride shall be heard no more at all in thee: for thy merchants were the great men of the earth; for by thy sorceries were all nations deceived.

"And in her was found the blood of prophets, and of saints, and of all that were slain upon the earth."

On earth, the merchants, leaders, and kings are busy wailing over their loss. They are inconsolable. Yet here we read the words "Rejoice over her!" All in heaven should rejoice because the greed that created Babylon (both the city and the system) has caused its death.

Because God has brought this city and system down to the ground, burning in ashes, we are told that God has brought His hammer of vengeance down once and for all. God is extremely patient, and in fact so patient that many come to think He's never going to do anything about their errant ways, but that is not true. God simply does things in His time and in His way.

Imagine a criminal walking into your home one day when you're not there and helping himself to your TV (good riddance you might say!).

He then lays low thinking you are going to call the police and report the incident.

After a number of days, he has heard nothing of any report that he thought you might have filed. Not long after that, he ventures passed your home just to see what is up and everything seems fine. You are out watering your lawn, the dog is playing with the kids – everything is just swell.

He waits a few more days, and then this time during broad daylight breaks into your home while you are at work. He helps himself to your microwave and some jewelry. After a few days, he hears nothing and sees you carrying on with life as if nothing has been stolen.

After this he becomes even more brazen, breaking into your home in the middle of the night. He carries off your stereo, some computer parts, and before he leaves, he helps himself to some food from your fridge. In other words, he has become careless, brazen, because he thinks either you don't care if he steals your belongings, or you are too dimwitted to notice anything is missing.

One day, though, he breaks into your home and you are waiting with a loaded gun and a phone. You force him to sit down on the floor, you call 911, and they come and cart the thief away. What he thought was stupidity on your part turned out to be patience, hoping either he would go away and not steal from you again, or you would simply bide your time until you could catch him in the act.

Apart from the fact that the previous illustration is not real (and a stretch), it serves to point out the fact that God is as patient as He needs to be. When He comes to the end of His patience, He does what He preordained that He would do.

This is how things will go for the Babylon system. It began with the Tower of Babel, and continued from that point. It will culminate with God destroying it.

The destruction of Babylon brings forth a joyful response from those who are in heaven. They rejoice because the Babylon system that killed the prophets and saints and led the nations astray and carried people away after the pied piper of greed is dead, defunct, never to rise again.

The last verse of chapter 18 explains in one sentence what greed forces people to do. They *kill*. People will kill because of greed. They will kill prophets and saints because they do not want to hear that they are sinning. They will kill the people of the earth who get in their way and attempt to stop them from making more and more money and controlling the world's commercial system.

Babylon is the symbol of unmitigated greed. This is the greed that decrees that people are worth nothing and greed is worth everything. Greed destroys the very soul, causing the person to act contrary to how human beings were originally made. Instead of glorifying God, greed causes people to strike out at God by killing those made in His image (*people*).

It does not take much of an imagination to realize how much bloodshed has occurred throughout the world and since the beginning because of greed. Greed is born of jealousy. You want something someone else has and you are angry or frustrated that they have it and you do not. Jealousy can often give birth to murder.

When there is nothing to be greedy for, the entire reason to be jealous goes by the wayside. If people are not jealous, they do not want to kill to protect what they have or to get something they do not have. During the first few years after the birth of the Church, authentic believers sold what they had to help other believers who did not have much (cf. Acts 2 and 4). This was simply a foretaste of what the Millennial Kingdom and beyond will be for those who are part of that time period on earth.

Babylon as a system is dead. The city or hub which may well wind up being the center of all business and commerce in the future is *dead* with it. There is no longer any reason to steal, connive, lie, cheat, or kill. No reason at all, except possibly for *hatred*.

REVELATION 19

Chapter nineteen of Revelation takes us to the throne room of God. God Himself has just destroyed Babylon. The system that began with Babel is finally gone and there is nothing but praise to our heavenly Father because of it, as we read in the first few verses.

Revelation 19:1-2

"And after these things I heard a great voice of much people in heaven, saying, Alleluia; Salvation, and glory, and honour, and power, unto the Lord our God:

"For true and righteous are his judgments: for he hath judged the great whore, which did corrupt the earth with her fornication, and hath avenged the blood of his servants at her hand."

God is praised for His judgment of a system that attempted to overthrow Him for thousands of years. His judgments are righteous and He is glorified through them and because of them. Those in heaven see the righteousness of His judgments and praise Him for it.

In this life, it is sometimes difficult to appreciate life from God's perspective, yet that is what we are called to do. When we arrive to heaven, our knowledge regarding God's decisions and judgments will be complete. We will fully understand why His ways, though not our ways here on earth, are the *only* ways. There will never be any more questions as to why God does what He does. It will simply be fully accepted.

Often people are too quick to condemn God for His judgments, and they usually offer the "*God is love*" as an excuse. If God is love, then how can He act in such a capricious manner? When God judges, He does *not* act in a capricious manner. Though the judgments themselves seem to come out of nowhere with unprecedented speed, God's timing is perfect, and judgments do not normally come until God has come to the end of His patience.

The reason He waits as long as He does has everything to do with the fact that He does not want anyone to perish (cf. 2 Peter 3:9). But consider the fact that though God may have waited *many* generations (or hundreds and even thousands of years) before enacting His judgments, people *live* and people *die* during that time.

So during that fateful generation when God finally sends the promised judgment, that particular generation may seem to think that God is capricious because of timing. It seemed to happen quickly and without warning. This is not the case, however, as God had spent generations warning people of what He would do. If people do not avail themselves of the information that He has provided in His Word that is not the fault of God.

Revelation 19:3-7

"And again they said, Alleluia. And her smoke rose up for ever and ever.

"And the four and twenty elders and the four beasts fell down and worshipped God that sat on the throne, saying, Amen; Alleluia.

"And a voice came out of the throne, saying, Praise our God, all ye his servants, and ye that fear him, both small and great.

"And I heard as it were the voice of a great multitude, and as the voice of many waters, and as the voice of mighty thunderings, saying, Alleluia: for the Lord God omnipotent reigneth.

"Let us be glad and rejoice, and give honour to him: for the marriage of the Lamb is come, and his wife hath made herself ready."

Now that the system and city of Babylon is destroyed, focus turns to Jesus and His Bride. An interesting phrase here is *"and his wife hath made herself ready."* This has meant a number of things to a number of people. It seems to be saying that the Bride has the responsibility of making herself ready for her Groom, Jesus.

People today say that the Church of Christ needs to be purified. They see persecution as a good thing because of its purifying effect. Many of these people are those who believe that the Church will go through the Tribulation because this, they say, is the act of God purifying the Church.

First, the Tribulation is specifically laid out for the nation of Israel and there are too many Scriptures to reference. Read the books of Joel, Ezekiel, Zechariah, Daniel, Isaiah, and others. Read the Olivet Discourse in Matthew 24, Mark 13, and Luke 21. The purpose of the Tribulation has nothing to do with the Church. However, for a moment, let's say it *does.*

All right, so if we say that the Tribulation is for the Church, then the Church will go through it. If the Church goes through it, then many will say, "That is how God is going to perfect and purify His Bride."

Does He? Where does it say in Scripture that as an authentic Christian, I NEED to be purified? Do we not learn in Romans 8 alone that *because* I am now *in* Christ, I am no longer condemned? There is *nothing* that God can or will condemn me for because *all of my sin,* past, present, and future, was dealt with at Calvary's cross. God says He will remember my sin no more (cf. Micah 7:9; Jeremiah 31:34; Isaiah 43:25, etc.).

Paul goes further and states without equivocation that I am already seated in heavenly places with Christ (cf. Ephesians 2:1-10). So, my sin is completely gone, I have Christ's righteousness that God the Father sees, and I am a new creation in Christ (cf. Romans 10:9-10; 2 Corinthians 5:17; Galatians 2:20; Ephesians 2:1; 1 Peter 1:23).

If I were to die right now, as I am writing this paragraph that you are reading, where do I go? Does not Paul say to be absent from the body is to be present with the Lord (for authentic Christians; cf. 2 Corinthians 5:8)? Well then, if I were to die right now, I would be immediately with the Lord. There is no "wait" period, or time of preparation, or purgatory that I go to where I will become purified. I am instantly transferred to His glorious presence. Would you agree? I hope so.

If that is the case, then it proves that I am already righteous. The only thing holding me back from living a sinless life now is that my sin nature remains with me, and will be with me until I depart this life. However, that is done in an instant. No amount of time dedicated to living a sinless life on earth will get me there. In fact, if all I am thinking about is living sinlessly, then chances are great that my eyes are focused on me, instead of Jesus.

Christ's Bride does *not* need to be prepared in the sense of removing our sin, because that already happened at the cross. The Bride is prepared by being changed into His glorious image and character, complete with the removal of the sin nature! That does *not* happen during persecution. What occurs during times of persecution is a realization that we need to let go of many things that we often cling to in this life. Doing so makes it easier to stay focused on Jesus.

In heaven we will have no problem focusing on Jesus, living the way He wants us to live, and glorifying Him every moment in our thoughts, words, and deeds. It will be so because we will no longer have the sin nature to contend with at all, not because we have somehow gone through hell on earth and we have learned to live sinlessly.

It is interesting that I took a break from writing to check my email and I had received an email post (to my blog at wordpress) about the "Fairy Tale" PreTrib Rapture. I have to approve any post before it goes up and this one I chose not to approve. For one thing, it was not simply a post, but a full-fledged article, consisting of just under 9,000 words. Yes, *nine thousand!* Secondly, he was way out there indicating that Obama was the False Prophet, and if you simply compare that with the touch tone phone and certain numbers, it becomes clear. Here is what he said,

> *"If you dial O-B-A-M-A on your touch phone the "O" + "M"*
> *are both 6's or 6+6 and the other 3 letters B + A + A are*
> *all 2's or 2+2+2 which equals 6 for a grand total of 6+6+6*
> *or 666. If you dial O-B-A-M-A you will dial 666!"*

How do you respond to that? Moreover, how do you take someone like that *seriously*? The implication, of course, is that *only* Obama's name comes up like that. This type of biblical illiteracy and guessing games is astounding! Why could we not just leave it as 6+6+2+2+2, which equals18? Well, if we did, it would ruin his theory. Why take the *three* 2s and turn them into *one* six? Why not take all the numbers, which are even, add them up, then divide by the sum total of Obama's birth date? It really gets ridiculous, but these are the type of people who say that I am the one who believes in fairy tales...*sheesh*.

The same writer points out a number of areas that concern Obama and finally sums up things by saying,

> *"OBAMAnable now is Commander in Chief and has com-*
> *plete control of the most powerful armed forces in the*
> *world. And so Obama meets all of the requirements to be*
> *the future False Prophet of 666 which makes it a very in-*
> *teresting speculation."*

Years ago, people did the same thing with Kissinger's name and a host of others. The reality is that we will not know who the Antichrist or the False Prophet is until they *reveal* themselves. For the Antichrist, this revealing will occur when he brokers peace with Israel. That is when the Antichrist is revealed to the world; though most will have no clue that he is the Antichrist. The False Prophet will be revealed when he comes alongside Antichrist and directs people to worship him.

You know, I believe Eschatology is very important; however, there is too much of an emphasis on Eschatology today. While it is important to know what you believe, people are routinely taking time out of the Great Commission to argue about this version of the Rapture or that version. Many people believe I am deceived because of my view of the PreTrib Rapture. Apparently, I only believe it because I do not want to be persecuted. Even if that was true (which is not), I would have to be an idiot to think that by believing it, it will become fact.

I do not care if I am here when the Tribulation starts and if the Rapture does not occur! I do not *care*. As far as I'm concerned, things are starting to take a huge downturn in our society today. It is starting to get really bad. Even IF the PreTrib Rapture is biblical fact, no one knows how bad it will get before it happens. Things could get very bad. Crime could go sky high. The economy could crash big time in a way that would make the Great Depression look like the Grand Illusion.

We simply do not know how bad things will get. Yet I hear people constantly putting PreTribbers in the same category as those good ol' Prosperity Preachers. You know, the name it-claim it people who deny that there are or should be hardships in this life. If you just claim things by faith, they become yours. Sorry, but that is New Age mysticism through and through. Most that follow that line of thought do not see it that way. The difference of course is that because they believe God is in the picture it makes it somehow different, but it doesn't. They have lowered God to t he level of a personal genie or butler. This is *not* who God is or why He is here. How *dare* anyone lower Him to anything! How dare they.

The guy who wrote me the stuff I quoted is way off base, in my opinion. He has little grip on the reality in which we live. He is looking for little green men with the label "PreTribber" on their foreheads.

He thinks he needs to spend time trying to convert them because they are not saved as they are in their beliefs.

My salvation is *not* based on my Eschatological view. It is based on the Person of Jesus Christ, who He is, and the work He accomplished on my behalf. That is the main thrust of Christianity.

Getting back to the Bride and the fact that she has made herself ready, let it be clearly understood that authentic Christians have a responsibility. This is without doubt. We obviously have a responsibility to actually *be saved*. We cannot simply be professors of the faith. We must be actually saved in the faith.

As authentic Christians, we must also understand that God expects certain things of us. He expects us to turn from sin, to seek His face, to accomplish His will. The wonderful thing about this is that though these are His expectations, He helps *fulfill* them in His children! He does not leave us to go it alone. We are told that Jesus is the Author *and* Perfecter of our faith, the beginning and the end. It starts with Jesus and it ends with Jesus. Without Him, there is not only no salvation, but also no growth, no spiritual development, no maturity in Christ.

It is the Bride's responsibility to *become saved*, to believe that Jesus Christ came in order to die, so that we might have eternal life. That is the Bride's first obligation. The second obligation is to give ourselves over to His purposes.

Keathley comments on this as well. *"Men must personally and responsibly believe in Jesus Christ as their Savior, and then, as believers and as part of the bride of Christ, **they must choose to walk by the Spirit of God according to the Word, by faith**, so they can bear fruit or reproduce good works. This is what is meant by the statement, "makes herself ready"."* (emphasis added)

The interesting and notable thing here is that what I have bolded should be done whether or not there is persecution, tribulation, or peril. In other words, to obediently choose to follow Jesus in all areas of my life *is* what it means to actively be a Christian. This is how the Christian life is lived in each authentic Christian, or *should* be. Too often it is not. People then believe that God sends persecution to those believers to wake them up, to get their attention, to move them out of their wrong lifestyles and attitudes and toward Him. He certainly may do that, but that is not necessarily the reason for persecution.

It seems clear enough that persecution comes because it is part of life (cf. John 16:33). Isn't this what Jesus means when He states that we *will* have persecutions in this world, but He has overcome it? This should give us great peace.

The fact that this world is corrupt and fallen makes the reality of persecution an expected commodity. Christians living in various parts of the world right now daily face harassment and even death simply because they are Christians. This is not necessarily God sending persecution (though He certainly allows it). It is the way the world is because the ruler of this world is Satan.

Jesus told us that the world hated Him and it will hate us (cf. John 15:18). That should be a given. We don't even have to do anything. The fact that God lives within us is readily seen by those demons in the spiritual world. They hate Jesus, so they hate us. They may inflict pain and suffering (as God permits) solely because of that fact alone. Was there any particular reason that God allowed Job to be so tormented? Certainly, as humble as Job was, there was always more room to become even more humble. Job was not an example of someone that need straightening out by God, so it was time to send some good ol' fashioned persecution his way! God did what He did to glorify Himself before Satan. This is not to say that Job was a pawn, because he was not. The difficulty though is that we are *in this Satanically ordered world*, and because we are not *of this world*, we will be on the receiving end of Satan's hatred. It is that simple.

To begin with, the Bride makes herself ready by *becoming saved*. Following that, God works within and guides every believer to bring them where He wants them to be. Authentic Christians cannot resist God's will, no more than the unsaved can resist His will.

The moment I die, I will have become perfectly ready for the marriage to Jesus Christ, because the last vestiges of *self* and *sin nature* will have been removed.

Revelation 19:8-9

"And to her was granted that she should be arrayed in fine linen, clean and white: for the fine linen is the righteousness of saints.

"And he saith unto me, Write, Blessed are they which are called unto the marriage supper of the Lamb. And he saith unto me, These are the true sayings of God."

Here we see a picture of the Bride dressed in fine linen. It was *granted* that she should be dressed in fine linen. The fine linen is the righteousness of the saints. This righteousness is not her own. It is Christ's righteousness. THAT is why the Bride is granted to be dressed in fine linens, because of the righteousness that is given to each authentic Christian that makes up the entire Bride of Christ at the moment of conversion.

The authentic Christian's faith allows him or her to *receive* salvation. God rewards that faith with eternal life *and* the righteousness that stems from Jesus' character. We *believe*, God *gives*, we *receive*. Those who are called to the marriage supper of the Lamb are truly blessed.

Revelation 19:10-16

"And I fell at his feet to worship him. And he said unto me, See thou do it not: I am thy fellowservant, and of thy brethren that have the testimony of Jesus: worship God: for the testimony of Jesus is the spirit of prophecy.

"And I saw heaven opened, and behold a white horse; and he that sat upon him was called Faithful and True, and in righteousness he doth judge and make war.

"His eyes were as a flame of fire, and on his head were many crowns; and he had a name written, that no man knew, but he himself.

"And he was clothed with a vesture dipped in blood: and his name is called The Word of God.

"And the armies which were in heaven followed him upon white horses, clothed in fine linen, white and clean.

"And out of his mouth goeth a sharp sword, that with it he should smite the nations: and he shall rule them with a rod of iron: and he treadeth the winepress of the fierceness and wrath of Almighty God.

"And he hath on his vesture and on his thigh a name written, KING OF KINGS, AND LORD OF LORDS."

John is so overwhelmed by this spectacle – and who would *not* be – that he literally falls at the feet of the angel near him to worship him. Unfortunately, he winds up attempting to worship an angel, instead of God Almighty. The angel immediately and firmly, yet gently, corrects John, telling him that he also is a servant of God and is not to be worshiped.

In other words, the angel tells John that he and John are on the same side, worshiping, serving, and adoring Almighty God of the universe. There is no more reason to worship the angel than it would be for the angel to worship John.

The angel points out that the testimony of Jesus is the spirit of prophecy. Currently, much is made of prophecy. It is important, obviously, but many of us tend to overemphasize it or underemphasize it. Jesus is the spirit of prophecy. His very being incorporates the essence of prophetic discourse. Jesus' entire life was a fulfillment of a multitude of prophecies and He has yet to fulfill numerous others, which He will do when He returns.

At this point, John sees the heavens *open* up. He sees a white horse and he sees One who sits on that horse named Faithful and True. In Jesus, there is no shadow of turning, nor is there even a hint of untruth. Everything that Jesus is, everything He says, everything He thinks, and everything He accomplishes all stems from absolute truth. He can do nothing less because in Him is truth and there is no darkness.

John sees the heavens open as Jesus, followed by His armies, prepares to descend to this planet, destroying those who stand in His way. If we stop to consider the fact that what John is seeing is nothing less than that of Jesus coming to the earth in all His glory, we should be awed.

In Matthew 16:27-28 we read the words, *"For the Son of man shall come in the glory of his Father with his angels; and then he shall reward every man according to his works. Verily I say unto you, **There be some standing here, which shall not taste of death, till they see the Son of man coming in his kingdom**."* (emphasis added)

Take a good look at the above two verses. Jesus is speaking to His apostles about the time when He will return to judge the nations and rule over the earth. He has just finished telling them that He must suffer and die and will be raised on the third day. Peter actually takes Him aside and tells Him that this will not happen! Jesus wastes no time in rebuking Peter, actually referring to him as Satan (cf. v. 23). This undoubtedly shocked Peter as it would all of us.

He then uses that as a jumping off point to explain the *cost* of following Him. It means that people will have to deny themselves and take up their cross. The cross we take up daily is that of setting our own will aside, replacing it with the will of Jesus. That is the cost, constantly having to decide to follow Jesus daily, moment by moment. This is not as easy as it may appear to some, because our own self-will often has a very strong hold on us. That coupled with our fallen sin nature makes it doubly difficult.

He finishes this section up with the statement that *not all standing there will see death until they see the Son of Man in His Kingdom*. Many attribute this to the event of the Transfiguration that takes place only six days later (cf. Matthew 17:1-3). Certainly, there is a point in which we see Jesus in His glory during this event. It serves to point ahead to the time when Jesus *will* return to earth to claim what is rightfully His.

However, the verse just before verse 28 in Matthew 16 specifically states, *"for the Son of man shall come in the glory of his Father with his angels; and then he shall reward every man according to his works"* (Matthew 16:27). Please note that this sentence really goes with the sentence after this and signifies that some standing there will not see death *until* they see Jesus coming in His power to the earth in order to set up His Kingdom.

I believe that this occurred and was fulfilled when John – in this vision of Revelation 19 – saw Jesus returning to earth in power, in glory, and with His army to take back what is rightfully His. Look at the description of the text. He will set up His Kingdom, He will judge the nations, and He will rule with a rod of righteous firmness. This is when the prophecy of Jesus was actually and fully fulfilled in John's life, because he was also one of the ones who saw the Transfiguration, and he was one of the ones who heard Jesus state that some "here" (there, hearing Him speak) would *not* die until he first saw Jesus returning to judge and rule the earth.

To me, this is a no-brainer, but Covenant, Reformed, and Preterist theologians believe something else. They believe that this is referencing A.D. 70, when Jesus allegedly returned "spiritually" during the destruction of the city of Jerusalem and the Temple. There is no need to allegorize Scripture like this when the answer to Jesus' prophetic utterance is found in Revelation 19!

All of Jesus' decisions emanate from His righteousness. It is from His righteousness that He judges. It is from this same righteousness that He makes war against those who are out to destroy Him. He does so *justly* because He knows the full truth of every situation.

In commenting on Psalm 9, Warren Wiersbe states, "*when God is the avenger, He has all the evidence He needs to find and punish rebellious sinners.*"[58] People are never in a position to judge perfectly because we cannot see the intentions of the heart. God of course is not limited as we are limited, therefore His judgments are fully righteous.

John describes Jesus:

1. *His eyes are like flames of fire*
2. *His head has many crowns*
3. *His Name is indiscernible by human beings*
4. *His clothing has been dipped in His own shed blood*
5. *His Name is called the Word of God*
6. *The armies of heaven – the saints – follow him clothed in spotless robes*

---

[58] Warren W. Wiersbe *Be Worshipful* (David C. Cook, 2004), 50

7. *A sharp sword comes out of His mouth – His Word cuts to the quick*

    a. *A word from Jesus destroys nations*

8. *He rules with necessary harshness because of the sin within man*

9. *Those that come under His judgments are trampled by His wrath*

10. *The Name King of Kings and Lord of Lords is written on His thigh*

We gather from looking at the above list that it is clearly impossible not to notice Jesus. Beyond this, it is equally clear that He is above all and Lord of all. There is no one who will stand in His presence, no one who will not do His bidding. Jesus is God and it is through His deity that He carries out righteous judgment on those who have stood opposed to His will.

When Jesus returns, a word from Him will destroy the Antichrist and his armies (cf. 2 Thessalonians 2:8). Out of His mouth comes truth like a sword, cutting down all those who stand against Him. They are nothing to the strength of His truth. They cannot stand and will be destroyed.

Revelation 19:17-21

"And I saw an angel standing in the sun; and he cried with a loud voice, saying to all the fowls that fly in the midst of heaven, Come and gather yourselves together unto the supper of the great God;

"That ye may eat the flesh of kings, and the flesh of captains, and the flesh of mighty men, and the flesh of horses, and of them that sit on them, and the flesh of all men, both free and bond, both small and great.

"And I saw the beast, and the kings of the earth, and their armies, gathered together to make war against him that sat on the horse, and against his army.

"And the beast was taken, and with him the false prophet that wrought miracles before him, with which he deceived them that had received the mark of the beast, and them that worshipped his image. These both were cast alive into a lake of fire burning with brimstone.

"And the remnant were slain with the sword of him that sat upon the horse, which sword proceeded out of his mouth: and all the fowls were filled with their flesh."

This section is stark because it offers us a preview of what will happen on the earth once Jesus arrives to take vengeance on all of those who have resolutely rejected Him. An angel stands and cries with a loud voice to all the carrion that flies in the heavens. He tells them to come and prepare to eat their fill. Death and destruction is coming.

This is called the *supper of the great God*. Unlike the marriage supper, this supper is the supper of victory over God's enemies. There will be tremendous carnage and the carrion is told that there will be plenty to eat. Those birds will dine on the flesh of kings, captains, and mighty men (warriors). They will have their choice of horses and all types of people from all walks of life.

There will be more flesh destroyed and available to eat than at any other time in history. Carrion will be able to eat until they can eat no more. Of course, this serves a two-fold purpose:

- *To provide food for the carrion, and*
- *For the carrion to dispose of the corpses*

What is interesting here especially is that the first to go are the Beast (Antichrist) and the False Prophet. They, as leaders of this coalition of anti-God forces, are culpable as two who have deceived the nations. They bear the brunt of responsibility because of their deceit, their lying, their vain babblings and boasts, and their successful attempts to steal people's allegiance away from the one true God so that the Antichrist would be worshiped.

It is interesting to note that both the Antichrist and the False Prophet are thrown into the Lake of Fire *alive*. There is no annihilation after this life. We do not just disappear into nothingness. Our spirits live on for all eternity. These two individuals were the first beings to inhabit the Lake of Fire, but there is room for plenty more.

Jesus then destroys the "remnant" with the sword. This sword is the Word from His mouth. In a word, His enemies are vanquished, defeated, and forever foiled. The word "remnant" here is specifically referring to those who have followed the Antichrist. If context means anything, then it means that those who follow the Antichrist are considered to be *his* remnant, doing his work, standing in opposition to the Living God.

It is amazing to me how often people will do word studies, yet they often ignore context. I know of no language where all words have only *one* meaning. Think only of English. There are a multitude of words that have many meanings. Most also have many synonyms as well. How then is the meaning of a particular word as it is used in a sentence determined? Certainly, word studies are very valuable, just like looking up the definition of a word. However, that is only part of the way we solve a puzzle. While we can learn the various meanings of a word, the context finally determines *the specific* meaning that the word is using.

In this context, the word "remnant" is associated with Antichrist, therefore we know that it cannot be referencing God's *Holy* Remnant. Therefore, this particular remnant is the unbelieving remnant that follows Antichrist to their own eternal death. That should be obvious, but it seems that to many, it is not. I have heard and read too many arguments from people who simply look up a word and believe that unlocks the meaning of a passage of Scripture. Certainly, it helps, but no one should stop at simply determining the meaning. The next step must be considered, and that is *context*.

In short, though Satan has mustered everything he has, even incarnating himself in the Antichrist and gathering his armies with all supernatural power, he is no match for Jesus Christ, the living God. He is no match at all! He is finite, created by the Infinite!

Amen! Praise God for His greatness, His infinite nature, His love, His justice, and His holiness. Praise Him for His unearned (and undeserved) love for us. Praise Him that He became a Man, while remaining God, in order to pay the penalty for our sin that we deserved to pay.

Praise God that He loves us as much as He does and that once we become His through the spiritual transaction we call salvation, He no longer remembers our sin. Beyond this, His righteousness becomes our righteousness.

Praise God! All praise goes to Him!

— 20 —

REVELATION 20

The twentieth chapter of the book of Revelation starts out with some wonderful news. Satan is placed into the bottomless pit for a period of one thousand years! This is good news for a number of reasons. Obviously, if Satan is bound and imprisoned, he cannot directly do harm to anyone, nor can he directly tempt anyone to sin. This does not mean that sin no longer exists. It means that this extremely intelligent and deceptive individual will not tempt people directly.

For one thousand years, people will know what it means to live without the devil's presence. Unfortunately, people will still have to deal with the world and the flesh.

The sin nature remains with Christians until they pass from this life to the next. When that happens, the sin nature is removed from every Christian's life. Once this takes place, the possibility of sinning is eradicated.

With the present sin nature, Satan uses that to his advantage. He knows our weak spots and he constantly attempts to push our buttons. He is too often successful, and with his success comes our failure.

During his imprisonment in the bottomless pit for one thousand years, he is not able to sway people or events. Yet people will sin because there will be many who did not die during the Tribulation and are ushered into the Millennial Kingdom of Jesus Christ. They remain human, complete with sin nature.

Revelation 20:1-3
"And I saw an angel come down from heaven, having the key of the bottomless pit and a great chain in his hand.

" And he laid hold on the dragon, that old serpent, which is the Devil, and Satan, and bound him a thousand years,

"And cast him into the bottomless pit, and shut him up, and set a seal upon him, that he should deceive the nations no more, till the thousand years should be fulfilled: and after that he must be loosed a little season."

Note the last phrase of the last sentence in paragraph three: *"and after that, he must be loosed a little season."* Why must he be loosed? God wants the overthrow of sin to be complete. In order to accomplish this, He allows sin to go to the end of itself.

There will be those who are born during the Millennial Kingdom. Those people who did not die, but lived through the Tribulation, will go into the thousand-year reign and marry (or will enter with their spouse). Many will have children and those children will grow up to marry and have children.

Since in each case the children are born to human parents, the sin nature is passed along to each newly born person. Because of this, each individual will need to come to terms with who Jesus Christ is for themselves. They will be born into a completely different world from the one we now live in.

They will be born into a world that is the closest thing to paradise here on earth. Yet they will also be born sinful and need salvation. Because they will need salvation, each will need to come to faith in Jesus Christ. Rejecting the salvation that is only found in Christ will have the same results that exist now – eternal damnation.

Because people will have the sin nature, the propensity to sin will always be present. People will have to make choices and will either make the right choices and not sin, or they will make the wrong choice, giving into temptation to sin.

Satan will be released and be allowed one final time to pull people away from Jesus Christ. He will, unfortunately, be somewhat successful. First, let's look at the other immediate result of Satan's imprisonment.

Revelation 20:4

"And I saw thrones, and they sat upon them, and judgment was given unto them: and I saw the souls of them that were beheaded for the witness of Jesus, and for the word of God, and which had not worshipped the beast, neither his image, neither had received his mark upon their foreheads, or in their hands; and they lived and reigned with Christ a thousand years."

What also takes place immediately prior to the Millennial Kingdom is a judgment. People here are judged according to their lives. Notice that many were *beheaded*, which, by the way, is one of the favored forms of execution in the Islamic world. These individuals were gladly willing to give up their lives because of Jesus Christ ("for the witness of Jesus"). They held nothing back, not even their lives.

These people are not being judged for their *works*. Their judgment is based on their life itself. Only authentic believers would be willing to submit to death for Jesus Christ. Professing Christians would have none of that. It is *because* these individuals were/are authentic Christians that they gave the ultimate sacrifice of their life. Because of this, they in turn *will reign* with Jesus for the duration of the Millennial Kingdom.

Once we learn the fate of those who gave up their lives for Jesus, the Bible immediately turns its attention to those who were not authentic Christians.

Revelation 20:5-6
"But the rest of the dead lived not again until the thousand years were finished. This is the first resurrection.

"Blessed and holy is he that hath part in the first resurrection: on such the second death hath no power, but they shall be priests of God and of Christ, and shall reign with him a thousand years."

God's Word tells us here that those who are not part of the martyrdom group spoken of in verse four are not raised until *after* the completion of the Millennial Kingdom. It is tempting to conclude that these individuals must have died without proper salvation, but that cannot be because of the next verse.

Admittedly, this is a difficult few verses, but it is not impossible to comprehend them. The sentence *"This is the first resurrection"* is actually referencing the previous martyrs, not the "rest of the dead" that were not raised until after the thousand-year reign was completed. That sentence – the rest of the dead lived not... – is a bit of a parenthesis. If you remove that parenthetical thought the text flows clearly, pointing to the first resurrection as referencing those who had died through martyrdom. The individuals on the thrones are more than likely the apostles (since the apostles are part of the foundation of the Church after Jesus) and the Church itself (cf. 1 Corinthians 6:2 3; 2 Timothy 2:12; Revelation 2:26 27; 3:21; see also Luke 22:29-30).

Immediately following *"This is the first resurrection"* we read the words *"Blessed and holy is he that hath part in the first resurrection: on such the second death hath no power, but they shall be priests of God and of Christ, and shall reign with him a thousand years."* It seems obvious then that the sentence referring to those dead who will not be raised until the end of the Millennium is without doubt parenthetical.

Those who are raised in the first resurrection are extremely blessed, for they will reign with Jesus for the duration of the Millennial Kingdom. This without doubt applies to the Church itself because of Jesus' promises to the Church (again, cf. Luke 22:29-30) that we will reign with Him.

Keathley points out that the resurrections of the saints do not all occur at once. *"But it is also important to note that in the first resurrection there is sequence and several phases, i.e., all the saints are not resurrected at the same time. This is evident from 1 Corinthians 15:20-24 and by the doctrine of the pre-tribulation rapture, a doctrine founded on an abundance of scriptural evidences and facts.*

First Corinthians 15:20-23 clearly teaches us that there is a time lapse or sequence, and a definite order to the resurrection program. Paul says "but each in his own order." The word "order" is the Greek tagma which means "a company, a troop, a battalion, or rank." This was a mil-

itary term used of ranks or troops of soldiers marching in sequence, with one order or troop following another. This word suggests sequence in the resurrection program of God. "His own" is the Greek idios which means "private, personal," and shows we all have a personal place or order in the resurrection according to the group to which we belong." [59]

Though we will not take the time to thoroughly research this aspect of future events here, the reader is encouraged to study others who have written extensively about this aspect of the future resurrection. Earl Radmacher, Charles C. Ryrie, John Walvoord, J. Hampton Keathley III and numerous others have all taken the time to more than adequately fill in any perceived difficulties with this section of Scripture. I will end this particular discussion with an extensive quote by Keathley that offers significant possibilities with respect to the future resurrection and return of our Lord.

"But there is another possibility with regard to the use of these Greek words used of the return of the Lord, or at least something to give some thought to. According to ancient usage, and especially as used of important persons like kings, parousia described a coming and a presence, or a coming which included the presence of the king after his arrival. The teaching of the Scripture is that our Lord comes for His bride (the church), and takes her up into the heavens (1 Thess. 4:13 17); a throne is set in the heavens, hidden for the most part from the world (but cf. Rev. 4:2; Dan. 7:9 with Rev. 6:14 16 where we are told that the sky will split apart and the world will have a view of this hea-venly throne). It is from this throne that the Lord pours out the Tribulation judgments upon the earth and also probably rewards His bride. But the point is this: could this not constitute Christ's presence? He has come and is in the more immediate heavens pouring out judgment (Rev. 6:16). For the most part, however, this is hidden from the world. Then at the end of the Tribulation (Rev. 19), He manifests His presence by

---

[59] J. Hampton Keathley III *Studies in Revelation* (Biblical Studies Press, 1997), 264

coming to earth. Second Thessa-lonians 2:8 may be translated "... and then that lawless one will be revealed whom the Lord will slay with the breath of His mouth and bring to an end by the manifestation (epiphaneia) of His presence (parousia)."

"So in this portion of the resurrection program (the first resurrection) there is sequence; first the resurrection of the church before the Tribulation, and then after the Tribulation the resurrection of Old Testament and Tribulation saints (Rev. 20:4 6; Dan. 12:1 2)."[60]

When we read the words "but the rest of the dead..." we see way into the future when the dead – those who died without Christ – will be raised to judgment. Their judgment is the Great White Throne Judgment, where they will be made fully aware of the reasons they are not going to be with Christ for all eternity, and will be cast from His presence.

This section discusses the future 1,000-year reign of Jesus Christ physically on earth. We need to understand this to be a *literal* situation that John sees and describes for us. There is great disagreement among theologians today, some who believe that the references to any actual physical reign of Jesus with a limited time span is merely figurative.

Some individuals believe that Jesus returned spiritually and in judgment at the destruction of Jerusalem and the Temple in A.D. 70. Since that time, they believe He has been reigning for the 1,000 years since. However, in order to arrive at that conclusion, His physical return must be allegorized so that it becomes a spiritual return. This flies in the face of the information provided by the two "men" (angels) in Acts 1 to the disciples who stood watching as Jesus was taken up to heaven. The angels informed the men that this same Jesus would return the very same way.

---

[60] J. Hampton Keathley III *Studies in Revelation* (Biblical Studies Press, 1997), 265

Jesus Himself stated in the Olivet Discourse (Matthew 24, Mark 13, and Luke 21) that He would return physically so that every eye would see Him. It is only when we ignore the literal ramifications of what Jesus as well as the angels said that we can look at this situation figuratively. If we choose to see the event figuratively, then in essence, the Bible can be made to say anything at all.

It is highly doubtful that when Jesus stated that during His return every eye would see Him, He actually meant that this would be something seen within the spiritual realm. Equally problematic is the assurance by the angels in Acts 1 indicating Jesus would return the same way He left, if it is meant to be taken in spiritual terms. There is nothing within either statement – by Jesus Himself or the angels – that allows us to take the statements allegorically.

Anyone who has studied Scripture for any length of time understands the reality of *legalities*. God is a God of order, and One who observes all the rules He has placed in effect. The reason God cannot simply *forgive* people, for instance, is because God's justice and holiness would not be satisfied. It is for this reason that God had to satisfy the requirements of the law.

Humanity broke God's law. He could no more simply set aside or choose to ignore that than He could Himself lie or sin. It is impossible. God had only two choices. He could do nothing for man and allow all of humanity to reap the consequences of sin, or God could Himself become the sacrifice for humanity, thereby satisfying the just and holy requirements of the law. The one thing God could not do was to simply act as if man had never sinned at all. We understand that God chose to become human Himself by being born of a woman and living a perfect, sinless life, one that pleased the Father at every step of the way.

Jesus finalized His life by fully satisfying the just requirements of the law. He suffered, bled, and died for something He Himself was not guilty of doing. He did this because of His great love for humanity. He literally became sin, though He Himself never sinned. As He hung upon the cross, the weight of the world's sin caused the Father to pour out His wrath and then turn away from His Son. This occurred when the sky above Jesus' cross turned black (cf. Matthew 27:45).

Through the unjust death of Jesus, the penalty of sin was paid. All that remained was for each individual person to acknowledge the death of Christ as payment for sin. Those who do that are saved with eternal salvation. Those who reject Jesus have nothing to rely on but themselves, and that does not hold up under God's scrutiny.

At every step of the way, we see that Jesus fulfilled the Law and the prophets. He did this because God is a God of law. The requirements for salvation were fully met and salvation could then be offered to all who would come to Him for eternal life.

At the beginning of the book of Revelation, we read that Jesus (the Lamb) was found worthy to open the seven-sealed scroll. Many theologians (this author included) believe that this represents God's wrath that is to be poured out during the Tribulation. It also represents the title deed to earth, which had been deceptively stolen from Adam and Eve in the Garden of Eden. There, Satan took what did not belong to him, and it was only when Christ died on the cross did God regain the deed to earth.

However, something else needs to occur in order to *show* ownership of this planet. In order for all things to be fulfilled, Jesus must actually sit in His "father" David's throne in Jerusalem and reign judicially from there over the entire earth.

It is only after Jesus physically reigns on the earth that He can then turn the title deed over to the Father. Everything will be done legally, and every jot and tittle will be fulfilled. This is the way God is – a God of holiness and justice. He can do nothing less.

Revelation 20:7-10

"And when the thousand years are expired, Satan shall be loosed out of his prison,

"And shall go out to deceive the nations which are in the four quarters of the earth, Gog, and Magog, to gather them together to battle: the number of whom is as the sand of the sea.

"And they went up on the breadth of the earth, and compassed the camp of the saints about, and the beloved city: and fire came down from God out of heaven, and devoured them.

"And the devil that deceived them was cast into the lake of fire and brimstone, where the beast and the false prophet are, and shall be tormented day and night for ever and ever."

Here are some of the saddest words in the Bible. The world having been free of Satan's direct tyranny will have to endure a final push from this master deceiver. It is clear that if anything, he has had 1,000 years to refine his ability to deceive, and does exactly that.

The text states that he goes out to deceive the nations from "the four quarters of the earth." This of course means that Satan goes out over the entire earth to gather people to his cause. His cause, of course, is one final attempt to overthrow God.

Satan manages to gather quite a throng together for battle. In fact, the text states that the number of individuals involved in this staging for the upcoming last battle is like the sand of the sea. Who can number the sand of the sea but God? To John's eyes (the human author of Revelation), the number was so large that the group could not be numbered.

This particular battle lasts but seconds, as God Himself does away with Satan and those who have chosen to follow him. Even though John uses the term "Gog and Magog," it is doubtful that this is the same Gog and Magog referenced in Ezekiel 38 and 39, often referred to as the Northern Invasion of Israel.

Keathley points out a number of reasons why this reference to Gog and Magog is not connected to the references in Ezekiel. He states, *"(a) The invasion in Ezekiel comes from the north, but this one comes from all directions; (b) Ezekiel's battle seems to occur about the middle of the Tribulation when the people of Israel are trusting in the treaty with the beast, but this battle occurs over a thousand years later, after Christ comes to earth; (c) In Ezekiel, Gog and Magog are the names given the ruler from the north and his land, a territory now occupied by Russia, but according to Ezekiel these will be decisively wiped out in the Tribulation."*[61]

Of course, the natural question is, why then does John use this reference if he is not referring to the same Gog and Magog? Keathley again: *"these names stand symbolically for a rebellious and war like people and for the nations in rebellion against God and His people (Psalm 2) who will be crushed."*[62]

This attempted assault on God's people and His holy city is Satan's very last stand. As all other attempts failed, so will this one, proving once and for all to Satan and all who follow him that his power is nothing compared to that of Almighty God. In fact, the quickness of defeat is designed to show Satan that any power he possesses came directly from God, and compared to God, Satan has little to none.

Keathley and other theologians rightly point out that this entire scenario of Satan attempting to overthrow Jesus and His saints in an environment that is perfect speaks against the idea that if only the ecological environment of the earth were perfect, and people lived in an environment of love, then war would be no more. The fact that Satan – after being imprisoned for 1,000 years – is released from his bond-

---

[61] J. Hampton Keathley III *Studies in Revelation* (Biblical Studies Press, 1997), 267
[62] Ibid, 276

age and gains a huge following of people who heretofore knew nothing of the world prior to the return of Jesus Christ, simply proves that nothing can help fallen man except the new creation that only comes from salvation gained by the work of Jesus Christ.

People living in a nearly perfect situation with Jesus as Ruler, who rules with justice, holiness, and perfection, are still capable of being deceived and lining up against the very One who came to save. The environment is nothing. While we should be good stewards of it, it will not save us.

Without God, love is nothing. In fact, apart from God, people cannot love at all, much less perfectly. The Millennial Reign of Jesus and the resultant large numbers of people who follow Satan in his final attempt to overthrow God is testament to the fact that fallen humanity does not know what right is, nor how to do what is right. Scripture, of course, says it best: *"There is a way which seems right to a man, but the end thereof is death"* (Proverbs 14:12; 16:25). In spite of the fact that the multitudes who choose to line up behind Satan firmly believe that they are doing the right thing, that way ends in their eternal death. They have not chosen correctly.

Revelation 20:11-15

"And I saw a great white throne, and him that sat on it, from whose face the earth and the heaven fled away; and there was found no place for them.

"And I saw the dead, small and great, stand before God; and the books were opened: and another book was opened, which is the book of life: and the dead were judged out of those things which were written in the books, according to their works.

"And the sea gave up the dead which were in it; and death and hell delivered up the dead which were in them: and they were judged every man according to their works.

End of the Ages

"And death and hell were cast into the lake of fire. This is the second death.

"And whosoever was not found written in the book of life was cast into the lake of fire."

These are also some of the saddest and most tragic words in the entire Bible. This Great White Throne Judgment is where all those who have spent their lives in one form or another rejecting Jesus Christ are being told why they will be cast into the eternal lake of fire.

Satan has twisted things so badly that many people in this life become angry at the mere mention of Jesus Christ. Have you ever been witnessing to someone and noticed that he or she reacts in anger? For whatever reason they believe they are fully justified to be angry. Either they see you as trying to force something on them they want no part of, or they see you as arrogant, or something else entirely.

They may not even understand why talking about Jesus makes them upset. Often, they wrongly believe that they will have to give up everything to become a Christian. Some think that they will have to become missionaries, or give up some of their hobbies or their friends. They feel defeated before they even truly understand what it means to be a Christian.

Yes, many things will change in a person's life after they receive Jesus as Savior and Lord. However, the Holy Spirit is the One who brings these changes about by recreating within us the character of Jesus Christ. To the unsaved person, it may seem that the demands of being a Christian are too much to bear.

All of the people who die without ever having received the only salvation available will be cast into the lake of fire. They will bear the same fate as Satan and his angels, who also rejected God and His rule over them.

340

Notice a couple of things in this section of Revelation. First, the books are opened up and each individual is judged by his or her own works. Their works are compared with only one other Person, and that is Jesus Christ.

In this life, we often fall prey to believing that we are better than others are because we compare ourselves with them. I have never murdered anyone, we say, therefore, I am not as bad as the man who actually did murder someone.

The problem of course is that when we stand before God, He is not going to compare our life with someone else's life with whom we might think we are better. He is going to compare our life with the life of Jesus Christ, who lived a perfectly sinless life. Having never sinned, He was eligible to become the propitiation for our sin. There is no one else that ever qualified.

Those who die without salvation are essentially saying that their life is good enough as it is to make it. They do not need God, nor His salvation. So when they are judged, it is their own life that will condemn them.

When the Christian stands before God, his or her own works do not judge him or her. That Christian is judged by only one thing: whether they trusted Christ for salvation or not. If they actually did trust Christ, then aside from being sealed with the Holy Spirit, God also washes away our sin, replacing our filthiness with the perfect righteousness of Jesus Christ.

Every authentic Christian is literally covered by the blood of Jesus Christ, which washes us clean from all unrighteousness. When I stand before Him, my works will not condemn me. Jesus' righteousness will vindicate me because of my trust in His efficacy through His death.

I look to Another to save me from eternal damnation. The individual who dies without Christ has only himself or herself to look to and that does nothing for them, since all have sinned and fallen short of the glory of God.

Notice also that no one escapes. The text says that the sea gave up its dead. Those who were residing in hell through physical death will rise up for this last judgment. Therefore, if a person drowned and their body was never recovered, it will be recovered at the Great White Throne Judgment. No one will escape. No one will hide. All will be seen and all will stand before the Judge.

This is so tragic, and if nothing else it should cause a great desire to evangelize to take root within each Christian. We need to tell the lost whether they listen or not, and we need to do that repeatedly. It is our job to tell them and it is God's job to open their eyes. Yes, He can and sometimes does do that without our help (as in the case of the thief on the cross), but He has deliberately included us in the process of evangelism. We must tell the lost that they are lost. We must tell them with our (or their) dying breath. God will hold us accountable.

— 21 —

REVELATION 21

We are closing in on the end of the book of Revelation and if the reader has not noticed, it has been a whirlwind. As the author has repeatedly stated throughout the book, this commentary was meant to touch on the book of Revelation in a way that makes it approachable for the average individual. No one book can answer all questions about this or any other aspect of the Bible, but if this particular commentary allows the reader to come away with a greater grasp of the book of Revelation, it has done its job.

In chapter twenty-one of Revelation, the reader is introduced to the coming eternal state. This, of course, is yet future for those living on this planet. However, the Lord is gracious enough to provide us with a glimpse beyond the curtain, allowing us to see what awaits us there.

When we speak of eternity future, we must realize that that is from our perspective. Prior to our *time*, there was eternity past. After time has completed its work, eternity future will commence. However, we need to be clear in understanding that God *exists* in the framework of eternity, not time. He Himself is eternal. While He can and has entered into man's timeframe, He is not governed by it. Time is something that affects us here, now. God, being completely outside the confinements of time, is not affected by time in any way, shape, or form.

Therefore, from a human's perspective, we see time as being linear, on a time line so to speak.

Revelation 21:1
"And I saw a new heaven and a new earth: for the first heaven and the first earth were passed away; and there was no more sea. "

This opening sentence of Revelation 21 is amazing because of its profound nature. Here, John sees two things: 1) a new heaven, and 2) a new earth. His description of this earth indicates that there is no more sea. The reason for the new earth is due to the fact that the first earth is gone, destroyed by the Lord.

There is no reason to believe that the sea John refers to is something other than the sea that currently covers much of this earth. There is nothing in the statement that would allow for an allegorical view of John's description.

For some reason, God has determined that there is no further need of a sea in eternity future. That gives pause to consider why God has chosen to eliminate the need of a sea in future eternity. The only real conclusion we can arrive at (since no real reason is provided in the text) is that our future glorified bodies will not require water as we do now. It could also very well point to the fact that Jesus is the Living Water and whoever drinks of Him will never thirst (cf. John 4).

Central to eternity is Jesus. All things will point to Him and stem from Him. There will not be one thing to detract from Him. Since He is the Living Water, then it is clear that we will not need to drink fluids, as we need to drink here. He will be our portion and we will be richly satisfied.

We should remember that what John is seeing here is not a picture of the Millennial Kingdom, but of the coming eternal order of the future. The Millennial Kingdom will have water because the earth is still this earth.

Prior to the beginning of the future eternal reign of Jesus, He will create new heavens and earth and that earth will not have water associated with it.

Revelation 21:2
"And I John saw the holy city, new Jerusalem, coming down from God out of heaven, prepared as a bride adorned for her husband."

John testifies to the fact that he was seeing these things himself. They were not simply being described to him. He saw them happen and this particular scene was breathtaking. It was so breathtaking that the only way he could describe it was to say that it was as a bride dressed for the wedding.

Note John declares that this New Jerusalem is utterly holy because it comes down directly from God in heaven. The city is not corrupt, and, as Keathley and any number of other commentators point out, is no longer like the Jerusalem that existed during the Tribulation, which is said to be like "Sodom and Gomorrah" (cf. Revelation 11:8). This is the very Jerusalem that was prepared by Jesus Christ for His own (cf. John 14:2). Here it lowers in its finished state from heaven to earth. It is the city made without hands. The very city that Abraham and all other saints look forward to entering. All saints from the Old Testament to the New Testament and through today will enjoy this city of Jerusalem. It will be the center of all activity throughout future eternity.

Revelation 21:3-8

"And I heard a great voice out of heaven saying, Behold, the tabernacle of God is with men, and he will dwell with them, and they shall be his people, and God himself shall be with them, and be their God.

And God shall wipe away all tears from their eyes; and there shall be no more death, neither sorrow, nor crying, neither shall there be any more pain: for the former things are passed away.

And he that sat upon the throne said, Behold, I make all things new. And he said unto me, Write: for these words are true and faithful.

And he said unto me, It is done. I am Alpha and Omega, the beginning and the end. I will give unto him that is athirst of the fountain of the water of life freely.

He that overcometh shall inherit all things; and I will be his God, and he shall be my son.

But the fearful, and unbelieving, and the abominable, and murderers, and whoremongers, and sorcerers, and idolaters, and all liars, shall have their part in the lake which burneth with fire and brimstone: which is the second death."

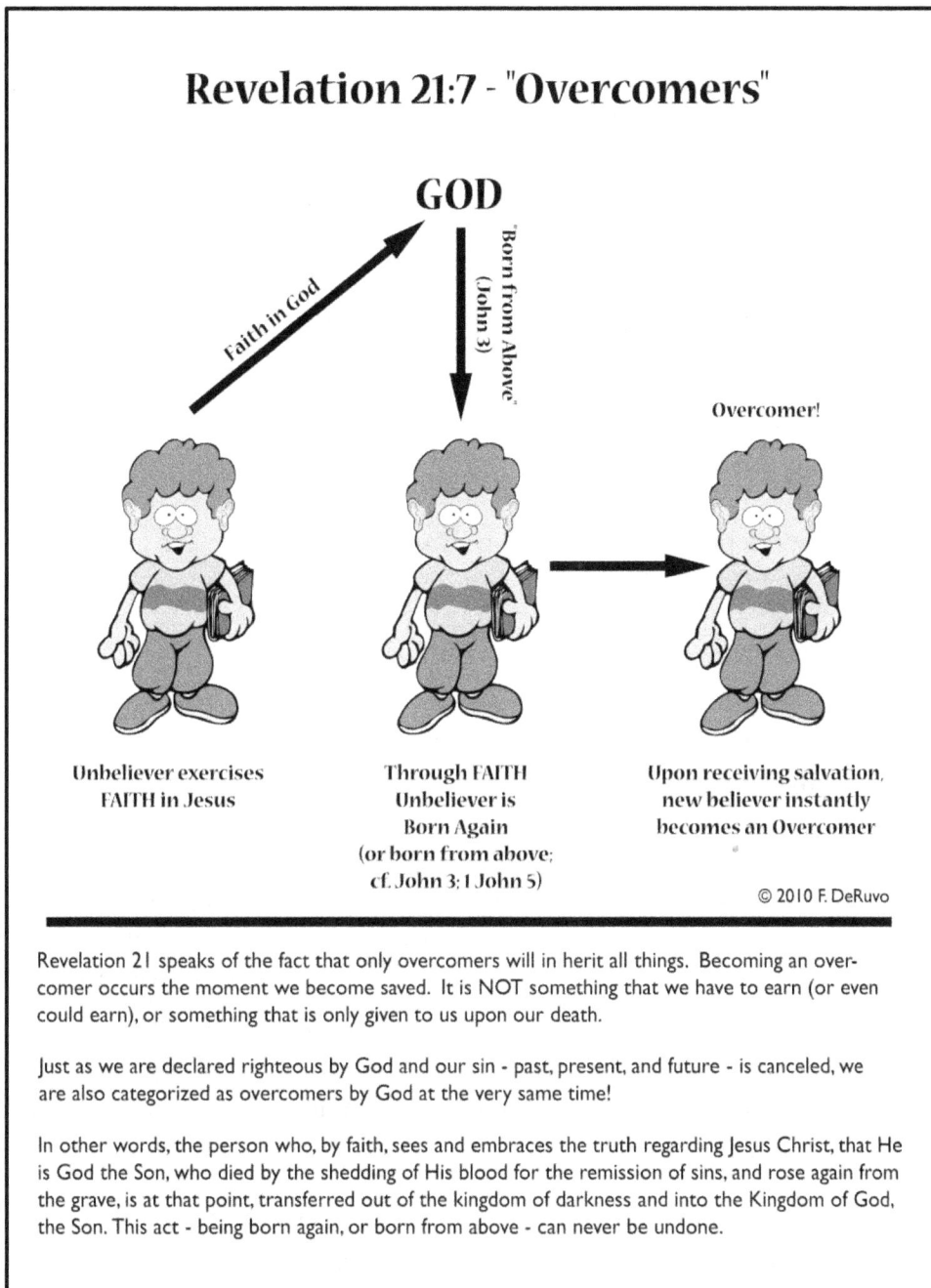

Overcomers

Revelation 21:7 - "Overcomers"

GOD

Faith in God

"Born from Above"
(John 3)

Overcomer!

Unbeliever exercises
FAITH in Jesus

Through FAITH
Unbeliever is
Born Again
(or born from above;
cf. John 3; 1 John 5)

Upon receiving salvation,
new believer instantly
becomes an Overcomer

© 2010 F. DeRuvo

Revelation 21 speaks of the fact that only overcomers will inherit all things. Becoming an overcomer occurs the moment we become saved. It is NOT something that we have to earn (or even could earn), or something that is only given to us upon our death.

Just as we are declared righteous by God and our sin - past, present, and future - is canceled, we are also categorized as overcomers by God at the very same time!

In other words, the person who, by faith, sees and embraces the truth regarding Jesus Christ, that He is God the Son, who died by the shedding of His blood for the remission of sins, and rose again from the grave, is at that point, transferred out of the kingdom of darkness and into the Kingdom of God, the Son. This act - being born again, or born from above - can never be undone.

The words just read contain great promise and hope for those who know and love Jesus. They contain terrifying words for those who do not.

This is a beautiful passage of God's love for His children. He will literally *tabernacle* with people. He will be thoroughly among us in the form of Jesus Christ, God the Son, the second Person of the Trinity. We can see how this passage builds upon itself. First, we hear the voice that announces the fact that God will dwell with people. All the people who will enjoy this new earth will be called His people.

It is precisely at this point that all distinctions between male and female, slave and free, Jew and Gentile are fully washed away in life. It is here that all become truly one in Him.

There appears here to be an interesting comment. We are given a list of things that God will do for His people:

- *wipe away all tears*
- *eliminate death*
- *eliminate pain*
- *make everything new*

The idea of trying to picture a place where there is no death or sorrow, no reason to cry, and nothing to *want* is something that is simply too difficult to picture in the here and now. This author certainly has difficulty trying to envision a place where sorrow, depression, frustration, sadness, pain of any kind, and death itself is never experienced. While we certainly understand the meaning of John's words, picturing a situation such as that which John describes is beyond the ability for most of us.

After Jesus has finished wiping away all tears, eliminating pain and death, He takes His seat on His throne and announces that all things are new. The reality here is that in one sense, this life from the beginning of God's Creation with Adam to the end of the Millennium has really been God's way of bringing glory to Himself – and why not? He is Creator of all things and far above them as well.

That is difficult for us to understand because we are corrupt. We would see that as self-aggrandizing behavior if/when we saw it in another human being. We know that no matter how good someone appears to be, there is still corruption there because none of us here have been completely cleansed of our sin nature. We *tend* to think this same thing about God, yet intellectually we know this cannot be true, if God is all that the Bible teaches us.

Therefore, for God to be above all things, Creator of all things, and perfect in all things, the idea that His actions are not in the slightest self-aggrandizing in the way a fallen human being's would be is difficult for us to grasp. Ultimately, God is love – though not *just* love. He is a faultless blend of love, holiness, omniscience, omnipotence, justice, and perfection in all ways. For Him to do things or to design His Creation so that at last He is seen for whom He is is something that we would expect from God, though we may certainly have trouble wrapping our brains around this concept.

For God, life on this planet (and the creation of it and all that it entails) is not a break in the continuum. It is the process through which He chose to display His flawless character to the entire universe. In essence then, because He is perfect, His plan is perfect. The culmination of His plan at some yet undisclosed future time is also perfect.

This chapter in the book of Revelation is the chapter where it all begins to come together. It is where the practical results of all that God is and all that He accomplished for humanity in the form of His matchless Son join to form the capstone of what the counsel of the Godhead declared even before this world was created. Here, in chapter twenty-one, John sees but a glimpse of it; but what a majestic glimpse!

People are often heard stating that if God is a God of love as Christians purport that He is, then how would it be possible for this God to allow human suffering throughout all of eternity? It is a good question, and one that John seems to answer indirectly in verse eight of this chapter.

"But the fearful, and unbelieving, and the abominable, and murderers, and whoremongers, and sorcerers, and idolaters, and all liars, shall have their part in the lake which burneth with fire and brimstone: which is the second death."

When considering the above verse, it is clear that there is something that is missed by people who point only to the attribute of love where God is concerned. Yes, as has been stated, God is absolutely (and absolute) love, but He is far more than that. Moreover, the people who ask that question are placing all the onus on God and ignoring the culpability of people.

In asking that question, people assume that once a person dies, their ability to sin *ceases*. From this verse alone, it is clear that this is not the case. People do not stop sinning after their death, simply because they now see God and realize the truth that they did not allow to rise to the surface throughout their earthly lives. Their individual sins continue.

To verify this, let us take a moment to look at a story that Jesus offered to His listeners about the rich man and Lazarus. We refer to the narrative found in Luke 16:19-31.

"19There was a certain rich man, which was clothed in purple and fine linen, and fared sumptuously every day:

"20And there was a certain beggar named Lazarus, which was laid at his gate, full of sores,

"21And desiring to be fed with the crumbs which fell from the rich man's table: moreover the dogs came and licked his sores.

"22And it came to pass, that the beggar died, and was carried by the angels into Abraham's bosom: the rich man also died, and was buried;

"23And in hell he lift up his eyes, being in torments, and seeth Abraham afar off, and Lazarus in his bosom.

"24And he cried and said, Father Abraham, have mercy on me, and send Lazarus, that he may dip the tip of his finger in water, and cool my tongue; for I am tormented in this flame.

"25But Abraham said, Son, remember that thou in thy lifetime receivedst thy good things, and likewise Lazarus evil things: but now he is comforted, and thou art tormented.

"26And beside all this, between us and you there is a great gulf fixed: so that they which would pass from hence to you cannot; neither can they pass to us, that would come from thence.

"27Then he said, I pray thee therefore, father, that thou wouldest send him to my father's house:

"28For I have five brethren; that he may testify unto them, lest they also come into this place of torment.

"29Abraham saith unto him, They have Moses and the prophets; let them hear them.

"30And he said, Nay, father Abraham: but if one went unto them from the dead, they will repent.

"31And he said unto him, If they hear not Moses and the prophets, neither will they be persuaded, though one rose from the dead."

The numerical references for the verses have been purposefully left in to make it easier for the reader to follow along. There is tremendous truth in the story, of course, and while some scholars believe it to be a type of parable and others believe that it was a true story that Jesus knew of, the point of the story should not be missed.

Here we see two individuals, a rich man and a beggar named Lazarus. During their lives, the rich man had everything he needed and wanted, while Lazarus had virtually nothing. Lazarus was completely dependent upon other people to meet his *needs*. Lazarus was a beggar undoubtedly because he was unable to walk and get around by himself. The text in verse twenty tells us that Lazarus "was laid at the gate" of the rich man and that Lazarus was "full of sores." In other words, his life was miserable.

Not so the rich man who enjoyed the best of everything. He probably assumed that he was rich because God blessed him and that Lazarus was not only poor, but lame as well, because he had sinned and God's curse was upon his poor miserable life.

One day, their individual lives on this earth ended and they both found themselves in the afterlife. The rich man found himself in the midst of torment, while the poor beggar Lazarus was actually being comforted. The point here is not that bad things happen to "good" people in the next life and good things happen to "bad" people. The point is far different from that.

Please note the attitude of the rich man. In this life, he had servants and he was highly respected because of the status he enjoyed. He was used to telling people what to do and they did it. Lazarus, on the other hand, had none of this and had likely spent years on the receiving end of all manner of ridicule, insults, and the like, solely because people viewed him as a "sinner."

In the afterlife, the rich man never stopped being "rich," in that his attitude of being haughty, obnoxious, and overbearing continued with him into eternity. Verse twenty-four tells us that in spite of the fact that he was in torment (cf. v. 23), he apparently felt he still had the status to make Lazarus serve him! He does this in verse twenty-four and twenty-seven, first by asking Abraham to send him with some water and then for Abraham to send him to his father's house to warn everyone.

It is difficult to believe that the rich man was truly concerned about his brothers or family. It almost gives rise to the idea that he was trying to show how concerned he was so that Abraham (or God, or whomever) would look at him and change his sentence. Nevertheless, the point here is that the rich man's haughtiness remained with him even after leaving this life and winding up with nothing. In other words, the rich man continued his sinful attitude even into eternity and in spite of the fact that he was in hell. His sin did not stop even after he understood the reality of his situation. It continued.

The people who leave this life without knowing Jesus as Savior and Lord do so with their sin counted against them. Because they have never had a spiritual transaction in this life – the one that Jesus explained to Nicodemus in John 3 about being born again, or born from above – their sin is never canceled. Because it has not been canceled in this life, it follows them to the next life. They also continue to have a sin nature because that has never been eradicated. A person with a sin nature cannot help but sin. Those who leave this life and retain the sin nature in the next will continue to follow its dictates, whether they like it or not.

This is the intended meaning of John's words in verse eight. He is pointing out that the individuals who are described by him in verse eight are appointed to the lake of fire because of their rejection of the Savior, Jesus Christ, and their continued lifestyle of sinning. It is not so much that the people who committed those individual sins will be part of the lake of fire. John is essentially referring to a *lifestyle* of sinning, promoted by following the dictates of the sin nature and the refusal to acknowledge Jesus Christ as Lord of Lords and to receive from Him the only salvation that is available. All people sin, and some people have murdered other people who are now in prison and will likely die there. The difference between him or her and another murderer has to do with their relationship to Jesus Christ. Even on death row, Jesus can and does save people. However, they at one time *did* murder someone, but that is no longer part of their life. They have received salvation from Jesus and He has washed away all of their sin.

Though they may die on death row or be executed for their crime in this life, the afterlife has something completely different for them because of their faith in Jesus Christ and the new birth they have received. It is easy for people to look at verses like this one and not truly understand what is being stated because of their own particular bias or misunderstanding. Those who *continue* to be murderers, thieves, sorcerers, liars, etc., in this life and never submit to Jesus Christ as Savior and Lord will continue sinning in the next life. It simply stands to reason. Because of their rejection of Jesus and the continued presence of the sin nature, they can do nothing else.

Revelation 21:9-11
"And there came unto me one of the seven angels which had the seven vials full of the seven last plagues, and talked with me, saying, Come hither, I will shew thee the bride, the Lamb's wife.

"And he carried me away in the spirit to a great and high mountain, and shewed me that great city, the holy Jerusalem, descending out of heaven from God,

"Having the glory of God: and her light was like unto a stone most precious, even like a jasper stone, clear as crystal;"

John moves from the people who will spend eternity in the lake of fire to a description of the New Jerusalem. The angel in the text has taken John to a high mountain, where from that vantage point John would be able to clearly see the sight that the angel wanted him to see. The angel refers to this New Jerusalem as "the bride, the Lamb's wife," which to us may seem weird considering we know the Bride of Christ to be His Body, His Church, of which all Christians are part. Why does the angel refer to Jerusalem as the bride of the Lamb?

"God calls new Jerusalem the bride, the wife of the Lamb, because as (a) the Lord is making his bride, the church, spotless and pure (Eph. 5:26 27), so he will make beautiful the new Jerusalem, (b) as marriage is permanent, so will be the new city, and (c) as a bride is beautiful and gloriously adorned, so will be the new city.

"Second, though the new Jerusalem will eventually be the home of all the redeemed, it will first be the home of the church, the bride of Christ, who will also be on display during the Millennium, the marriage feast. Remember, this is the home that He is preparing for us (John 14:2 3).[63]

It seems reasonable to conclude that the New Jerusalem is connected to Christ's Bride because of purity and eternality. Since Christ's Bride (His Body) will be residents in this city, it makes sense then that there is a connection between the two entities.

This version of Jerusalem is not only new but also holy, and to ensure that it is and remains holy it was obviously built not with human hands, but by God, since it comes down to the earth from heaven.

This particular Jerusalem is one that glorifies God fully, and it is clear that John understood that the light emanating from it was none other than God's glory. This is very different from the Jerusalem of our day in which there is nothing but acrimony and fighting.

Scripturally, the Bible declares unreservedly that Jerusalem was given to the nation of Israel. Yet the Bible also tells us that the Gentiles would trample this same city until the end (cf. Luke 21). This city to-

---

[63] J. Hampton Keathley III *Studies in Revelation* (Biblical Studies Press, 1997), 279

day is a far cry from the Jerusalem that God Himself will build and float down to the earth in preparation of the real new world order of the future. Though Satan has been trying to build a new world order of which he is king, God will allow him to try, and he will be successful for a short time. However, Satan's rule will only last for a short time. God will with finality completely overthrow
Satan and all who follow him, replacing his dark rule with God's eternal rule.

The New Jerusalem will never become sullied by sin because in the eternal order of the future, all of God's enemies will have been permanently vanquished, including death and sin. Sin will never again darken any gate of this new city, or any other part of God's Creation.

Revelation 21:12-14

"And had a wall great and high, and had twelve gates, and at the gates twelve angels, and names written thereon, which are the names of the twelve tribes of the children of Israel:

"On the east three gates; on the north three gates; on the south three gates; and on the west three gates.

"And the wall of the city had twelve foundations, and in them the names of the twelve apostles of the Lamb."

Here, John begins to describe for us the city itself, and we begin to see how all things come together here. There are at least two things of great interest here. First, note how there are twelve gates with a high wall that surround the city. Each gate has one of the names of the twelve tribes of Israel engraved thereon. Note also that the city itself is built on twelve foundations, and on each of these foundations there is the name of one of the twelve apostles.

The question arises, *which* twelve apostles? There were actually *more* than twelve. Aside from the original twelve (which included the Judas who betrayed Jesus), we know from Acts 1 that Matthias replaced Judas, and then later in Acts 9, Saul became the apostle Paul after his conversion.

It is difficult, if not impossible, to know until we get there. The main point of this section seems to be that Israel and the Church continue to be two different groups of people, one represented by the twelve tribes (gates) and the other represented by the twelve apostles (the foundations). In spite of this, both groups share equally in the perfection of God's holiness and love, which is part and parcel of their lives forever.

Revelation 21:15-17
"And he that talked with me had a golden reed to measure the city, and the gates thereof, and the wall thereof.

"And the city lieth foursquare, and the length is as large as the breadth: and he measured the city with the reed, twelve thousand furlongs. The length and the breadth and the height of it are equal.

"And he measured the wall thereof, an hundred and forty and four cubits, according to the measure of a man, that is, of the angel."

Here John defines the size of the city and it turns out to be a very large city! It is a perfect square (length is as large as the breadth) measuring up to 1,500 miles on each side (depending upon how this dimension is interpreted).

One scholar has indicated that a *"comparison in land area notes that the coverage would equal the combined areas of all the states in the United States except Montana, Utah, Nevada, Arizona, Washington, Oregon, California, Alaska, and Hawaii."*[64]

---

[64] Robert L. Thomas *Revelation 8-22 An Exegetical Commentary* (Chicago: Moody Press 1995) 467

It is difficult to know what is actually meant here in the text, which causes some to move into the allegorical realm, taking the meaning to be reflective of size, but not literally that large. However, there is no reason to move into the allegorical realm here because these numbers are specific and would eliminate the need to take them figuratively.

The diagram below shows the size and breadth of Jerusalem, The Temple, and surrounding area during the Millennial Kingdom reign of Jesus. The New Jerusalem that floats down from the heavens *after* the Millennium and at the beginning of the future eternal order will

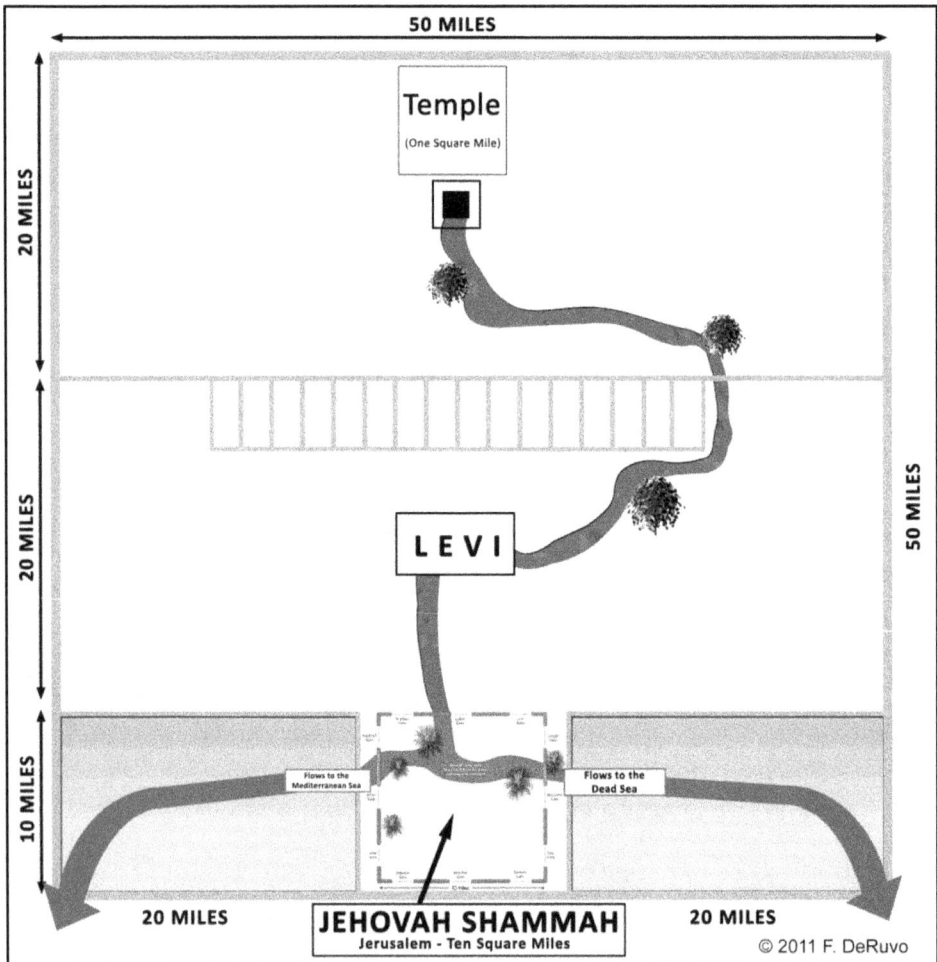

Jerusalem in Millennium (A)

dwarf this one in size and breadth. The next diagram (on the next page) highlights only Jerusalem during the millennial period.

Many biblical scholars believe that what John is seeing and experiencing in chapter twenty-one is a *cube* shape. Others believe that this New Jerusalem will be in the shape of a three-dimensional triangle.

Regardless, the point of this section of text is that the city will be extremely large and stand as the centerpiece of eternity future with all activity emanating out from there. It is difficult for our minds to pic-

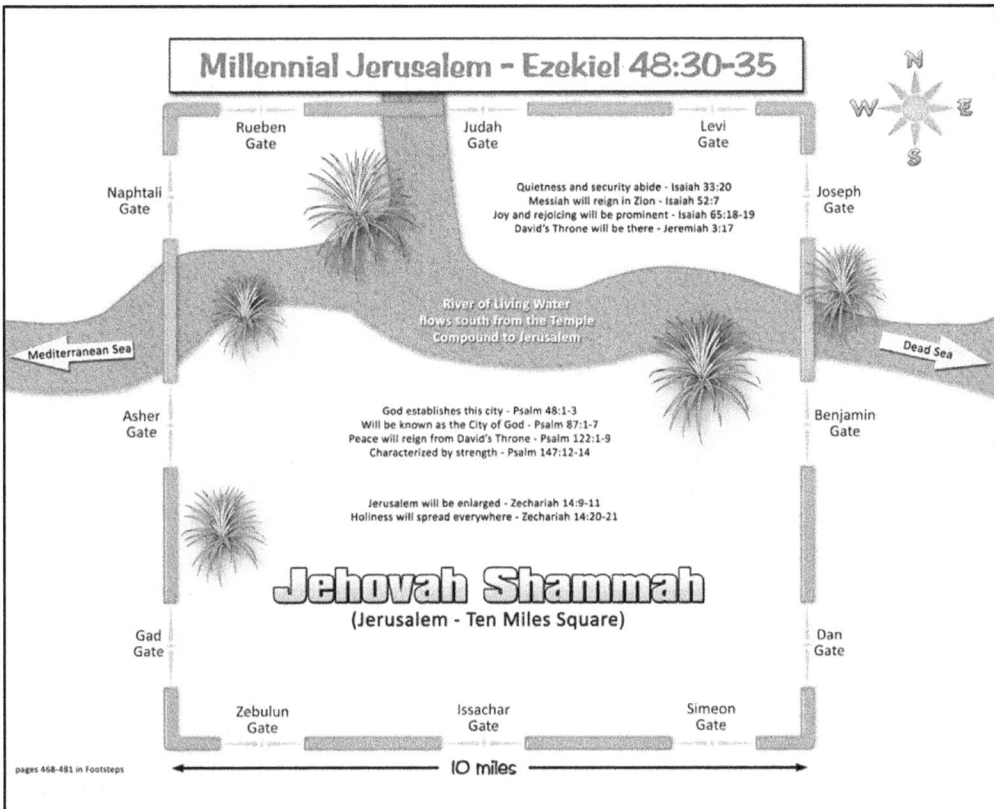

Jerusalem in Millennium (B)

ture much less embrace something that is so huge, simply because of the divisions within the United States for instance. These boundaries, though invisible to the naked eye, are nonetheless something we recall when thinking of particular states. It is no easier picturing the size of this New Jerusalem than it is gaining a handle on the size and breadth of eternity!

Revelation 21:18-21

"And the building of the wall of it was of jasper: and the city was pure gold, like unto clear glass.

"And the foundations of the wall of the city were garnished with all manner of precious stones. The first foundation was jasper; the second, sapphire; the third, a chalcedony; the fourth, an emerald;

"The fifth, sardonyx; the sixth, sardius; the seventh, chrysolyte; the eighth, beryl; the ninth, a topaz; the tenth, a chrysoprasus; the eleventh, a jacinth; the twelfth, an amethyst.

"And the twelve gates were twelve pearls: every several gate was of one pearl: and the street of the city was pure gold, as it were transparent glass."

Here again, it is difficult to picture these scenes in the mind; however, what *is* clearly discerned is the fact that there is a good deal of *shine* to this city and translucent coloration to the portions of it. The city is a translucent gold, something this reader has never seen. The foundations of the city were replete with "all manner of precious stones," each foundation sporting a unique stone for that section.

The twelve gates were made of pearls and the fascinating thing here is that each gate, according to John, *is one pearl.* We all know what a pearl looks like, but trying to imaging a pearl so large that it could be a gate is interesting to say the least.

The street (note it says *street* in the singular) is also of the same type of translucent gold that describes the city itself. Do you get the sense that this city, though glittering with light, is not blinding to the eye? Imagine eternity, where we will see in actual 3-D, something that scientists say we do not really do in this life (each eye sees in 2-D and our brain constructs the scene in 3-D from those two separate images). Imagine the smells, the tastes, and the beauty that will always be before us. Imagine your favorite fruit here in this life, and then try to imagine what it will taste and smell like in the next.

The beauty and splendor of eternity future is a direct result of God's full and unimpaired glory, which will never be veiled, but will remain visible for all His children to enjoy and literally bathe in.

Revelation 21:22-27

"And I saw no temple therein: for the Lord God Almighty and the Lamb are the temple of it.

"And the city had no need of the sun, neither of the moon, to shine in it: for the glory of God did lighten it, and the Lamb is the light thereof.

"And the nations of them which are saved shall walk in the light of it: and the kings of the earth do bring their glory and honour into it.

"And the gates of it shall not be shut at all by day: for there shall be no night there.

"And they shall bring the glory and honour of the nations into it.

"And there shall in no wise enter into it any thing that defileth, neither whatsoever worketh abomination, or maketh a lie: but they which are written in the Lamb's book of life."

We now begin to grasp a more complete picture of this New Jerusalem. Unlike the Jerusalem and surrounding compound during the millennial reign of Jesus, this New Jerusalem has no temple at all. The need for sacrifice is gone, and Jesus Himself (the Lamb) is the temple. He will be worshipped in spirit and in truth for that which He is – King of King and Lord of Lords. There is no longer any need to go to a particular place of worship, as Jesus will be the center of worship in eternity future as He should be now.

John's description gets even more interesting here because we learn about the source of the light that makes all of the various elements shine as they do. It is Jesus Himself. He is the glory of God that provides constant light. It is neither reflected (as the sun reflects off the moon), nor is it slowly growing dark (as is our sun). The sky never grows dark in New Jerusalem.

God's glory is permanent, constant, and effectively provides all the light needed for the citizens of the New Jerusalem. Note also that we will finally walk fully in the light as He is in the light, something we have only been able to do badly here in this life. With the sin nature gone, there is no chance of sin, and therefore no chance of ever breaking our fellowship with God.

When this author was growing up in the small town of Hobart, NY, it was not uncommon to leave doors unlocked. There was little to no fear of any criminal breaking and entering. That is not the case today. Doors and windows are double-locked and precautions are taken to at least make it difficult for thieves to break in and steal.

The New Jerusalem boasts a safety that nothing can compare with in this life. The gates will remain open, and of course, any city that never shuts its gates means that it has no fear of being attacked. Since all of God's enemies are permanently gone, so is the chance of war. Citizens of New Jerusalem will come and go as they please without a thought about danger.

Notice that there are still *nations* included in this picture of eternity future. Whether this is symbolic or not it is difficult to know, and may be descriptive of the variety of people from all the nations, but could also mean that there are groups of nations though there is no separation or disparity between groups.

The last verse of this section confirms to us that nothing which is less than perfect will ever enter into New Jerusalem. In fact, the only ones who will enter and have access to New Jerusalem are those whose names are written in the Lamb's book of life! What a picture. Can you see it?

Do you want that? Without Jesus, you have no chance of reaching that goal. There is no chance that upon your death, you will awake to enjoy the life that John describes. This is reserved only for those who trust in Jesus as Savior and Lord.

If you do not know Jesus, you *can* know Him. You must believe that Jesus is who He said He is (God, the Son), that He came and lived a sinless life here on this planet, and gave Himself for your sin (the very sins that keep you out of heaven) by dying a gruesomely brutal death on Calvary's cross. It did not end there, though, because three days later, He rose from the dead. He rose because death itself had no claim on Jesus and therefore was unable to keep Him in the grave! This author would implore you not to go another moment without receiving the salvation that Jesus holds out to you.

This is not easy-believism. It is not simply saying a few words, and then living the life you want to live without worrying about reper-cussions. The life referred to herein is the *new* life that becomes yours as you trust Jesus for salvation. Reaching out to Jesus for the salvation that He offers is what grants you this new life. The Holy Spirit will come into your life, dwell there, seal you unto the day of redemption, then begin to create within you the character of Jesus

Christ. You will find yourself moving away from the things that you used to enjoy, but turns out were sinful and you did not even know it.

Becoming a Christian is not simply going through certain actions – praying, going to church, reading the Bible, tithing, etc. – it is a complete change in your life brought about through faith in the finished work of Jesus Christ.

Please, get right with God today. You have absolutely no clue when you will breathe your last, and while you may think you have plenty of time left, you do not know that. Your life could end today, even before you finish reading this book.

The book of Revelation shows us the future. Is it a future of which you want desperately to enjoy? Maybe you are thinking of holding off or waiting before making a decision about Jesus. You are not sure yet, so you need time to think about it. However, do you actually know if you *have* the time? Do you know that for *certain*?

If you die now without having received salvation from Jesus, your fate is the same as the rich man who was in torment. He had no way out of it and there was no chance of overturning the conviction. Please, do not wait. Talk to God now because your life *does* depend upon it.

22

REVELATION 22

In this last chapter of the book of Revelation, we see that everything has come full circle. What began in Genesis with an earthly paradise ends in Revelation with another paradise. The difference, of course, is that this new paradise highlighted in Revelation 22 is such that it can ever be sullied through sin.

In this new world of the future, there is nothing to detract from God. There is nothing that will take away from His Creation, and nothing that will ever cause anyone to ever sin again. The picture John paints under the inspiration of the Holy Spirit is one that is certainly difficult to imagine, though very real nonetheless. It makes this author pause, consider, and reflect.

When we consider the fact that for many of us, loved ones have already gone to eternity, we are left to continue living for the Lord and waiting for His personal call to us. Our friends and loved ones who enjoy that eternal experience now very likely look back at this life (if it is even remembered, which is doubtful) thinking that it was little more than a dream or vague memory. If the next life could be compared with this one, it is easy to imagine that everything there has far greater depth than anything here does in this life. Whether we are talking about smells, sights, sounds, or touch, being there and experiencing all that eternity future has to offer makes this life appear as though it has been but a dream. In this last chapter of Revelation, let us look and consider whether we can even begin to comprehend all that awaits those who love the Lord and look forward to His coming.

Revelation 22:1-2

"And he shewed me a pure river of water of life, clear as crystal, proceeding out of the throne of God and of the Lamb.

"In the midst of the street of it, and on either side of the river, was there the tree of life, which bare twelve manner of fruits, and yielded her fruit every month: and the leaves of the tree were for the healing of the nations."

The same angel that has been highlighting one splendid sight after another is now here pointing out a river that proceeds directly out of God's throne. John describes the river first as the *water of life*. It has life-giving properties to it.

"The words "the river of the water of life" are literally "a river of water, of life." This entire phrase is anarthrous, without any articles. As such it stresses the quality and character of this river above all other bodies of water. "Of life" points out what kind of river it is, a life-giving river. This

symbolically portrays the abundance of life which God and the Lamb will provide in the eternal city."[65]

This particular river is central to the New Jerusalem and it reminds us of what Jesus Himself told the woman at the well in John 4. The conversation Jesus had with this woman highlights a number of things about Jesus, and one of those things testifies to the fact that He is that from which living water flows (cf. John 4:10). Jesus is the Living Water, the Word of Life, and a hundred and one other phrases that describe His splendor, His majesty, and His ability to save.

Here in the New Jerusalem, this living water will serve to remind us forever of He who saves, renews, and recreates. This is Jesus, King of Kings and Lord of Lords. He is the One to whom all glory will be given. He is the One whose shoulders bore the pain and weight of our sin. He is the One from whom all life flows as Creator. He is the One through whom salvation is extended to a lost world. Are you one of His, or are you still floundering with the rest of the lost?

This river of life is there in New Jerusalem and it is crystal clear, which stresses its purity. Who does not want to drink water that is clear, as opposed to water that has a film, or is polluted with bacterial matter?

It reminds me of the movie "Back to the Future" when main character Marty McFly went back to the Old West to look for his friend, Doc Brown. While there, he stayed with his distant relatives, where dinner was hunted daily and the water was slightly brownish-looking. Who would willingly drink it unless they either knew no better or were literally dying of thirst?

Please note that on both sides of this river are fruit trees of all sorts, and we also see the tree of life. You will recall that in the Garden of Eden, there were also various trees that Adam and Eve could have

---

[65] J. Hampton Keathley III *Studies in Revelation* (Biblical Studies Press, 1997), 284

eaten from while there. Recall also that there was the tree of knowledge of good and evil, as well as the tree of life.

Unfortunately, our first parents chose to eat of the tree of knowledge of good and evil *instead* of from the tree of life. Had they chosen the tree of life *first*, they likely would never have even desired the fruit of the tree of knowledge of good and evil.

Yet here in this future garden paradise stands another tree of life. This particular tree of life gives life to twelve different types of fruits, not merely one! Every month, instead of once per year, the fruit from this tree is available to eat. John notes also that the leaves themselves contain healing powers. Again we read of "nations" that will be in New Jerusalem.

The question of course arises whether we will be required to eat of this tree, or for that matter any tree or food, in order to continue to live. That is doubtful simply because we know that while Jesus *did* eat after His resurrection, it does not appear to be necessary. So it may well be with us. We may eat if we desire to, but are not required to do so to remain alive. Remember, there is no death here because death along with hell itself was thrown into the Lake of Fire. Death no longer occurs. It is no longer the enemy of glorified humanity.

Could the tree of life also be part of a memorial? It is possible. It would seem that there might well be things in this paradise – New Jerusalem – there for our enjoyment and choice.

Revelation 22:3-4
"And there shall be no more curse: but the throne of God and of the Lamb shall be in it; and his servants shall serve him:

"And they shall see his face; and his name shall be in their foreheads."

How powerful is what has just been stated by John? There is no more curse! The curse that God placed on people, on animals, and on the earth itself is removed! The curse that results in old age, feeble mindedness, sickness, and ultimately death is gone, once for all. That is wonderful news.

Do you ever get tired and need sleep? Of course we do, because we are human. However, it is not simply being human that causes us to become tired. It is part of the curse that was placed on life here. Our bodies are constantly winding down regardless of how well we may believe we care for them. Certainly, healthier people may get by with less sleep than those who are infirm or older, but the process of dying is part of this life. Sleeping renews our bodies and minds. Without sleep, we would die infinitely sooner than most people do now.

Sleeping allows us to become and/or remain healthy. It allows us to renew our minds and bodies. We need sleep because we are dying and we are dying because of the curse. It is the same reasoning behind the fact that when God pronounced His curse on the earth, He stated that it would be by the sweat of our brows that the earth would give forth its food (cf. Genesis 3). Why is that? It is a blessing in the midst of the curse.

Those who never exert themselves become overweight, listless, sloppy, unable to think clearly, sickly, and much worse at times. Physical effort keeps our bodies healthier than if we did nothing. Manual labor exercises our muscles, including our heart, and strengthens our bodies. Physical work or exercise allows us to become and remain healthy.

This was not the case prior to our first parents' fall from grace. Work was not tiring or even exhausting. Try to imagine what it must have been like for Adam and Eve. One day, they knew what life was like *prior* to their sin. They enjoyed the smells of the garden, ate the food offered to them by the trees and plants, and were not afraid of any of the animals. They never stubbed their toe, never knew what pain was, and certainly were not aware of how sickness felt.

Then one day, they sinned and from that point on began to die. Their bodies started to age, as did their minds. What they previously gave no thought to now required effort, stamina, and a good deal of sweat. The animals that were never afraid of them now shied away from them. Adam and Eve also now began to fear the animals. Their sounds now seemed foreign, fear inducing.

They now also were introduced to pain, something they could not have described prior because they never experienced it. Now, it was becoming a daily experience. If their muscles were not tired and fatigued, they accidentally struck their head on a low hanging branch, or they stubbed their toe while walking in unfamiliar territory.

Consider as time went by – in fact, decades and centuries – life continued its downward spiral. In the Garden of Eden, they had enjoyed perfect health and no sign of tiredness or aging. Now, with each passing decade, they were feeling less chipper than they had prior to it. This slow death was not at all appealing.

Adam and Eve are the only two human beings who fully understood what it was like to be perfectly in tune with all of God's Creation one day, and out of tune with it the next, until their physical death. No other human being can relate to that. Of all the things that made their sin so *sinful* and bad, having experienced perfection and then sliding into daily degradation simply made their sin and the result of it that much more painful.

Imagine seeing how much life changed. Imagine giving birth to children, watching them grow only to see your first two sons argue, resulting in the death of one of them. Imagine living long enough to see that sinful people can become terribly bad. In our society, we understand how bad things can get, but we can only *imagine* how perfect life will be.

We might look at other people and shake our heads because of their sinfulness. We are comparing them with ourselves, but we are unable to compare them (or even ourselves) with the perfection that Adam and Eve knew through daily living. Consider the tragedy of being Adam and Eve!

In New Jerusalem, all of the Lamb's servants will serve Him and serve Him gladly. We will know no such thing as fatigue, or anger, or frustration, or anything else that was created through sin. We will know only love, adoration, unbroken fellowship, and absolute perfection.

Our greatest unfulfilled desire in this life as authentic Christians is to be able to serve our Lord with the type of consistency and fervor that we will live in eternity future. There, in New Jerusalem, we will never fall short of that goal. So great will be our capacity to serve Him that we will never ever grow tired of it. We will truly exist to serve Him and will be glad because of it.

Probably the greatest aspect of New Jerusalem is the ability to see Jesus' face! Isn't that what His children want, to see Him as He is, to look into His eyes, to be on the receiving end of His smile? In this life, it is by faith. In the next, it will be by experience.

We will *see* Him! We will have the privilege of serving and worshiping Jesus whom we will see and adore with our eyes! Will there be anything greater?

Notice that His Name will be on our foreheads. We will be fully His, owned by Jesus. As Owner and Chief Shepherd, He will spend eternity future caring for each of us as only He can. Unlike the evil of the Tribulation when the Antichrist will force all to accept his mark on the forehead or the right hand, we will walk and live proudly proclaiming for each other to see that we belong to Him who gave His life in order that we might enjoy the paradise that He created us to enjoy!

We belong to Him. We are His and we will spend eternity reflecting His glory perfectly one to another. He will be lifted up and glorified in all that we say, all that we think, and in all that we do; something that is fully desirable, but also impossible here.

Revelation 22:5

"And there shall be no night there; and they need no candle, neither light of the sun; for the Lord God giveth them light: and they shall reign for ever and ever."

As the last chapter of the last book begins to wrap up, John reminds us that there will never be any darkness. There will never be any need to reach for a match to light a candle, or reach for the switch to turn on the light, or look to the sky to see the sun. God's glory will provide all the light that is needed, and He will be our light forever and ever, without end.

The darkness will be gone. It will never interact with us or any part of God's Creation again. It is as if it will be vanquished. God is light and in Him is no darkness at all (cf. 1 John 1:5).

Revelation 22:6-7

"And he said unto me, These sayings are faithful and true: and the Lord God of the holy prophets sent his angel to shew unto his servants the things which must shortly be done.

"Behold, I come quickly: blessed is he that keepeth the sayings of the prophecy of this book."

The angel testifies to John that what John has seen and heard is true. The fact that God has sent His holy angels to tell John these things proves that it is true. Note also that the angel says that these things must happen *shortly*. Of course, students of the Bible and scholars argue a great deal about these things, but it seems that the arguments occur because we view words and phrases like this from our temporal plane. Here, we are guided by time. We cannot get away from it. Even if we could successfully find a way to go back in time, we would still be *using up some time*. We can never, in this life, separate ourselves from time.

In eternity of which the spiritual realm is part, time is, at the very least, different. It may well be that time does not exist at all and something else exists. If the angel and John are in a spiritual dimension as John has been shown all of these things, it stands to reason then that the idea of something happening "shortly" has more to do with the eternal realm than this temporal one. This is not to say that what happens in the eternal spiritual realm does not affect us here in this physical realm. It is to say that just as the cross of Christ is always before God, so also is the concept of things occurring quickly, or soon.

On one hand, the spiritual realm may only be one or two dimensions separate from us, and it is clear that angelic beings (as well as demons) can come into our dimension. However, the passage of any length of time may be far different from one another if we were able to compare these separate, yet somewhat connected, realms.

It is this author's suggestion that as far as God is concerned, when all of the things that John saw and wrote about do occur, they will have happened *soon*. To us it seems like an eternity because of the way the concept of time works on and against us. It can seem interminable on occasion.

It is also worth considering that regardless of what we think of time in our dimension and any type of time in the spiritual dimension, we should all be constantly aware of the fact that our death is always one breath away. Because I do not know when my death will occur, it is always imminent and could very well happen *soon*. We should probably spend a good deal less time arguing about intended meaning with things like this and simply understand that time is short for everyone on this earth. Not only do we *not* know when our own death will occur, but also we are completely unaware of the timing of anyone else's death. It is for this reason alone that evangelism should be our first priority as we serve our Lord.

Having said that, please note the last verse in the text above. It says, *"blessed is he that keepeth the sayings of the prophecy of this book."* What does that mean? Well, for one thing, it means that people who take this book of Revelation seriously are blessed through the study of it. The reason has to do with the fact that in order to properly study the book of Revelation, it is advisable to study a number of other books found in the Old Testament, such as (but not limited to) Daniel, Ezekiel, Joel, Amos, Zechariah, Zephaniah, Isaiah, and the Psalms. These are just for starters.

If we study His Word sincerely desiring to know *His* meaning, rather than what we might *think* He is saying, He will bless us with the truth that is important for us to live this life now. It provides us with a different perspective for this life. It shifts our focus from ourselves to God and the lost He died to save.

As Christians, we tend to be caught up in the things of this world, and when that occurs we lose sight of our goal. Of course, it is understood that Satan loves it when we start focusing too much on this life because it keeps us from noticing all the lost and dying people around us.

When studying the book of Revelation, whether we agree with one another on all the various points is not really the main point. The thing that matters most is that we understand the importance of the fact that Jesus is going to return some day and human history will end. Moreover, it is equally important to understand that we may not be living at the time He does return. We may have already died and gone to be with Him in heaven. Taking the book of Revelation seriously means that we begin to see our lives for what they are – a vapor that is here today and gone tomorrow (cf. James 4:14; see also Psalms 39:5; 102:3; 144:4; Job 7:7).

Considering the fact that our life truly is so short (compared to eternity), should we not focus on those things that have *eternal* meaning? This is the overall meaning of Revelation. Through the apostle John, Jesus wants us to understand that He – as God the Son, Creator of all things, King of Kings, and Lord of Lords – should be our *continual* and *absolute* focus. It is only when we bring Him into the center of attention do we truly begin to understand what it means to live for *Him* instead of for *ourselves.* Understanding that the end of this world is eventually coming, that Jesus Christ will be returning, and that all things will be made new is one of the best ways to achieve this type of attitude and demeanor.

Most people go through life unaware that their death could easily be right around the corner. Most of us believe that we will live to be old, our life will have been fulfilled, and then we will simply die in our sleep. The problem, of course, is that while everyone may think that, it does not happen to a large percentage of people in this world.

We do not know when our death will occur, nor are we told ahead of time in what manner we will die. It would be best for us to be aware of the fact that not only the timing of our death but the method of our death is in God's hands. If we adopted this attitude, we would be that much closer to appreciating the fact that Jesus is King of Kings and Lord of Lords as well. Our failure to grasp the simple truth of our imminent death keeps us from grasping the concept that Jesus is in full control of all things and this world, far from being about us, is truly about Jesus Christ and Him only.

Revelation 22:8-9
"And I John saw these things, and heard them. And when I had

heard and seen, I fell down to worship before the feet of the angel which shewed me these things.

"Then saith he unto me, See thou do it not: for I am thy fellows-ervant, and of thy brethren the prophets, and of them which keep the sayings of this book: worship God."

John makes a mistake and is quickly – but gently – chided for it by the angel. The angel makes it clear that he is a fellow servant of this very same God and all worship should go only to Him.

Considering it, who can blame John? Think of all that he has seen, felt, and vicariously experienced through the numerous visions that he was shown. In the final analysis, *seeing* Jesus not only come to this earth in all His glory, but rule over all things in holiness, righteousness, and justice, while all enemies are handily dispatched, would make anyone fall down to worship.

Think of it. John lived to see Jesus return in His glory just as Jesus said he would. In Matthew 16:27-28, Jesus tell us, *"For the Son of man shall come in the glory of his Father with his angels; and then he shall reward every man according to his works.*

"Verily I say unto you, There be some standing here, which shall not taste of death, till they see the Son of man coming in his kingdom."

If we look at this verse, Jesus is specifically saying that some with Him at that point would not see death until he (they) see the Son of man coming in His Kingdom. Since His disciples were with Him, it is plausible to conclude that John was one of them.

Preterists and others have a field day with this passage because since Jesus has not physically returned yet, they conclude that He must have meant something that should be taken allegorically. However, if we understand Revelation, it certainly seems that prior to John's death (as he had been imprisoned on the island of Patmos), John *did* see Jesus returning to the earth in all His glory. If not, how would he have been able to describe the event for us?

This author believes the literal meaning of Christ's words was fulfilled in the book of Revelation, when John saw the vision of Jesus' return to earth as King and Ruler. By understanding Jesus' words in this way, it does not do any damage to the text whatsoever, and fulfills them as well.

John was privileged to see and hear things that we can only imagine. We were not there with him, so it is impossible in *some cases* to be dogmatic about meaning. The point though is that he literally went behind the veil that keeps us from seeing all the activity in the spiritual realm that is constantly happening. Not only this, but he saw things that were of a decidedly *future* perspective, things that it was fortunate for us he was able to write down and share with us.

John was witness to the power, the glory, and the coming reign of our Savior and King, Jesus. John saw *beyond* this as well, into eternity *future*, when all things will be made new. John *witnessed* the return of the King to the earth that He created. He saw it and it was not a dream. It was the playing of a future event as it happened, and since at that point he was outside of time, the constraints that play on us did not exist.

John saw the coming King. That cannot be denied, so why some people have such a difficulty with Jesus' words in Matthew 16 is because they are not comparing Scripture with Scripture. This and taking Scripture out of context are the two biggest reasons people make such large mistakes when it comes to doctrine and prophetic utterances.

John has seen firsthand what our life will be like when Jesus – the rightful Owner – returns to earth to claim what is His. Additionally, there is no way John could have seen these things without *experienc-*

ing them as well, even from a slight distance. It is no different from when we go to see a movie and parts of that movie bring us to tears or cheers, depending upon the scene. In essence, we are living the same thing vicariously, through the actors in the movie. The acting is so good and the script so believable that we have left our world and entered that world. This is what John experienced.

John saw the King, he saw the judgments, he saw the throne room of God, and he then saw Jesus literally return to earth in complete and total victory and everything that happened after that. This is why the book of Revelation is the last book of the Bible. It culminates with the victorious rule of Jesus Christ, King of Kings and Lord of all.

The angel who spoke to John sums up the one overriding call to all of us from the book of Revelation: *worship God*. There is nothing higher that we as created human beings can do. This is in fact why we were made, to worship our Creator in spirit and in truth throughout all eternity and that begins in the *here* and *now*.

Revelation 22:10-15

"And he saith unto me, Seal not the sayings of the prophecy of this book: for the time is at hand.

"He that is unjust, let him be unjust still: and he which is filthy, let him be filthy still: and he that is righteous, let him be righteous still: and he that is holy, let him be holy still.

"And, behold, I come quickly; and my reward is with me, to give every man according as his work shall be.

"I am Alpha and Omega, the beginning and the end, the first and the last.

"Blessed are they that do his commandments, that they may have right to the tree of life, and may enter in through the gates into the city.

"For without are dogs, and sorcerers, and whoremongers, and murderers, and idolaters, and whosoever loveth and maketh a lie."

Here John is commissioned to tell the world the things he has seen and interestingly enough, from A.D. 95 unto the present, we have these words. What is our response to them?

John is told that those who are unjust will continue to be unjust. Those who are righteous will continue to be righteous. It appears that what John is being told is that many will read these words and they will have no impact on those who are destined for hell. Those who are righteous because of the shed blood of Jesus and faith in His death will continue to be righteous because this book will confirm for them the reality of what is coming our way.

When Jesus says to John that He is coming quickly, again, we must realize that this refers to imminency. Jesus is just beyond the wall of our dimension (in physical appearance), though God is everywhere at once. He will return when that moment arrives and it will take the world by surprise because most will not be ready for it, including many who have read this book of Revelation and believe it to mean something it does not mean.

Jesus presents His credentials to John as being the Alpha, the Omega, the First, and the Last. Jesus is "I Am," the One who never changes, from which all things flow, and to which all things culminate. Because of who He is, those who do what is commanded of them are blessed. Why are they blessed? Simply because by *doing* what is commanded of us, it becomes obvious that we *believe* that He is who He says He is and the proof is seen in our actions.

Anyone can say that they are Christian (and many do), but we know that not all who say it are, in actuality, truly saved. The proof is in the pudding so to speak, and likewise, those who belong to Jesus willingly do what He commands. Those who are truly saved *will* enter in through the gates to the New Jerusalem. Jesus is not saying that works save people. He is simply saying that the works that a person does from the heart, based on a deep love for Jesus, is because that person has received authentic salvation from Jesus. Because of that fact, the truth or veracity of that person's salvation is seen in their actions, though not perfect.

Revelation 22:16-21

"I Jesus have sent mine angel to testify unto you these things in the churches. I am the root and the offspring of David, and the bright and morning star.

"And the Spirit and the bride say, Come. And let him that heareth say, Come. And let him that is athirst come. And whosoever will, let him take the water of life freely.

"For I testify unto every man that heareth the words of the prophecy of this book, If any man shall add unto these things, God shall add unto him the plagues that are written in this book:

"And if any man shall take away from the words of the book of this prophecy, God shall take away his part out of the book of life, and out of the holy city, and from the things which are written in this book.

"He which testifieth these things saith, Surely I come quickly. Amen. Even so, come, Lord Jesus.

"The grace of our Lord Jesus Christ be with you all. Amen."

Again, Jesus presents His credentials, verifying that He and He alone is the rightful Owner and Ruler because His lineage goes back to King David. Jesus is the "bright and morning" star. Lucifer in all his brightness was never as bright as Jesus was then and remains. Lucifer's brightness depended upon God because Lucifer is a created being. Not so with Jesus, who has always been God the Son, the Eternal Son, the Second Person of the Godhead. He outshines all others!

Notice also that Jesus Himself warns those who would either add to or detract from the words of this book. It is *that* important that when studying the book of Revelation, students of the Bible insist on finding God's meaning, not their own or what they believe to be God's meaning.

It also appears that Jesus is saying that those who do detract from or add to will experience the plagues found within because they are not truly His, though they may believe themselves to be. Only authentic Christians would strive to submit themselves to God to determine His meaning in this book. Does that mean that all authentic Christians are correct about all these things? That cannot be, since authentic Christians *do* disagree about certain aspects of Revelation.

What it likely means is that above all things, we need to approach the book of Revelation with a bit of fear and trembling, knowing that we are playing with fire. We need to grasp the fact that these are God's Words to us through John. Too many today are way too flippant about what they believe the text in Revelation means, often ridiculing those with whom they disagree. Not only is this not good, but it proves an attitude of superiority or pride, something that God is never pleased with in any portion of His Creation.

The book ends on two uplifting notes. First, Jesus reiterates that He is coming quickly, and then we hear the doxology that His grace should be with all of us. Amen , or *so be it*.

Authentic believers would do well to note that this book is extremely important. This is not to say that any other portion of Scripture is of less value. It means that the importance of Revelation cannot be overemphasized as to its inherent ability to provide a thorough and clear picture of what lies ahead, as no other book in the Bible does.

Anyone who approaches the book of Revelation *only* to gain knowledge of future events, though, is approaching it in the wrong frame of mind. Studying the book of Revelation should bring us to a number of stark facts:

1. *Jesus alone is worthy, and*
2. *Everything in Revelation should direct our attention to Him*

If we are able to read Revelation without arriving at the two conclusions above, then we have wasted our time and should start all over again, this time with the proper frame of reference. Jesus is to be adored and worshiped above all things and creatures. The book of Revelation is *the* book that highlights Jesus as He is *now* and as He will be when we finally see Him, whether on earth after the Tribulation or in heaven due to our death.

Part of the reality of the book of Revelation is the fact that without Jesus, we are forever and completely lost. To leave this earth without knowing Him as Savior means we enter eternity forever separated from Him. A lost condition in eternity means it will never change.

It is here in this life that we are given opportunity to see and embrace the truth about Jesus Christ. It is not enough to simply *see* the truth about Jesus. We need to go beyond that and actively *embrace* that truth. Without embracing that truth, though seeing it, we will be able to walk away from Him.

The book of Hebrews speaks of this very thing throughout its contents. The writer encourages his readers to *enter into the rest* that God provided through Jesus Christ. In chapter six of Hebrews, the writer becomes very explicit. He states, "*For it is impossible for those who were once enlightened, and have tasted of the heavenly gift, and were made partakers of the Holy Ghost, and have tasted the good word of God, and the powers of the world to come,*

"If they shall fall away, to renew them again unto repentance; seeing they crucify to themselves the Son of God afresh, and put him to an open shame" (Hebrews 6:4-6).

It seems clear that the writer is warning his readers that having tasted of the heavenly gift through knowledge of the truth, though not fully embracing that truth, could cause some to fall away. If they fall away after they have begun to understand the truth related to Jesus, it is impossible for them to return since it will be as though they have crucified Jesus a second time.

The writer of Hebrews is not speaking of sinning, then repenting. We all sin, even authentic Christians. That will unfortunately continue in this life until God removes our sin nature in the next life.

The writer of Hebrews is referring to the fact that it is possible to gain an *appreciation* for Jesus through knowledge of Him. However, it is only when that knowledge is fully *embraced* is salvation given. Simply *knowing* or *understanding* aspects of Jesus' life is not good enough. It is required to fully *believe* in all that He is and all that He has accomplished for the lost. Believing in Jesus indicates a willingness to follow Him. Following Him is where the rubber meets the road because it also means sacrificing your will for His will.

Have you done this? Do you believe that Jesus is God and that He died for *you*? That is an excellent place to start, but you cannot stop there. Demons believe that Jesus is God, and though they tremble at that truth, it does not save them (James 2:19). Knowing or believing certain things *about* Jesus does not equate to receiving salvation. It is only when we believe *what His death accomplished* for us and the fact that He rose from the dead are we on the way to receiving salvation.

If you do not know Jesus, please do not put down this book without deliberately believing that He is God, that He died for you by the shedding of His blood on the cross, and that He rose three days later because death could not keep Him. Do you believe that? If you do not yet believe it, do you *want* to believe it? If so, then simply ask God to help you come to believe all that Jesus is and all that He has accomplished for you. God will answer your prayers, and you may either receive instantaneous awareness of all that Jesus is and has done, or it may be a *growing* awareness over time. In either case, it is the most important decision you will ever make.

Turn to Him now and pray for knowledge of the truth and an ability to embrace it. Please. He is waiting for you.

Ask Yourself:

1. Do you *know* Jesus? Are you in *relationship* with Him? Have you had a spiritual transaction according to John 3?
2. Do you *want* to receive eternal life through the only salvation that is available?
3. Do you believe that Jesus is God the Son, who was born of a virgin, lived a sinless life, died a bloody and gruesome death to pay for your sin, was buried, and rose again on the third day? Do you *believe* this?
4. Do you *want* to *embrace* the truth from #3?
5. Pray that God will open your eyes and provide you with the faith to begin believing the truth about Jesus. Ask Him to help your faith embrace the truth, realizing that you are not good enough to save yourself and that your sin will keep you out of God's Kingdom without His salvation.
6. Pray as if your life depended upon it, because *it does*!
7. If you have prayed to receive Jesus as Savior and Lord, please write to me. I want to send you some materials at *no charge or obligation*. Write to me at **fred_deruvo@hotmail.com** and sign up for our free bimonthly newsletter at **www.studygrowknow.com**

Bibliography (Printed Sources)

- Bible, King James Version
- Fruchtenbaum, Arnold *Footsteps of the Messiah*
- Keathley, III, J. Hampton *Studies in Revelation*
- MacArthur, John D. *The MacArthur Study Bible*
- Strong's Exhaustive Concordance
- Wiersbe, Warren W. *Be Worshipful*
- Thomas , Robert L. *Revelation 8-22 An Exegetical Commentary*

Bibliography (Internet Sources)

- http://dictionary.reference.com
- http://net.bible.org
- http://www.kingdomofjesuschrist.org
- http://www.independent.co.uk
- http://cnn.com
- http://www.space.com
- http://www.ag.ndsu.edu
- http://www.astrobio.net
- http://www.unionoffaiths.com
- http://ronaldweinland.com
- http://en.wikipedia.org
- http://www.brillig.com

Listen to our radio program, **Study-Grow-Know** on the following stations:

- **AM950 KAHI** or listen on their Website **www.kahi.com** Saturdays at Noon
- **Live365.com** and search for Study-Grow-Know

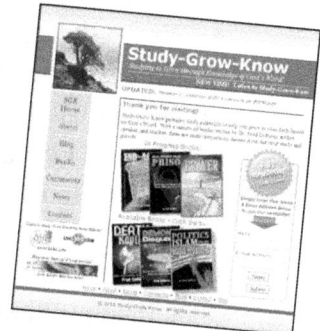

All of our programs are archived at our own Web site **www.studygrowknow.com** on our **BLOG** page from the MENU

Glossary

- **Allegorical Hermeneutic** – normally interpreting prophetic passages of Scripture as metaphor, with underlying meaning
- **Antichrist** – a name for the final human dictator who opposes God; also called the man of sin
- **Beast** – the name given to the final human dictator who opposes God and also called the man of sin or Antichrist. Also refers to the geo-political system that began with Babylon
- **Book of Revelation** – the last book of the Bible, the Apocalypse, and the final words of Jesus Christ
- **Day of Jehovah** – the period of time (not merely a day) which incorporates the Tribulation, Great Tribulation, and Second Coming
- **Day of the Lord** – an alternate phrase for "day of Jehovah"
- **Eschatology** – the study of prophecy related to the End Times or Last Days
- **False Prophet** – the Antichrist's number one fan, who directs worship and attention to the Antichrist
- **Great Tribulation** – the last three and a half years of the Tribulation when everything becomes markedly more evil
- **Lamb** – the name given to Jesus because He became the sacrificial lamb through His sinless death on the cross
- **Literal Hermeneutic** – interpreting the meaning of Scripture in its most plain and ordinary sense. Context dictates meaning.
- **Man of Sin** – a name for the final human dictator who opposes God; also called the Antichrist
- **Millennial Reign** – Period of 1,000 years in which Jesus reigns from David's throne in Jerusalem after Second Coming
- **PreTrib Rapture** – the gathering of Christ's Bride (the invisible Church) in the air prior to the beginning of the Tribulation; not to be confused with Second Coming of Jesus
- **Second Coming** – the return of Jesus to earth to judge the nations and begin His 1,000-year reign (Millennium), all of which takes place at the end of the Tribulation
- **Tribulation** – a period of seven years consisting God's intense judgment/wrath poured out on the earth and its inhabitants

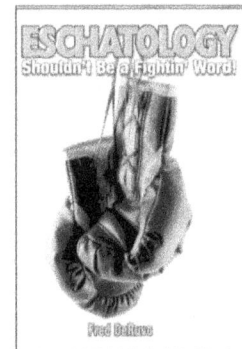

www.studygrowknow.com or wherever quality books are sold!

We are looking up, Deb!

www.ingramcontent.com/pod-product-compliance
Lightning Source LLC
Chambersburg PA
CBHW080509090426
42734CB00015B/3008

* 9 7 8 0 9 7 7 4 2 4 4 9 8 *